Persian Cooking

for dummies®
A Wiley Brand

Persian Cooking

by Najmieh Batmanglij

Persian Cooking For Dummies®

Published by: **John Wiley & Sons, Inc.,** 111 River Street, Hoboken, NJ 07030-5774, www.wiley.com

Copyright © 2022 by John Wiley & Sons, Inc., Hoboken, New Jersey

Published simultaneously in Canada

No part of this publication may be reproduced, stored in a retrieval system or transmitted in any form or by any means, electronic, mechanical, photocopying, recording, scanning or otherwise, except as permitted under Sections 107 or 108 of the 1976 United States Copyright Act, without the prior written permission of the Publisher. Requests to the Publisher for permission should be addressed to the Permissions Department, John Wiley & Sons, Inc., 111 River Street, Hoboken, NJ 07030, (201) 748-6011, fax (201) 748-6008, or online at http://www.wiley.com/go/permissions.

Trademarks: Wiley, For Dummies, the Dummies Man logo, Dummies.com, Making Everything Easier, and related trade dress are trademarks or registered trademarks of John Wiley & Sons, Inc., and may not be used without written permission. All other trademarks are the property of their respective owners. John Wiley & Sons, Inc., is not associated with any product or vendor mentioned in this book.

LIMIT OF LIABILITY/DISCLAIMER OF WARRANTY: WHILE THE PUBLISHER AND AUTHORS HAVE USED THEIR BEST EFFORTS IN PREPARING THIS WORK, THEY MAKE NO REPRESENTATIONS OR WARRANTIES WITH RESPECT TO THE ACCURACY OR COMPLETENESS OF THE CONTENTS OF THIS WORK AND SPECIFICALLY DISCLAIM ALL WARRANTIES, INCLUDING WITHOUT LIMITATION ANY IMPLIED WARRANTIES OF MERCHANTABILITY OR FITNESS FOR A PARTICULAR PURPOSE. NO WARRANTY MAY BE CREATED OR EXTENDED BY SALES REPRESENTATIVES, WRITTEN SALES MATERIALS OR PROMOTIONAL STATEMENTS FOR THIS WORK. THE FACT THAT AN ORGANIZATION, WEBSITE, OR PRODUCT IS REFERRED TO IN THIS WORK AS A CITATION AND/OR POTENTIAL SOURCE OF FURTHER INFORMATION DOES NOT MEAN THAT THE PUBLISHER AND AUTHORS ENDORSE THE INFORMATION OR SERVICES THE ORGANIZATION, WEBSITE, OR PRODUCT MAY PROVIDE OR RECOMMENDATIONS IT MAY MAKE. THIS WORK IS SOLD WITH THE UNDERSTANDING THAT THE PUBLISHER IS NOT ENGAGED IN RENDERING PROFESSIONAL SERVICES. THE ADVICE AND STRATEGIES CONTAINED HEREIN MAY NOT BE SUITABLE FOR YOUR SITUATION. YOU SHOULD CONSULT WITH A SPECIALIST WHERE APPROPRIATE. FURTHER, READERS SHOULD BE AWARE THAT WEBSITES LISTED IN THIS WORK MAY HAVE CHANGED OR DISAPPEARED BETWEEN WHEN THIS WORK WAS WRITTEN AND WHEN IT IS READ. NEITHER THE PUBLISHER NOR AUTHORS SHALL BE LIABLE FOR ANY LOSS OF PROFIT OR ANY OTHER COMMERCIAL DAMAGES, INCLUDING BUT NOT LIMITED TO SPECIAL, INCIDENTAL, CONSEQUENTIAL, OR OTHER DAMAGES.

For general information on our other products and services, please contact our Customer Care Department within the U.S. at 877-762-2974, outside the U.S. at 317-572-3993, or fax 317-572-4002. For technical support, please visit https://hub.wiley.com/community/support/dummies.

Wiley publishes in a variety of print and electronic formats and by print-on-demand. Some material included with standard print versions of this book may not be included in e-books or in print-on-demand. If this book refers to media such as a CD or DVD that is not included in the version you purchased, you may download this material at http://booksupport.wiley.com. For more information about Wiley products, visit www.wiley.com.

Library of Congress Control Number: 2022942044

ISBN 978-1-119-87574-1 (pbk); ISBN 978-1-119-87575-8 (ePDF); ISBN 978-1-119-87576-5 (epub)

SKY10035369_071922

Contents at a Glance

Recipes at a Glance

Appetizers

Main Dishes

Desserts

Drinks

Table of Contents

Introduction

Cooking Persian food is based on a philosophy reaching back to ancient times. Thousands of years ago, Zoroaster elaborated the ancient myth of the twins. One became good; the other, evil. One, the follower of truth; the other, of falsehood. This concept of duality is typically Persian, and it extends beyond moral issues. Persians often balance light and darkness, sweet and sour, hot and cold. The philosophy is both a science and an art. Increasingly, science is discovering links between food and health. And although the ancient Persian system of balance does not eliminate the need for doctors, it is an excellent nutritional adjunct to good health. For Persians, food is medicine. In fact, the word for a spice mix in Persian, *advieh*, means "medicine."

These days, you can find Persian kitchen staples at almost every grocery story. For example, recently, I've found rose water and pomegranate molasses at my local supermarket! And what's more, with the Internet, you can complete your Persian pantry with the click of a button. Hooray!

This book is intended for those who are new to Persian food, as well as for those who enjoy having creative fun in the kitchen. I hope it will serve as a key that unlocks all the secrets of Persian cooking for you. I'm excited for you to get together with family and friends and use this book to cook, tell jokes, and eat and drink as Iranians have done for thousands of years.

PERSIA OR IRAN?

Iran and *Persia* refer to the same place. These days, the word *Iran* is used to refer to the country and the word *Persia* or *Persian* is used to refer to the culture (like Persian carpets, Persian cats, and, of course, Persian food). Persian, also called Farsi, is the language of Iran.

About This Book

If you haven't eaten Persian food and you'd like to give it a try in your own kitchen, but you don't know where to begin, this is the book for you! Come join me on a voyage of culinary discovery, along a path that stretches through the ages, across Iran from the Caspian Sea in the north to the Persian Gulf in the south. In this book, I help you master basic techniques, use spices delicately, and stock your pantry with key ingredients that may be new to you.

In this book, you discover how to cook rice, the jewel of Persian cooking, with a golden crust, known as *tahdig*. You become confident about the building blocks of *khoresh*, a Persian braise that has a depth of flavor. I also show you how to cook a range of different Persian vegetarian dishes that can be served as side dishes to the main course, creating a feast! If you're vegetarian or vegan, I offer options at the end of many of the recipes throughout this book, too.

This book includes my family's favorite recipes — I hope they become yours, too! The recipes in this book help you put together various menus to please everyone. Think of this book as a road map that will guide and lead you to your destination of a perfect Persian meal. You can refer to it on a need-to-know basis and skip through pages to learn about Persian food culture.

Here are my recommendations to guide you through this book:

>> Stock your pantry with the basic ingredients you need for cooking Persian food. Some of the recipes in this book need special ingredients that can be found at Persian markets or on the Internet. Good news: You need only three basic seasonings for Persian cooking — salt, pepper, and turmeric — along with a Persian spice mix called *advieh* (see Chapter 6). **Note:** You don't need to make homemade *advieh* every time you cook; store-bought *advieh* (including my own, called Najmieh's Advieh, and available at https://persianbasket. com/advieh-najmieh-batmanglij-s-persian-spice-mix.html) works, too.

>> Read the entire recipe before you begin to cook to make sure you have all the ingredients. If you don't have some ingredients, no need to panic — you can easily find replacements in your kitchen. For example, you can substitute yellow split peas for mung beans because they have similar cooking times. Fresh tomatoes can be replaced with canned tomatoes, and fresh sour cherries can be replaced with dried or frozen ones. You can even replace dried barberries, a specialty of Persian cooking, with dried unsweetened cranberries.

» Setting out your prepared ingredients (known as *mise en place* in French) is standard practice in professional kitchens, but I recommend it for anyone who wants to cook with less hassle. If the recipe calls for, say, peeled tomatoes or chopped herbs, you'll be more efficient if you have these items prepared and ready to go before you begin cooking.

» You'll need basic equipment for Persian cooking, including a nonstick pot for cooking *tahdig,* a good skillet or frying pan, and a wooden spatula to prevent scratching nonstick pots. (Chapter 2 walks you through all the tools you need.)

» Personalize the recipes to suit your tastes. This practice comes naturally when you have confidence in the kitchen. If you're new to cooking in general, give yourself time — you'll get there!

» An everyday Persian meal is made up of rice, braise, and small side dishes, such as yogurt-based salads. A platter of fresh herbs, cheese, and flatbread always accompany a Persian meal. Most of my recipes are made for four to six people — you'll have plenty of food, but if you're planning to cook for more than six people, you can scale up your recipe. As a rule, if you're doubling a recipe, double the spices as well. If you're more than doubling a recipe, I recommend initially going easy on the spices and then adjusting them to your taste at the end of your cooking.

» All recipes have English titles followed by the original Persian titles in parentheses.

» All oven temperatures are in Fahrenheit, but the Appendix at the back of the book provides conversions to Celsius.

🍅 Vegetarian recipes are marked with the tomato icon in the Recipes in This Book (after the Table of Contents), as well as in the Recipes in This Chapter list (at the beginning of every chapter). For nonvegetarian recipes, when possible, I include tips on altering the recipes to make them vegetarian — you can find that information at the ends of the recipes.

Finally, within this book, you may note that some web addresses break across two lines of text. If you're reading this book in print and you want to visit one of these web pages, simply key in the web address exactly as it's noted in the text, pretending as though the line break doesn't exist. If you're reading this as an e-book, you've got it easy — just click the web address to be taken directly to the web page.

Foolish Assumptions

In writing this book, I made a few assumptions about you, the reader:

>> You've tasted Persian food at a Persian restaurant and you want to make it in your own kitchen.

>> You're interested in cooking and you have some experience with it. (If you're totally new to cooking, I recommend starting with *Cooking Basics For Dummies,* 5th Edition, by Bryan Miller and Marie Rama [Wiley].)

>> You're curious and want to learn about Persian food and interested in familiarizing yourself with unfamiliar ingredients.

Icons Used in This Book

Throughout the book, you see icons in the margins. Here's what each icon means:

TIP

The Tip icon highlights information that will make your life easier — in the kitchen, at least!

REMEMBER

Whenever I tell you something so important that you should commit it to memory, I use the Remember icon.

WARNING

When you see the Warning icon, be extra careful — the information here will help prevent something from going wrong.

CULTURAL
WISDOM

Persian food is an integral part of Persian culture. I use the Cultural Wisdom icon to highlight some cultural information that can enrich your experience of Persian cuisine.

Beyond the Book

In addition to what you're reading right now, this book comes with a free access-anywhere Cheat Sheet that includes tips on how to buy key Persian ingredients (such as good-quality basmati rice, dried barberries, saffron, pomegranates, grapes, date molasses, and yellow split peas), Persian cooking tools and techniques, and how to build a *khoresh*. To get this Cheat Sheet, go to www.dummies.com and type **Persian Cooking For Dummies Cheat Sheet** in the search box.

Where to Go from Here

If you're new to Persian cooking, I recommend starting with Part 2, which is all about common Persian cooking techniques, how to use Persian ingredients, how to build a *khoresh,* and how to bring a meal together. Parts 3 and 4 guide you to building your own menus — you'll find everything you need, from appetizers to desserts.

You don't need to create a feast the first time you make a Persian meal. Just try one recipe, and then build on your repertoire from there. The key is to have fun!

I hope this book serves as a key that unlocks all the secrets of Persian cooking for you. I'm excited for you to get together with family and friends and use this book to cook, tell jokes, and eat and drink as Iranians have done for thousands of years. *Nush-e joon!* (This traditional wish in Persian is similar to bon appétit in French. It means, "May the food be nourishing.")

1
Getting Started with Persian Cooking

Look at the history of Persian cooking.

Discover the essential kitchen tools for Persian cooking and how to use them.

Stock your kitchen with the special ingredients needed for Persian cooking and find out how to use them.

Chapter **1**

Exploring Persian Culture through Food

Every country expresses itself in food — the meals and casual delights created from what grows in its soil, swims in its seas, and grazes on its fields. Yet food is so much more than sustenance. In ways both subtle and powerful, it maintains bonds of family, friends, communities, and entire societies.

I was born in Iran, but I've lived away from it for the past 40 years, researching and writing cookbooks about Persian cuisine in exile. A few years ago, I wanted to renew my ties directly and went back to Iran to see and see again the amazing markets; meet cooks and restaurateurs; and share kitchens, tables, tastes, and scents that convey the very essence of Persian cooking. This book is the simplified, yet authentic result.

You know more about Persian food than you may think. When you ask for oranges, pistachios, spinach, or saffron, you're using words derived from Persian that refer to foods either originating in the region or introduced from there, because Persia was a great trading center of the ancient and medieval worlds. The land was the first home of many common herbs, from basil to cilantro, as well as scores of familiar preparations, including sweet-and-sour sauces, kabobs, and almond pastries.

In this chapter, I walk you through the long history of Persian cooking (in just a few pages!) and introduce you to the way in which Persian meals are served.

Going Back to the Beginning

Kingdoms had risen and fallen for thousands of years before the Persians arrived in the plateau known as Iran. Ancient Persians inherited the civilizations of the past; they absorbed and transformed the arts of Mesopotamia, Assyria, Babylonia, and Elam (present-day southwestern Iran).

The Persians had their kings of the fifth and fourth centuries BCE to thank for their famous royal kitchens and love of food. Darius the Great paid attention to agriculture and urged the transport of seeds and plants. To feed the famed Persian horses, alfalfa seeds were exported to Greece. To feed humans (and for pleasure), plants were transported from province to province — rice was imported from China and India, sesame from Babylon to Egypt, fruit trees from Persia to Anatolia, and pistachios from Persia to Syria.

We know from the fifth century BCE Elamite clay administrative archives discovered in the 1930s in southwestern Iran, that ancient Persians used many herbs and spices, such as cardamom, celery, cumin, dill, mustard seeds, saffron, and sesame. The ration register also includes both fresh and dried fruit and nuts, such as almonds, apples, dates, figs, mulberries, pears, and pistachios, which confirms Iranians' love and use of these herbs, spices, fruits, and nuts for more than 2,500 years.

The royal courts of two ancient Persian empires, a thousand years apart, were famous for their cuisines. Today, we would call them "foodies." What we know about Persian food is from archaeological kitchen tools; architecture, miniature painting, and poetry; linguistics; and old texts and cookbooks. Several cookbooks were written in Arabic during the tenth century, but we know that many of the recipes were borrowed from Persian royal kitchens of the sixth century and later taken to Europe by the Arabs.

The great ancient trade routes that are now called the Silk Road connected China to Italy with Iran at its center. As a result, Iran looked both east and west and became the trading center of the ancient world. Thus, Persia both influenced and was influenced by the culture and cuisines that existed between the Mediterranean in the west and China in the east.

Having some give and take with China, India, and Turkey

Rice, which was cultivated in China and India 5,000 years ago, seems to have reached Persia only in the 4th century BCE, but it did not become an important part of Persian cooking until the 15th century. Since then, rice has become not so much the anchor of a meal (the way it is in China), but the basis of festive and elaborate dishes called *polows.* Like other popular dishes, *polows* have spread far beyond their Persian source. Under such related names as *pullao, pilavi, pilaf,* and *pilau,* they grace celebrations from Afghanistan to Albania, and from India to Turkey.

Noodles and noodle dishes are often associated with Chinese and Italian cooking. In fact, according to legend, Marco Polo brought noodles from China to Italy in the 13th century. Today, however, food scholars agree that pasta probably originated in Persia. In fact, it was the Arabs who introduced noodles, and the hard durum wheat necessary for making it, from Persia to Italy in the ninth century via Sicily and Genoa. No one knows exactly how the technique for making pasta reached China. What can be said with certainty is that before the Han Dynasty in the second century BCE, China lacked the mills, which the Iranians had, for large-scale grinding of the durum wheat used to make pasta.

In the second century BCE, a Chinese imperial guard called Zhang Qian, was sent west on a diplomatic mission. In Persia, he discovered and took back to China not only the domesticated seeds of grapes (for making wine) and alfalfa (for feeding horses), but also such exotica as broad beans, coriander, cucumber, pomegranates, sesame, and walnuts.

Later, Persian cooking, already international, helped to influence the conquering Arabs of the 7th century and the Mongols of the 13th century. Between the 13th and 15th centuries, the Mongols, who later ruled parts of India, took both Persian cooking and the Persian language to India. Today, kabobs, *koofteh, biriyani,* and korma in Indian cooking all show the influence of Persian cooking.

During this period, Persian cooking also greatly influenced the cuisines of Mughal India and Ottoman Turkey. We know that the Ottoman Empire invited Persian chefs to cook in their royal kitchens. Today, what is called "Ottoman cuisine" in Turkey is very similar to Persian cooking, and many of the names of dishes still show their Persian origins.

Seeing how the Arabs introduced Persian food to North Africa and Europe

You might think that the conquest of Persia by the Arab armies in 637 would end the rich Persian civilization and trade, because the desert warriors were rough men and nomads. But instead, within a few generations, the conquerors were building new cities in the circular style of the Persians, constructing buildings with the vaulted domes and courtyards, absorbing and extending Persian scholarship, wearing Persian-style clothes, drinking Persian wine, eating Persian food, and writing cookbooks that included Persian recipes in Arabic. Persia provided the model for the splendid centuries known as the Golden Age of Islam (from the 8th to the 14th centuries). The Arabs introduced Persian cooking ingredients and techniques to North Africa and Europe. These exchanges formed a culinary bond — a sign of early and peaceful communication — that linked distant and sometimes hostile cultures.

Identifying the influence of Islamic dietary restrictions

Before the Arabs arrived, Persians were Zoroastrians (followers of one of the world's oldest religions — one that influenced not only Judaism, Christianity, and Islam, but also Buddhism and Greek philosophy) and were wine makers and drinkers.

Wine was an integral part of the Persian culture, and all Zoroastrian ceremonies included drinking wine. However, with the arrival of Islam, wine was forbidden, and Islamic dietary restrictions were imposed on Persians. The consumption of alcohol, pork, and some seafood were forbidden for believers of the faith. Additionally, the concept of *halal* (an Islamic method of slaughtering animals, very similar to kosher in Judaism) was introduced to Persians.

Recognizing the similarities and differences from region to region

Iran is a big country, highly diverse in climate and terrain, with mountain ranges, grasslands, and deserts. Seas lie to the north and south. Here and there are great cities where many cultures mingle. These regions have distinctly different climates, and until the advent of modern transportation, each had its own local ingredients and food culture.

Every region in Iran has its own style of cooking. But certain basic themes remain. For instance, yogurt and its by-product, *kashk* (fermented sun-dried yogurt) is used all over Iran, but in northwest Iran, yogurt is more prevalent, whereas in central Iran *kashk* is more common. Fruit and its molasses are used in recipes all over Iran, but pomegranate and citrus are the souring agent of choice in northern Iran, whereas tamarind and dried lime are popular in southern Iran and vinegar is popular in central Iran.

Understanding the philosophy behind Persian cooking

Thousands of years ago, Zoroaster elaborated on the ancient myth of the twins. One of the twins became good and the other, evil; one, the follower of truth and the other of falsehood. This concept of duality is typically Persian, and it extends beyond moral issues. We often balance sweet and sour in cooking. For Persians, food is also classified as *garmi* (hot) and *sardi* (cold). Dates and grapes, for instance, are hot fruits; oranges, peaches, and plums are cold. This classification of ingredients has nothing to do with the temperature or spiciness, but rather the nutritional properties of the ingredients. This concept of balancing dishes is similar to the Ayurvedic diet in India and yin and yang in China.

Eating Persian-Style

Traditionally, Iranian meals are served on a *sofreh* (a cotton cover embroidered with prayers and poems), which is spread over a Persian carpet or a table. Besides the main course, a Persian meal at home always includes *Nan-o Panir-o Sabzi Khordan*, a platter of bread, cheese, and whatever vegetables and herbs are freshest in the garden or market that day. Added to this are small dishes called *mokhalafat* or *mazzeh,* which often include yogurt-based salads, pickles, egg *kukus* (an egg, herb, or vegetable omelet much like an Italian frittata), seasonal fresh fruits like melon, puddings and custards, and dried fruit such as dates. They're spread out for the family and friends or any uninvited guests who may appear.

All those sitting around the *sofreh* are asked to help themselves to what they like, before, during, and after the meal. There is no rule or order that governs the way you eat the meal, unlike the idea of first course, second course, and so on found in western meals.

Chapter **2**

Tools of the Trade

I n order to make the recipes in this book, you'll need some tools — everything from pots and pans to knives, cutting boards, and more. Many of these items you probably already have; others may be unfamiliar to you. In this chapter, I walk you through everything you'll need so you can take an inventory of your kitchen and make a list of the tools you may want to add.

Pots and Pans

No matter what you're cooking, using the right pot or pan is important. In this section, I list all the pots and pans you'll want to have on hand.

TIP

You may see the terms *reactive* and *nonreactive* used when referring to cookware. These terms refer to the type of metal from which a container is made. Aluminum, cast iron, and copper are all reactive. Stainless-steel, ceramic, glass, and metal cookware with enamel coating are all nonreactive.

Nonstick pot

A nonstick pot is essential for creating a rice with a golden crust, known as *tahdig*. Use a deep, nonstick pot with a lid to allow the rice grains to swell properly and a good crust to form without sticking. I use a 5-quart pot that measures 11¼ inches in diameter and 3¼ inches deep.

When steaming rice, be sure to wrap the lid of the pot in a clean dish towel to absorb any condensation and prevent the rice from becoming mushy. Figure 2-1 illustrates how to do it.

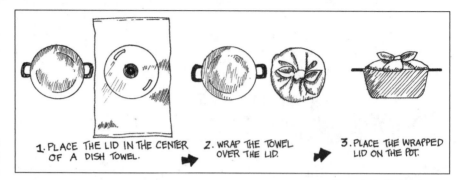

FIGURE 2-1:
Wrapping
a pot lid.

1. PLACE THE LID IN THE CENTER OF A DISH TOWEL.

2. WRAP THE TOWEL OVER THE LID.

3. PLACE THE WRAPPED LID ON THE POT.

TIP

Nonstick pots scratch easily. Look after yours by using a silicone spatula or wooden spoon when touching the bottom of the pot.

Note: You *can* use a stainless-steel pot for making golden *tahdig*, but it may not come out whole and some of it may stick to the bottom of the pot.

Braiser

An enameled cast-iron braiser with a cover (see Figure 2-2) is best for making a *khoresh* (a Persian braise). Your braiser should be wide enough so that the ingredients aren't lying on top of one another while they're being sautéed, but deep enough to contain the broth. Le Creuset makes a very good braiser, but you can find a less expensive option made by Lodge.

MEDIUM-SIZED ENAMELED CAST-IRON BRAISER WITH COVER

FIGURE 2-2:
Braiser.

Saucepan with lid

A small saucepan is necessary for boiling ingredients. It's also great for cooking eggs, potatoes, grains, and legumes. You can find saucepans in various sizes — for example, 1½ quarts, 2½ quarts, or 3 quarts. If you don't own a saucepan, I recommend 1½ quarts, but if you already have one in another size, as long as it has a lid, you'll be fine.

Wide skillet

Wide skillets are good for caramelizing onions, toasting spices and nuts, cooking patties and meatballs, and searing meat and fish. You can find skillets in various sizes — 10 inches and 12 inches are common. If you're in the market for a skillet, I recommend 12 inches, but if you already have a 10-inch skillet, you'll be able to make any of the recipes in this book.

Crêpe pan

Crêpe pans are great for making lavash (a large, thin flatbread). I use an 11-inch round nonstick crêpe pan without sides. If you don't have a crêpe pan, any wide nonstick skillet will do the job.

Roasting pan

A roasting pan is essential to make roasts and casseroles. I recommend an All-Clad traditional roasting pan with a rack. Small or large will work.

Sheet pan

I use rimmed sheet pans (instead of ones without rims) because they prevent the juice from dripping off. I have a rimmed half sheet pan for baking and a rimmed quarter sheet pan for making egg *kukus* (herb and vegetable omelets similar to Italian frittatas).

Knives and Other Cutting Tools

Knives are sacred to all chefs. Some chefs even carry their knives with them when they're invited to cook in other kitchens. In general, you really only need three knives:

» **An 8-inch chef knife:** For chopping and dicing.

» **A paring knife:** For peeling fruits and vegetables. I also like to use a paring knife for peeling fruit and vegetables, but you can use a good, sharp peeler if you aren't comfortable using a knife.

» **A long serrated knife:** For slicing thin-skinned vegetables, such as tomatoes, and for bread.

In addition, you may want to have on hand the following:

» **Vegetable peeler:** Although I use a paring knife for peeling vegetables, a sharp vegetable peeler can come in very handy.

» **Fillet knife:** For skinning fish and cutting meat.

» **Cleaver:** For chopping herbs.

» **Mandoline:** Although I use a knife for slicing, a mandoline is a wonderful tool for thinly slicing onions, cucumbers, or any firm vegetables. Just be very careful, and always wear a mandoline glove.

» **Microplane:** I like to use a microplane to grate garlic, lime, and orange zest.

» **Stainless-steel box grater:** For grating onions and tomatoes.

CARING FOR KNIVES

Knives should be stored in a knife block on the counter or in an in-drawer knife block. I don't recommend those magnetic knife holders attached to the wall, because they may fall and damage the knives or, even worse, hurt someone.

Never put a knife in the dishwasher. Instead, hand-wash them with a soft sponge and soap under warm water and dry them immediately.

Sharpen your knives frequently with a knife sharpener. Sharpening your knives regularly will make slicing and dicing much easier. A sharp knife will also bring fewer tears to your eyes when chopping onions. After sharpening your knife, be sure to rinse it with warm water and wipe it with a clean dish towel.

REMEMBER

I've seen chefs who exclusively use a cleaver for all their cutting needs, and I was astonished when I met a home cook in southern Iran who used only a paring knife to prepare *everything.* All that matters is that you use whatever knife *you* are comfortable with.

Other Miscellaneous Tools

Make sure to have on hand the following miscellaneous kitchen tools. You'll use them everything you cook, not just for Persian recipes:

- » **Cutting boards:** I use three high-quality cutting boards — one is for vegetables and onions, one is for fruit, and one is for raw meat and fish. I keep my vegetable and fruit cutting boards separate so the fruit doesn't absorb the flavor of the onions and garlic.

- » **Measuring cups and spoons:** All the recipes in this book call for precise measurements using measuring cups and spoons. Keep them handy while cooking to ensure you add the correct measure of all ingredients to the recipes.

- » **Scale:** Scales are often needed for weighing meats and vegetables.

- » **Ice-cream scoop:** In addition to using an ice-cream scoop for ice cream, I use one for scooping up even amounts of paste for meatballs — this way, all the meatballs come out the same size.

- » **Skewers:** You need skewers for making kabobs. I like to use metal skewers that are anywhere from a ¼ inch to ½ inch wide and about 12 inches long.

- » **Press juicer:** A press juicer can be used for juicing limes, lemons, oranges, and even pomegranates. It's easy to use, but be sure to wash it and wipe it dry right away after using to prevent the acids from damaging the juicer.

- » **Pot holders and dish towels:** Pot holders and dish towels are essential in any kitchen. But in a Persian kitchen clean dish towels are also used to wrap the lid of the pot used for making rice (refer to Figure 2-1, earlier in this chapter).

- » **Timers:** Use timers to prevent overcooking or burning your food. I have multiple timers in my kitchen. They're essential when you have several dishes cooking at the same time.

- » **Colander:** In a Persian kitchen, you need a stainless-steel fine-mesh colander with a base, especially for draining rice.

- » **Sieve:** Use a sieve with a handle to immerse in a container of water when soaking rice or barberries (or anything else).

>> **Salad spinner:** I use a salad spinner to soak my herbs when washing them. Then I lift up the interior basket, dump the water, and repeat this process twice. Finally, I spin the herbs to dry them. Herbs must be totally dry before chopping.

>> **Rolling pin:** A rolling pin is necessary for rolling out dough. A thin one is especially useful for rolling out the dough for baklava and lavash.

>> **Mixing bowls:** Every kitchen needs at least two mixing bowls, preferably of different sizes. You can use a mixing bowl to make bread dough, as well as for tossing vegetables and marinating kabobs.

>> **Whisk:** I use a whisk to dilute starch in water, to whisk flour, and to prevent curdling in puddings.

>> **Offset spatula:** An offset spatula makes it much easier to turn over patties in a skillet and transfer them to serving plates. It's also great for removing cookies from sheet pans.

>> **Skimmers and slotted spoons:** I use a fine-mesh skimmer to skim froth and check the grain of the rice while parboiling to make sure it's tender before draining it.

>> **Wooden spoons and silicone spatulas:** Wooden spoons and silicone spatulas will prevent scratching the bottom of your nonstick pot.

>> **Ladles:** I prefer stainless-steel ladles for soups.

Kitchen Appliances

The following appliances will make cooking faster and easier (which means you can get to the eating even sooner!):

>> **Food processor:** A food processor is a must in a Persian kitchen. You have so many herbs to chop and nuts to grind, and a food processor will expedite this process. It's also great for mincing onions used when making meatballs and kabobs.

>> **Rice cooker:** Rice cookers are a wonderful invention for cooking rice Persian-style because the nonstick coating allows for the creation of the *tahdig* and the unvarying temperature produces consistently good rice. However, to make the best *tahdig,* buy a rice cooker from a Persian market — their thermostats are set for making the golden crust (Japanese rice cookers won't do this).

>> **Spice grinder:** My mother had a huge stone mortar and pestle in her kitchen, which she used for grinding everything from rock salt to nuts. In addition to a small, marble mortar and pestle, I use an electric spice grinder and absolutely love it!

WARNING

Never put anything moist in the spice grinder. Moisture affects the quality of the spice, causes it to mold, and, worst of all, can give you an electric shock if you put your finger inside when removing the ground spice. (I speak from experience.)

>> **Electric stand mixer:** I use an electric stand mixer to make dough.

>> **Electric handheld mixer:** An electric handheld mixer is very useful for partially pureeing the grains in a soup while it's cooking.

>> **Multicooker:** Using a multicooker (like an Instant Pot) can reduce the cooking time for braises by half, especially when you have bone-in meats and legumes. Be sure to follow the manufacturer's instructions for the multicooker that you're using.

IN THIS CHAPTER

» **Picking the perfect meat, poultry, and fish**

» **Gathering dairy products and eggs**

» **Perusing the produce section**

» **Choosing the right fat**

» **Stocking your pantry**

» **Finishing it off with flavorings and garnishes**

Chapter **3**

Shopping for Essential Ingredients

The easiest way to begin your Persian cooking journey is to have a well-stocked kitchen. If you're lucky enough to have a Persian grocer or market nearby, check it out! Exploring various ethnic food cultures by visiting their grocery stores is a fascinating and educational experience for anyone who loves to cook. I encourage you to go to the Persian market and shop for all the specialty ingredients used in Persian cooking. Whenever fresh tarragon and dill are out of stock at my local supermarket (which is often these days), I can rely on the Persian market to have them. Fresh fava beans in the pod (in season) or frozen fava beans that are double peeled are always available at Persian markets. You'll also find Persian basil, a relative of lemon basil that's more tender than Thai basil and has a delicate taste, perfect for accompanying Persian food. *Narenj* (sour orange); fresh, young grape leaves; and fresh *ghureh* (unripe grapes) are only available at Persian markets.

In this chapter, I fill you in on the ingredients you'll want to have on hand and what to look for when shopping for them.

Meat, Poultry, and Fish

Traditionally, lamb and veal have been used in Persian cooking, but you can also use beef (beef eye of round, cut into cubes is good for braising). However, lamb is my preferred meat these days because, in the United States, it's the least likely to have added hormones and antibiotics.

Braises are typically made with red meat, but I give you the choice to make them with chicken, too. I prefer to use chicken thighs rather than breasts because they have more fat and, as a result, are more flavorful and less likely to become dry. The favorite fish in Persian cooking are striped bass/rockfish or branzino. I've also found that salmon works very well.

Lamb

I prefer to use boneless leg of lamb or goat for making braises, but you can replace it with beef or veal if you prefer. If you aren't familiar with cooking lamb, the recipes in this book will help you grow to love it.

TIP

When buying lamb to use in braises, look for some marble in the meat — you want to see some parts with fat. This is important because braises can take up to two hours to cook, and the fat on the meat will keep it tender.

Chicken

I often buy organic, boneless, skinless chicken thighs for Persian cooking — it's tastier and juicier than chicken breast. Plus, chicken thighs are good not only for kabobs but also for braises that need to simmer for a long time.

Fish

Atlantic salmon, which is often most readily available fresh, works very well in Persian cooking. If you're lucky enough to find fresh, wild striped bass or rockfish, get it! These fish come closest to the taste of the renowned Caspian Sea whitefish called *kutum*. Grouper is another fish good for Persian cooking — it's close to the Persian Gulf's famous *hamour*.

Dairy and Eggs

Persians have used all kinds of dairy products in their cooking since ancient times. Yogurt is cherished, and often you'll find a bowl of it on the table as an accompaniment to a meal. Adding *kashk*, a sundried sour yogurt, gives Persian noodle soup a distinctive and delicious flavor. White sheep or goat cheese (like feta) is popular for breakfast; it's also often included in the indispensable fresh herb platter on the Persian table. Soft-boiled eggs are popular breakfast fare, but a favorite way to eat eggs is as a *kuku*, which is an egg, herb, or vegetable omelet similar to an Italian frittata.

TIP

Be sure to look at the expiration date when buying all your dairy and eggs.

Milk

I use whole milk in my recipes (though you can use low-fat or skim milk). You can also use plant-based milks such as almond or oat milk as a nondairy substitute.

Yogurt

In Iran, yogurt is always plain and often drained to make it thicker and richer (*mast-e kisehi*). It's available in Persian markets (or you can drain your own). Good equivalents, available in traditional supermarkets in the United States, are known by names such as Greek strained yogurt, labneh, or kefir cheese. I also like Cream Top Plain Whole Milk Yogurt from Brown Cow (www.browncowfarm.com/products/cream-top/plain).

CULTURAL WISDOM

A well-known story goes like this: A desert nomad, possibly Persian, was carrying some milk in his goatskin canteen. During his journey, heat and the right bacteria (*Lactobacillus*) transformed the milk into yogurt. The nomad took his chances and drank the mixture. Much to his astonishment, he found a sour, creamy, and pleasant taste. When he didn't get sick, he shared his discovery with others. And that's how we got yogurt!

Kashk

Kashk is a by-product of fermented and sun-dried sour yogurt. In Iran, it's used in cooking as a high-protein, fat-free replacement for cream. Traditionally, *kashk* is sold as a solid and dissolved in water to use in cooking. These days, it's also available in jars as a liquid. Or you can make your own (see Chapter 4).

Cheese

Panir (Persian cheese) is curdled, boiled milk cut into blocks. It's made simply with whole milk — sheep, goat, or cow — and lime juice. *Panir* is often eaten for breakfast with bread and herbs. You can make your own *panir* easily using the recipe in Chapter 4, or find it (often called *feta*) at your local grocery store. It can be flavored with fresh or dried herbs, nigella seeds, or sesame seeds, or served plain. My preferred *panir* these days is cheese made with goat's milk.

Eggs

In northern Iran, they love to use duck eggs, a delicacy of the region. The rest of Iran, however, uses chicken eggs, and I always use organic, free-range eggs in my own cooking. In the recipes in this book, I use large eggs.

Produce

Traditionally Iranians went to market every day to buy fresh produce of the season for cooking the meal for that day. I still prefer to use fresh ingredients, but nowadays, some frozen ingredients, such as peas and spinach, can be very good, especially when they're picked and frozen at peak season, preferably on-site.

Fruits

Popular fruits used in Persian home cooking — but not often used by home cooks in the United States — are quince (available in the autumn), sour orange (available in the autumn and winter), and sour cherry (available in the summer). Shop for them when in season at farmer's markets, gourmet grocers, and Persian markets.

TIP

In Persian cooking, I prefer to use limes instead of lemons. Lemons tend to be sweeter, whereas limes are more sour with a touch of bitterness that enhances the flavor of the dishes.

Since ancient times, Persians have also used dried fruits to create a sweet-and-sour flavor in dishes. Dried fruits are commonly used in braises, stuffings, and soups; they're also eaten as a dessert or as a snack with nuts. Dried fruits frequently used in Persian cooking include apricots, dates, and raisins, all of which are readily available in supermarkets (though I recommend the long, golden Iranian raisins available at Persian markets). Dried Persian limes and dried barberries are usually only available at Persian markets or on the Internet.

Vegetables

Potatoes and tomatoes are necessities for Persian cooking. Although they come from the new world and are not native to Iran, they're very commonly used in Persian cooking. I use starchy potatoes such as russet and Yukon gold for Persian cooking because they're good for roasting, mashing, and frying.

Another essential vegetable in Persian cooking is eggplant. The Persian market carries several types of eggplant. You need firm, seedless eggplants for preparing Persian dishes. Chinese and Japanese eggplants (which are long and slender) are perfect for braises and aren't bitter. If you use an Italian eggplant (which is deep purple and not slender), be sure to remove the bitterness using the method included in this book (see Chapter 4). I use seedless Italian eggplant for smoking over a flame.

Spring onions (scallions) are another popular ingredient in Persian cooking. I usually use all the white and green parts (in addition to adding to the taste, it's not wasteful). They not only add great taste and a certain freshness to dishes, but also have good health properties.

Herbs

Commonly used herbs in Persian cooking are cilantro, mint, parsley, and tarragon. For cilantro and parsley, I only cut off 1 inch of the stem and use the rest (in addition to being more nutritious, it's less wasteful).

I suggest shopping for fresh herbs whenever possible, but if you can't find fresh, dried or frozen herbs are okay to use.

I also recommend using dried fenugreek and mint leaves because they're more potent than the fresh leaves. Buy your dried herbs from Persian markets, though, because they sell a lot, which means you're getting fresher dried herbs of much better quality.

Fats

In the recipes in this book, I give you the option to use olive oil, butter, or *ghee* (clarified butter) — you can use whichever you prefer.

I like to use olive oil for all my cooking these days, even for pastries, because it's one of the least processed oils and it gives your dishes a wonderfully light taste.

Ghee has been traditionally used in Persian cooking, especially for rice. It's available in stores, or you can very easily make your own (see Chapter 4).

WARNING

There are two kinds of ghee — the kind made with butter and the kind made with hydrogenated vegetable oil. The kind made with hydrogenated vegetable oil is cheaper and has more trans fats, which are very unhealthy. Be sure to get ghee made from butter from grass-fed cows.

TIP

I recommend making your own ghee and keeping it in the fridge, but if you have store-bought ghee, be sure to keep it in the fridge after opening.

Pantry Items

Stock your pantry with some basic ingredients for Persian cooking, particularly items that are harder to find in your local supermarket. Make sure you always have dried limes, ground Persian hogweed seeds, dried barberries, dried fenugreek and mint leaves, and dried Persian shallots (all available from local Persian markets or online).

Flour

In Persian cooking, in addition to unbleached all-purpose flour (which is used for making pastries and bread), flour is often used as a thickening agent for soups and meatballs.

Other flours such as sprouted wheat flour (available on the Internet or in Persian markets, where it's called *sen*), rice flour, chickpea flour, and almond flour are commonly used in Persian cooking and good to have in your pantry.

For lavash bread, I use 00 flour (also called *pizza flour*). You'll also need rice starch and cornstarch for some recipes in this book.

TIP

Keep flour in airtight glass containers.

Rice

Indian basmati rice, long-grained and wonderfully aromatic (its name comes from the Sanskrit word *vasmati*, meaning "fragrant"), is excellent for Persian cooking. It's widely available in the United States, even in supermarkets, but not all types are of the same quality. Persian and other Middle Eastern grocers, as well as Amazon, have several brands of basmati rice. My favorite these days is the Khazana brand, which sells both the regular basmati and a smoked version.

TIP

If you're using aged Indian basmati rice, follow the instructions for soaking and rinsing (see Chapter 4) because it greatly improves the wonderful aroma.

I use jasmine rice for some of the pudding recipes in this book. It should be readily available at your regular grocery store, but if it isn't, you'll easily be able to find it at a Middle Eastern market or on the Internet.

Noodles

Persian noodles are not made with eggs — only salt, water, and flour. They're flat, similar in shape to Italian fettuccini or tagliatelle, but without eggs. In Persian cooking, noodles are toasted and mixed with rice or boiled in soups. Rice-stick noodles (available in Persian or Asian stores) are also used for the renowned Persian sherbet.

TIP

Keep noodles in airtight glass containers.

Legumes

Red kidney beans, chickpeas (also called *garbanzo beans*), white beans (also called *cannellini*), and fava beans (with the second skins removed and available in frozen packets under the Shams brand at Persian markets or online) are the essential legumes in Persian cooking. Also used are pinto beans, mung beans, and yellow split peas. I prefer to use dried legumes and soak them before use, but canned legumes work fine, too.

TIP

Soaking, draining, and rinsing dried legumes reduces their cooking time and makes them easier to digest (see Chapter 4).

Tomato and tamarind pastes

Persian recipes sometimes call for tomato paste. You can find it canned or in tubes, but I prefer to use the paste that comes in a tube because it's easier to use.

REMEMBER

Refrigerate tomato paste after opening it. If you're using canned tomato paste, transfer any remaining paste to an airtight glass container and keep it in the fridge.

Tamarind paste, also used in Persian cooking, is available at Persian and Middle Eastern markets. I like the Golchin brand.

Molasses

Pomegranate, grape, and date molasses are essential for Persian cooking. All Middle Eastern markets carry them, but I've recently noticed that Whole Foods carries them, too.

Nuts

The Persian pantry requires a variety of nuts. Almonds, walnuts, and pistachio kernels are used for garnish in many Persian dishes, including soups, rice, braises, and pastries. Slivered pistachios are best bought at Persian markets or online, while almonds — whole, blanched, and slivered — and walnut halves are readily available at supermarkets.

Pickles and preserves

Pickles and preserves are often placed on a Persian spread as an accompaniment to the meal. You can make your own from the recipes in this book, or you can buy them from Persian markets.

Three famous favorite Persian pickles are *sir torshi* (garlic pickle), *torshi-e liteh* (eggplant and vegetable pickle), and *piaz torshi* (onion pickle).

The most popular Persian preserves are *moraba-ye beh* (quince preserve), *moraba-ye albalu* (sour cherry preserve), and *moraba-ye anjir* (fig preserve).

Canned goods

Canned peeled tomatoes, when tomatoes are out of season, are good to have on hand. The same goes for canned grape leaves. Canned *ghureh* are called for in some recipes; you can find them at Persian markets or on the Internet. Canned legumes are good substitutes for reducing cooking time.

TIP

If you're using canned legumes, be sure to rinse them thoroughly in a fine-mesh colander to get rid of any off smell or taste from the can.

Aromatics

Rose water and orange blossom water are must-haves in the Persian pantry. I use Cortas or Sadaf brands, available at Persian and Middle Eastern markets and in many supermarkets as well.

Don't buy the pharmacy versions — they aren't meant for cooking.

Tea and coffee

For Persian tea, use Do Ghazal brand black Ceylon tea, available at Persian markets (buy the blue and black label version) or Earl Grey. For Persian coffee, use the very fine-grind coffee known as *Turkish coffee*.

Flavorings and Garnishes

Persian cooking is delicately spiced with a range of spices and ingredients that include not only edible leaves and flowers but also various sweetening and souring agents.

Spices

The good news is that for cooking Persian food, you don't need lots of spices. For most Persian dishes, you need a basic seasoning, such as salt (I use fine-grain sea salt) and spices such as freshly ground black pepper, turmeric, and, of course, saffron, which, in addition to adding a delicious flavor and aroma, adds a glorious color to your dishes.

Coarse-grained salt adds less flavor because there are fewer grains in a given measure. Ordinary Morton's iodized salt tends to add more flavor. The amount of salt you use is up to you, but rice dishes in particular need the minimum recommended amount of salt for both taste and texture. For "finishing" the flavor upon serving, or for adding texture (for kabobs, for example), I recommend a delicate sea salt flake such as a *fleur de sel* or Maldon Sea Salt Flakes (https://maldonsalt.com).

Ground Persian hogweed seeds, called *golpar*, is a frequently used spice in Persian cooking. It's mostly available in Persian markets or online, so you'll have to go out of your way to find it, but its unique taste makes it well worth the trouble.

You can make many dishes with these basic spices and add other good-quality spices such as cardamom, cinnamon, cloves, coriander, cumin, and ginger to your pantry as you start to cook more.

A spice that is also favored in Persian cooking is sumac. Dried sumac berries are ground to a powder and available at Persian markets. Sumac is used as a spice, mostly on kabobs, but also in soups and in meatball broth. I've also used it with fish — check out the delicious Sumac Grilled Fish (Mahi-e Kababi ba Somaq) in Chapter 16.

A basic Persian spice mix called *advieh* literally translates to "medicine," perhaps because spices used in Persian cooking have a healing power. Every region in Iran has a different *advieh*, and I've developed my own, which you can use whenever a recipe calls for it in this book. You can make my *advieh* at home (see Chapter 6) and keep it in an airtight glass container, or you can buy my premade spice mix, called Najmieh's Advieh, from your local Persian market or online at https://persianbasket.com/advieh-najmieh-batmanglij-s-persian-spice-mix.html.

Ground spices have a short shelf life (anywhere from six months to a year), and it's important to use them while they're fresh. I recommend, whenever possible, buying spices whole and grinding them at home in small quantities as needed.

TIP

Keep spices away from light and humidity in an airtight glass container. Use them within a year after they're ground — they lose their nutritional properties and aroma with time.

Sugar

You can use granulated sugar to add sweetness to dishes, but ancient Persians used grape or date molasses or honey as a sweetener.

Vinegar

Many Persian dishes call for vinegar to create a sweet-and-sour balance. I use mostly apple cider vinegar or wine vinegar when cooking.

I also recommend using a splash of distilled vinegar in a container of water when soaking herbs.

Verjuice

Verjuice (unripe grape juice) is a souring agent used in some Persian recipes. It's available bottled at Persian or Middle Eastern stores and gourmet markets, as well as online.

Edible leaves and flowers

Grape leaves are used as a wrapper for stuffing in a dish called *dolmeh.* If you can find fresh young grape leaves, available in season at Persian stores, use them. However, canned grapes leaves are also okay and available in many grocery stores.

Edible dried rose petals are used frequently in Persian cooking, both as a garnish and for jams. They're available at Persian markets or online. Buy the dried petals and not the buds for Persian cooking. I recommend the Khasana brand of rose petals.

2

Getting Comfortable in the Kitchen

Master common Persian kitchen techniques.

Find out how to use the staple ingredients of Persian cooking.

Discover how to use spices the Persian way.

Bring it all together in a personalized Persian meal.

Chapter **4**

Common Persian Kitchen Techniques

Throughout this chapter, I show you the easiest way to peel vegetables, explain how to caramelize ingredients like orange peel, and more. Think of this chapter as the foundation upon which all the recipes are built. When you understand the techniques in this chapter, you'll be able to make Persian recipes with ease.

Peeling Away the Unappealing Parts

Fruits and vegetables with thick skins, such as butternut squash, need to be peeled for cooking, but these days I like to peel all my fruits and vegetables, even though the peels may be full of nutrients. (Peeling makes them easier to digest and prevents exposure to pesticides.) I usually use a paring knife or a sharp peeler to remove the unwanted skin of fruits and vegetables. However, a few fruits and vegetables, such as tomatoes and butternut squash, are easier to peel in other ways. In this section, I show you how.

Tomatoes

Tomatoes are a fairly recent addition to the Persian pantry.

CULTURAL WISDOM

In northern Iran, because of the Italian and Russian influences, tomatoes are called *pomodor*, whereas in southern Iran, because of the Portuguese influence, they're called *tamata*.

I peel a tomato using one of two methods. The first method is to blanch the tomatoes to loosen the skin from the flesh. Follow these steps:

1. **Bring a large pot of water to a boil and place a large bowl of ice on the counter next to you.**

2. **Use the point of a paring knife to remove the tomato stems and cut out the hard circular area where the stems were connected.**

3. **Drop the tomatoes in the boiling water until the skin lifts off slightly, about 30 to 60 seconds.**

   The time required will depend on the type of tomatoes and how ripe they are.

4. **Remove the tomatoes with a strainer or a slotted spoon and submerge them in the ice water.**

5. **When the tomatoes are cool, remove the skin using a paper towel or your fingers.**

6. **Use immediately or store in an airtight glass container up to 3 days.**

The second way of peeling a tomato is a bit faster, but also messier! Follow these steps (see Figure 4-1):

1. Horizontally cut a ripe tomato in half.

2. Place a grater, large-hole-side up, over a bowl and grate the tomato, cut-side-down, into the bowl, until only the tomato skin is left in your hand.

3. Discard the skin.

FIGURE 4-1:
Peeling a tomato by grating it.

Butternut squash

Many Iranian recipes use pumpkins or butternut squash. I prefer to use butternut squash, which is readily available throughout the year in supermarkets. Here's an easy way to peel and dice it (see Figure 4-2):

1. With a heavy cleaver, slice the squash crosswise into 1-inch rings and remove the seeds with a spoon.

2. Use the cleaver to peel the squash by placing one of the rings, flat side down, on a cutting board and chopping off the skin of the squash.

3. Cut each squash into 1-inch cubes, rinse and drain, and pat dry.

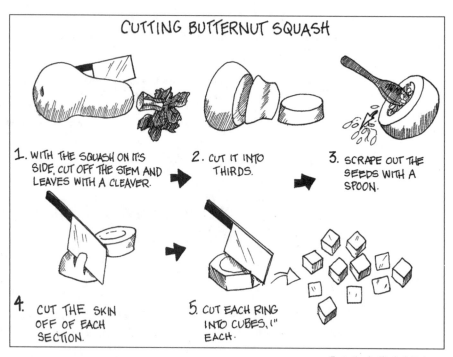

FIGURE 4-2:
Cutting butternut
squash.

Illustration by Elizabeth Kurtzman

Eggplants

Persian eggplants resemble Italian eggplants. They're small and have bitter skin that can be removed with a sharp peeler. However, the hat, or *calyx*, of an eggplant is sometimes considered a delicacy in Persian cooking and should be left on.

Ginger and garlic

Ginger adds a wonderful taste to many dishes, but it needs to be used properly. I use a small spoon to remove the very thin skin of ginger. I keep the ginger in a glass container or resealable bag in the freezer for up to 3 months and grate some of it whenever I need it. (It's easier to grate ginger when it's frozen.)

Garlic and onion, caramelized together are essential to many Persian dishes. Knowing how to use garlic is a good technique to know. Follow these steps:

1. **Choose bulbs with no blemishes.**

   Don't worry if there are green shoots.

2. **Place the bulb on your cooking surface, root-side up, and press down on the root with both hands (or use the butt of a chef knife to whack it).**

   This separates the cloves from the root.

3. **Cut off the top and root of each clove, remove the skin, and use a clean dish towel or paper towel to thoroughly dry each clove.**

I store my garlic in an airtight glass container in the refrigerator up to 3 weeks. The bulbs can be used whole, sliced, or grated using a microplane.

Cutting Vegetables Like a Pro

Not a day goes by when I don't slice, chop, dice, or mince something. That's how important these techniques are when preparing Persian recipes.

TIP

What's the difference between chopping, dicing, and mincing? It's not always obvious, but technically the word *chop* is used for larger pieces, *dice* is used for smaller pieces, and *mince* is used for very small pieces (in particular, in Persian cooking, for onions used in meatballs and kabobs).

The most important thing to keep in mind when cutting anything — whether you're chopping, dicing, or mincing — is to make sure that everything is the same size so the pieces cook evenly. Also, be sure to use a knife that's sharp and that you're comfortable with.

When cooking Persian braises, the size of the vegetable pieces is very important. Vegetables like butternut squash, quince, or eggplant should be chopped into relatively large (1½-inch) pieces so that they can keep their form. On the other hand, onions should not be the focal point of your dish, so you'll want to cut them smaller.

In the recipes in this book, I guide you to slice and chop vegetables and meat and delicately spice them to maintain their integrity by keeping them intact and making sure the spice doesn't overpower the flavor.

If you haven't done a lot of chopping, you'll feel awkward at first as you try to get your fingers and the knife and the vegetables in the right places. But as you spend more time chopping, you'll get more comfortable with it, and soon you'll be a pro! Practice makes perfect.

When you're chopping onions, you need to start by thinly slicing along the grain. I use the smallest yellow onions I can find for slicing. If you're using a large onion, be sure to make a horizontal cut before slicing along the grain. The following steps explain how to slice an onion with the grain to help it become integrated into the dish (see Figure 4-3):

1. **Place the onion on a cutting board, and use a sharp knife to cut off the stem; then cut the onion in half through the root.**

2. **Peel off the skin and place one of the halves flat on the cutting board.**

3. **Make parallel lengthwise cuts along the grain, without cutting through the root end.**

4. **Cut horizontal slices from the top to the bottom.**

5. **Cut through the onion at a right angle to the cutting board, making pieces as thick or as thin as desired.**

6. **Finally, cut off the root and discard.**

Onions are typically sliced as thinly as possible for Persian cooking. You can also use a mandoline, but must be very careful and wear a mandoline glove to protect your fingers.

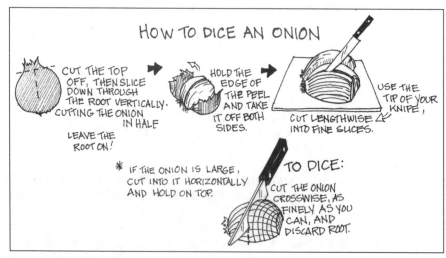

FIGURE 4-3:
How to dice
an onion.

Illustration by Elizabeth Kurtzman

TIP

Dicing is a more precise form of chopping. Persian salads and braises often call for diced onions and other vegetables, which are all diced into equally sized 1/2-inch pieces. A large dice is 3/4 inch, a medium dice is 1/2 inch, and a small dice is 1/4 inch.

When you're making meatballs or ground meat kabobs, I recommend mincing your onions. Minced onions are very finely diced to less than ¼ inch. You can either use a sharp knife to dice the onion into the smallest pieces possible or mince the onion in a food processor by pulsing.

Washing and Drying Fresh Herbs

To wash fresh herbs, follow these steps:

1. Pick over the fresh herbs and remove any wilted or yellowed sprigs.

2. Place the herbs in a container (or the bowl of a salad spinner) filled with water and add a splash of distilled vinegar.

3. Allow the herbs to soak for 10 minutes.

4. Lift up the herbs, leaving any sediments or impurities behind.

5. Repeat Steps 2–4 one more time.

6. Place in a colander, rinse, and dry thoroughly.

Before chopping washed herbs, be sure that they're thoroughly dry. I like to use a salad spinner to remove excess water. Then I wrap the herbs in a clean dish towel to remove any trace of moisture before chopping. This is especially important when chopping herbs for Fresh Herb Kuku (Kuku Sabzi Chapter 9) to prevent it from becoming soggy.

Cleaning and Washing Barberries

Zareshk (barberries) are a popular ingredient in Persian cooking. The tart berries are cultivated in northeastern Iran. In the United States, barberries are usually only available as dried berries — you can find them at Persian groceries.

TIP

Be sure to choose red ones (dark, brown berries may be old and from earlier seasons).

Barberries have very sharp, short stems that must be removed before washing and cooking. To clean and wash the berries before using, follow these steps (see Figure 4-4):

1. Spread the barberries on a sheet pan lined with parchment paper and pick over any impurities, stems, or visible sand.

2. **Place the barberries in a fine-mesh sieve, and immerse the sieve in a bowl of cold water.**

   Let it rest for 20 minutes, allowing any dirt to sink to the bottom of the bowl.

3. **Lift the sieve out of the water, run fresh cold water over the berries, and give it a shake.**

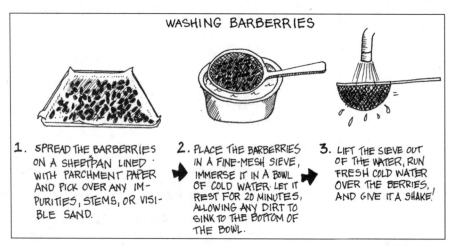

WASHING BARBERRIES

1. SPREAD THE BARBERRIES ON A SHEETPAN LINED WITH PARCHMENT PAPER AND PICK OVER ANY IMPURITIES, STEMS, OR VISIBLE SAND.

2. PLACE THE BARBERRIES IN A FINE-MESH SIEVE, IMMERSE IT IN A BOWL OF COLD WATER. LET IT REST FOR 20 MINUTES, ALLOWING ANY DIRT TO SINK TO THE BOTTOM OF THE BOWL.

3. LIFT THE SIEVE OUT OF THE WATER, RUN FRESH COLD WATER OVER THE BERRIES, AND GIVE IT A SHAKE!

FIGURE 4-4: Washing barberries.

Illustration by Elizabeth Kurtzman

TIP

Fresh barberries come in clusters. If you're lucky enough to find fresh ones, you only need to stem and rinse them before cooking.

TIP

Barberries are sour, so caramelizing them with a little water and sugar will bring out the best in them. Check out the following section for instructions on how to caramelize barberries.

Caramelizing Ingredients for Flavor

Caramelizing ingredients is an excellent way to bring out their natural sweetness. Caramelizing is popular in Persian cooking. In the following sections, I walk you through caramelizing orange peel, barberries, and onion.

REMEMBER

In the recipes in this book, when something needs to be caramelized, I provide the steps for you to follow.

Orange peel

To caramelize orange peel, follow these steps:

1. **Scrub and wash 3 large oranges.**

2. **Peel the oranges with a paring knife, keeping some of the pith on the peel.**

   Save the fruit for orange juice.

3. **Cut the orange peels into thin slivers (about ¼ inch × 2 inches).**

4. **To remove the bitterness, place the peels in a medium saucepan, cover with water, bring to a boil, and then immediately drain in a colander and rinse with cold water.**

   If you're using *narenj* (bitter oranges) repeat this step 5 times, because the rind is quite bitter.)

5. **Place the orange peels back in the saucepan and add 1½ cups orange juice (you can use the juice from the 3 large oranges you used in Step 2), 1 cup sugar, and 1 tablespoon orange blossom water.**

6. **Bring to a boil, reduce the heat to medium, and simmer uncovered until caramelized, about 16 to 18 minutes.**

7. **Use immediately or store in an airtight glass container in the refrigerator for up to 3 weeks or in the freezer for up to 3 months.**

Barberries

To caramelize barberries, follow these steps:

1. **In a wide skillet, place 1 cup washed and drained barberries, 2 teaspoons grape molasses or sugar, 2 tablespoons olive oil, and ¼ cup water.**

2. **Stir-fry over medium-high heat until caramelized, about 4 minutes.**

WARNING

   The barberries will become brighter and shinier as they cook. Barberries are quite fragile, and it's best not to overcook them. Undercooking is okay, so err on the side of undercooking rather than overcooking.

3. **Use immediately or store in an airtight glass container in the refrigerator for up to 3 days or in the freezer for up to 3 weeks.**

Onions

Caramelizing onions brings out the sugars in them, adding another dimension to the flavors of your dish. To make slow-cooked, caramelized onions, follow these steps:

1. Peel and thinly slice (along the grain) 4 small onions. Set aside.
2. In a wide nonstick skillet, add 2 tablespoons of oil, butter or ghee. Warm the pan over low heat, until hot but not smoking, about 10 minutes.
3. Add the sliced onions to the pan, and sauté, stirring occasionally, until golden brown and caramelized, about 30 to 40 minutes.

Caramelized onions can be stored in an airtight glass container in the refrigerator for up to 5 days or in the freezer for up to 3 months.

Toasting Nuts and Noodles

Toasting draws out the natural oils of nuts, and adds flavor to the dish. Toasting noodles gives them not only a nutty flavor and a heavenly aroma but also a crunch that takes a dish to another level.

Nuts

I toast nuts to make them more flavorful and crunchy. You can do it on the stovetop or in the oven.

To toast nuts on the stovetop, follow these steps:

1. Add the nuts to a skillet without any oil.
2. Toast over medium-high heat, shaking the skillet constantly, until the nuts are golden brown and the aroma rises, about 3 to 4 minutes.
3. Remove from the heat.

Toasted nuts can be stored in an airtight glass container in the refrigerator for up to 3 weeks.

To toast nuts in the oven, follow these steps:

1. **Place the rack in the center of the oven and preheat the oven to 350 degrees.**

2. **Line a rimmed baking sheet with parchment paper.**

3. **Spread the nuts on the parchment paper, and toast until lightly darkened, about 7 to 10 minutes.**

   WARNING

   Be careful — nuts burn easily.

4. **Remove from the oven.**

Toasted nuts can be stored in an airtight glass container in the refrigerator for up to 3 weeks.

Noodles

Persian noodles are flat, more like fettuccini than spaghetti. They're available, already toasted, at Persian markets. When used inside rice dishes, they're broken up, but they're kept as ribbons for noodle soup.

To toast your own noodles and make them more flavorful, follow these steps:

1. **Break the noodles into 4-inch pieces.**

2. **In a wide skillet, spread the noodles evenly.**

3. **Heat the skillet over medium-high heat, shaking constantly, until the noodles are lightly golden, about 2 to 3 minutes.**

   WARNING

   Be careful not to burn them.

4. **Remove from the heat.**

Although you can store toasted noodles, you're better off toasting them as needed for the recipe you're making.

Frying Onions

Adding *piaz dagh-e chipsi* (crispy fried onions) to a dash adds another layer of texture and flavor. I make these once a week and store them in an airtight glass container in the fridge to use as needed. They're wonderful mixed with rice or for topping a *khoresh* (Persian braise) just before serving.

To make crispy fried onions, follow these steps:

1. Peel and thinly slice (along the grain) 4 small onions. Set aside.
2. Fill a medium saucepan halfway with water and bring it to a boil.
3. Add the onions, stir twice, and bring back to a boil.
4. Drain the onions in a sieve and allow to sit for 10 minutes to dry out.
5. Wipe the saucepan dry.
6. In the same saucepan, add 4 cups of oil (filling the pan no more than halfway) and warm over medium-high heat for about 4 minutes.
7. Add the onions to the pan and cook until golden, stirring frequently to ensure even cooking, about 8 to 10 minutes.

   The onions will continue to cook and become darker after removing them from the oil, so avoid overcooking.

8. If you like, add ¼ teaspoon turmeric or ⅛ teaspoon ground saffron threads and stir.
9. Drain the onions in a sieve over a bowl, and allow to sit for 5 minutes so all the oil drips through.
10. Line a sheet pan with parchment paper and spread the onions out on the parchment paper; allow to cool.
11. Use immediately or store in a covered glass container in the refrigerator up to 1 week or in the freezer up to 3 months.

Making a Mint Garnish

Mint garnish (*na'na dagh*) is a flavorful, savory garnish that is added at the end of the cooking process. It adds umami to soups and eggplant spreads.

To make your own mint garnish, follow these steps:

1. Peel and grate 5 cloves of garlic. Set aside.
2. In a small skillet, add 2 tablespoons of oil.
3. Warm the oil over medium heat and add the garlic.
4. Stir-fry the garlic until golden, about 2 to 3 minutes.
5. Add ½ teaspoon of turmeric and stir-fry for 1 minute.

6. Remove the pan from the heat.

7. Crumble 2 tablespoons of dried mint flakes in the palm of your hand and add to the garlic, mixing well.

The mint garnish can be stored in an airtight glass container in the refrigerator for up to 3 weeks.

Removing Bitterness

Some ingredients, such as the black Italian or Persian eggplant and orange skins are bitter. Removing the bitterness brings out their flavor. In the following sections, I show you how to remove the bitterness from eggplant and orange peel.

Eggplants

The Italians and French call some eggplant dishes "the poor man's caviar." Eggplant dishes can be delicious, and eggplants aren't difficult to use in cooking, but you have to prepare them properly.

There are two ways to remove the bitterness from eggplants. Follow these steps for the first method:

1. Peel and slice the eggplants according to your recipe.

2. To a large container, add 8 cups of cold water and 2 tablespoons of fine sea salt.

3. Add the eggplant to the container of water and let stand for 30 minutes.

4. Drain, rinse thoroughly, and blot dry completely.

If you prefer, you can follow these steps:

1. Peel and slice the eggplants according to your recipe.

2. Place the eggplant in a colander in your sink and rinse.

3. Rub each piece with plenty of salt and allow to stand for 30 minutes.

4. Rinse again and blot dry completely.

TIP

The long purple Chinese and Japanese eggplants don't have bitter skins and can be used in recipes without this process.

Orange peel

Orange peel is used in several Persian dishes because it can add a deliciously subtle flavor to the dish. To remove the bitterness from orange peel, follow these steps:

1. **Peel the oranges with a peeler or paring knife, and cut the peels into slivers.**

2. **Drop the slivers into a saucepan of boiling water and bring back to a boil.**

3. **Drain in a colander and rinse under cold running water.**

TIP

If you're using *narenj* (bitter oranges) repeat this step 5 times, because the rind is quite bitter.

Blanching a good supply of orange peel saves time. Store in small 1-cup portions in resealable bags in the freezer up to 3 months, using as needed.

Seeding and Juicing Pomegranates

Pomegranates have been part of Persian cooking since ancient times. Iranians love to use fruit in their cooking — in fact, the concept of sweet-and-sour was a known specialty of Persian cooking by the ancient Greeks.

A bowl of pomegranate *arils* (the red seeds inside a pomegranate) makes a wonderful dessert on its own with a little salt and *golpar* (Persian hogweed); with a thick yogurt or labneh; or with saffron ice cream. The arils are also essential for garnishing the beloved Chicken, Walnut, and Pomegranate Braise (Khoresh-e Fesenjoon; see Chapter 13).

Seeding a pomegranate

To seed a pomegranate, follow these steps (see Figure 4-5):

1. **With a sharp paring knife, slice off the crown.**

2. **Make a superficial spiral cut in the skin around the pomegranate.**

3. **Press both thumbs into the open crown and pull the fruit apart.**

4. **Hold each half, one at a time, seed-side down, over a bowl and tap the skin with a heavy wooden spoon to dislodge the arils from the membrane that holds them.**

   The arils will fall through your fingers into the bowl. Some of the membrane may get into the bowl. Be sure to pick over the seeds and remove the white membrane.

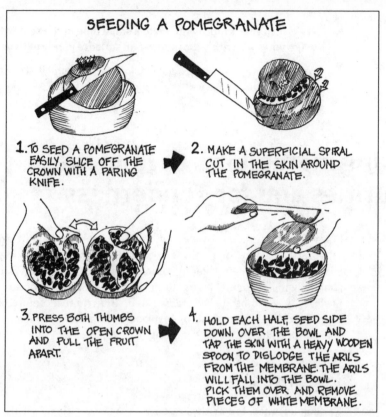

FIGURE 4-5:
Seeding a
pomegranate.

Illustration by Elizabeth Kurtzman

Juicing a pomegranate

This was one of my favorite ways to juice a pomegranate in its skin during my childhood in Iran:

1. **Choose a good-looking pomegranate with no blemishes or holes in the skin.**

2. **Hold the pomegranate in both hands with one thumb over the other.**

3. **Gently squeeze one of the raised parts of the fruit (there are usually four or five hills and valleys).**

   The idea is to squeeze the seeds inside the skin without bursting the skin. Do this gently and systematically, going around the pomegranate until the whole fruit is soft and squishy.

4. **Press it to your mouth and make a small hole in the skin with your teeth while you suck with your mouth and squeeze gently with your hands.**

   You'll get a very refreshing burst of juice in your mouth that's both delicious and sensual. Continue working around the fruit, squeezing and sucking, until you've drunk all the juice.

Soaking Ingredients to Remove Impurities and for Tenderness

Many dried ingredients used in Persian cooking benefit from soaking and rehydrating before using in a recipe. For example, soaking legumes before cooking reduces their cooking time and makes them easier to digest. Persian shallots which can only be found in the United States as dried shallots in Iranian markets, need to be soaked, rehydrated, and trimmed before using. When using large quantities of dried herbs instead of fresh herbs, I recommend that they be soaked for a short time before using.

Legumes

To soak legumes, follow these steps:

1. **Add the legumes to a large bowl, and fill with water.**

   There should be about three times as much water as legumes (the water should be about 2 inches above the legumes in the bowl).

2. **Soak overnight or up to 24 hours.**

3. **Drain and rinse thoroughly before cooking.**

For chickpeas, I also add ½ teaspoon baking soda and ½ teaspoon salt to the water for soaking. This tenderizes them, gives them texture, and makes them cook more quickly. Some people add salt as well, making it a baking soda brine.

Persian shallots

I think of *musir* (Persian shallots; see Figure 4-6) a bit like truffles. They grow wild in the foothills of the Zagros Mountains and have to be found and dug out of the earth by dedicated artisans. They're especially delicious when mixed with yogurt. They taste like a cross between elephant garlic and regular shallots. Dried

Persian shallots are available in Persian markets, and they're well worth the effort it might take to find them.

FIGURE 4-6:
Persian shallots.

To use dried Persian shallots, follow these steps:

1. **Add the dried shallots to a large bowl, and fill with water.**

   There should be about three times as much water as shallots (the water should be about 2 inches above the shallots in the bowl).

2. **Soak for 4 to 24 hours in the refrigerator.**

3. **Drain, rinse in cold water, and pat dry.**

4. **Inspect the soaked shallots, cutting off any stems that remain hard after soaking, and chop finely before using.**

TIP

I like to store my chopped shallots in an airtight glass container and freeze them up to 3 weeks. That way, I have them ready to use whenever I want to mix them with yogurt.

Dried herbs

I like to use fresh herbs whenever possible, but sometimes fresh herbs aren't available and I need to use dried herbs. When using dried herbs, use one-third of the required fresh measure.

TIP

If you're using more than 3 tablespoons of dried herbs in a recipe, place the dried herbs in a sieve and immerse it in a bowl of cold water. Allow to soak for 20 minutes. Then lift the sieve and shake it to drain thoroughly before using it in the recipe.

Dried Persian limes

Dried Persian limes add a very distinctive, earthy, tangy taste to a dish that's quite different from fresh limes. They're becoming more and more popular as an ingredient in the United States and can be found in Persian and Middle Eastern markets.

To use dried Persian limes, start by piercing the limes with the point of a knife in several places and soaking in a cup of cold water for 30 minutes. Don't drain — use the limes and their juice. This soaking method helps to soften the limes and reduce cooking time.

To make ground hearts of dried Persian lime, follow these steps (see Figure 4-7):

1. **With a knife, crack open the limes, halve them, and remove any seeds.**

2. **Grind the dried limes to a powder in a spice grinder and store in an airtight jar.**

In some Persian markets, you can find hearts of dried lime so you don't have to make them yourself.

TIP

HOW TO MAKE GROUND HEARTS OF PERSIAN LIME

1. DRIED PERSIAN LIME.

2. CUT IN HALF

3. DISCARD THE SEEDS AND REMOVE THE HEARTS.

4. GRIND THE HEARTS TO A POWDER.

FIGURE 4-7: How to make ground hearts of Persian lime.

Illustration by Elizabeth Kurtzman

Making Kabobs Sizzle

Since the discovery of fire, cooks have known that meats are imbued with a wonderful flavor when grilled over an open flame. The Persian word for grilled meat, *kabab*, has entered the West's culinary vocabulary.

Kabobs, convenient and virtually foolproof, are very popular. The meat is marinated, covered, and kept in the refrigerator until it's ready to cook. Then, when it's nearly time to eat, the meat is threaded onto metal skewers (traditionally, a small piece of lamb-tail fat is placed between every two pieces of meat) and cooked over glowing charcoals for a subtly perfumed flavor. Kabobs are best when marinated for at least 24 hours and up to 3 days before grilling.

There are also some versions of kabobs cooked in pans and called *panned kabobs.*

Kabobs are best eaten hot off the grill; they suffer if kept warm for any length of time after they're done. When you make a meal that involves kabobs, be sure everything else for serving is ready before grilling the kabobs.

The method for preparing and cooking kabobs differs from traditional American barbecuing. Long, flat metal (preferably stainless steel) sword-like skewers are used. Different widths are used for different types of kabobs. For best results, ground meat kabobs should not be cooked on the grill surface; instead, they should straddle the coals and be supported at either end by the grill edges or bricks.

Start a bed of charcoal at least 30 minutes before you want to cook and let it burn until the coals glow. When the coals are ready, arrange the skewers of meat on the grill. The skewers should be turned frequently and gently and the meat brushed with the baste mixture of butter, lime juice, salt, and saffron just before removing from the grill. The kabob is cooked just long enough to be seared on the outside and juicy on the inside.

REMEMBER

The secret to a good kabob is a very hot fire.

To serve the kabob, begin by spreading lavash or flatbread on a serving platter. Place the kabob on the bread and brush it again with the remaining baste. Cover with another piece of lavash bread to keep it warm. Keep the kabobs on the skewers until just before serving to keep them warm. Remove the meat from each skewer by placing a piece of lavash bread over the meat to hold down the meat while you pull off the skewers.

Kabobs require a marinade to make the meat moist, tender, and delicious. Most Persian marinades contain salt, pepper, turmeric, onion, garlic, fat, and some kind of souring agent (such as lime juice, sour orange, vinegar, pomegranate molasses, or juice, dried lime powder, sumac powder, or tomato juice). These souring agents are used to tenderize meats. I like to marinate chicken for kabobs for at least 24 hours and up to 3 days to make the chicken flavorful and tender. I use turmeric for all kabobs to elevate the taste. I use ground saffron diluted in rose water to add another dimension to the taste and create a heavenly flavor. To balance the marinade, I use a combination of oil, yogurt, or buttermilk with a souring agent such as lime, sour orange, pomegranate, tamarind, or vinegar.

There is another type of marinade, a specialty in northern Iran, that uses herbs, walnuts, and pomegranate juice. This sweet-and-sour marinade is my favorite.

Here's an overview of what you need to make a good Persian marinade for kabobs (I give you specific ingredients and measurements in the recipes in Chapter 14).

1. Choose a large, nonreactive container, preferably one with a cover.

2. Add spices such as salt, pepper, turmeric, and saffron to add color and flavor.

3. Add sour agents to tenderize.

4. Add oil, whole plain yogurt, or buttermilk to moisturize.

5. Stir so that the ingredients are well combined and adjust the seasoning to your taste before adding the meat.

6. Rinse the meat thoroughly with cold water, pat it dry, add it to your marinade, and toss well; cover tightly and refrigerate.

7. Turn the meat twice while it's marinating.

Discard the marinade after use.

Smoking Vegetables

Smoking vegetables is one of the secrets of many Persian dishes, and it helps to know how to do it easily. In this section, I walk you through how to smoke eggplants and butternut squash.

Eggplants

To smoke eggplants, follow these steps:

1. Over the flame of a charcoal grill or a gas cooktop, smoke the eggplants on all sides until the skin is burned and completely blackened, turning frequently, about 3 to 5 minutes.

2. Transfer the eggplants to a rack on a rimmed sheet pan and make a slit in the eggplants to allow any bitter juice to drain.

3. Transfer the eggplants to a cutting board and leave until cool enough to handle.

4. Cut off the crowns.

5. Use your hands or a dish towel to remove and discard the skins, and finely chop the eggplants to use in the recipe.

Here's another method that takes longer but needs less attention:

1. Preheat the oven to 450 degrees.

2. Prick the eggplants in several places with a fork to prevent them from bursting during cooking.

3. Place the eggplants on a rack in a rimmed sheet pan and smoke in the oven for 50 minutes.

4. Remove from the oven and make vertical slits in the eggplants to allow any bitter juices to drain.

5. When cool enough to handle, use your hands or a dish towel to remove and discard the skins.

6. Transfer to a cutting board and finely chop.

Butternut squash

To smoke butternut squash, follow these steps:

1. Preheat the oven to 450 degrees.

2. Cut the butternut squash in half lengthwise and scoop out the seeds with a spoon.

3. Brush a rack with 1 tablespoon oil and place it in a rimmed sheet pan.

4. Arrange the butternut squash halves, face side up, on the rack.

5. Brush the tops of the squash with another tablespoon of oil.

6. Bake in the oven for 1 hour.

7. Remove the squash from the oven and leave until cool enough to handle.

8. Scoop the flesh out of the skin to use in a recipe.

Making and Using Ghee

A staple in Persian, Indian, Afghan, and Uzbek kitchens, *ghee* (clarified butter) gives a delicious nutty taste to rice and pastries and has a higher scorching point than regular butter. It's sold in specialty food stores, but you can easily make it at home. Just follow these steps:

1. In a small saucepan, add 1 pound of unsalted butter and melt over low heat.

2. Let it simmer until most of the bubbling and foam that forms subsides.

3. Turn off the heat and let it cool in the pan for 5 minutes.

4. Drain the liquid through one layer of muslin or three layers of cheesecloth to separate the clear butter fat from the milk solids that you can discard.

5. Store in an airtight glass container in the refrigerator up to 6 months.

Making Panir

Panir is a soft fresh cheese made by curdling goat, sheep, or cow milk. It's most commonly eaten for breakfast in Iran, with hot bread and sweet black tea. Cheese, bread, and tea are a meal for many Iranians facing food insecurity.

To make *panir*, follow these steps:

1. Line a strainer with three layers of cheesecloth and place it in a large container.

2. In a large saucepan, add 8 cups of plain whole milk and bring to a boil over high heat.

3. Add ½ cup fresh lime juice and 1 tablespoon fine sea salt and stir once.

4. **Reduce the heat to medium and boil until the milk's color turns yellowish and curds appear, about 3 to 5 minutes.**

5. **Remove the pan from the heat and allow to sit for 15 minutes.**

6. **If you like, add 1 teaspoon dried thyme and 1 teaspoon nigella seeds.**

7. **Immediately pour the milk mixture into the cheesecloth; allow it to drain for several minutes.**

   Hold the ends of the cheesecloth; bundle and tightly tie together to enclose the cheese. Save the liquid in the container for later use.

8. **Place the cheese bundle in the center of the strainer and place a heavy weight on top of the bundle; allow to stand for about 2 hours to get rid of excess liquid and to set.**

9. **Remove the cheese from the cheesecloth.**

   It's ready to use at this stage.

10. **Serve the cheese with bread and a fresh herb platter.**

You can use the whey to store the cheese in; any excess can be discarded.

To store, place the cheese in an airtight glass container. Add about 1 cup of the strained liquid/whey from Step 7. Cover tightly and refrigerate until ready to serve. You can keep it for up to a week in the fridge.

Making and Thickening Yogurt

Yogurt is one of the older foods known to mankind. Regional records of ancient civilizations from Egypt to Iran refer to the healthful properties of yogurt. The word yogurt comes from *jaghurat* — from central Asian Sogdian, a branch language of old Persian. The word *jaghurat* is still used in parts of Iran to refer to yogurt.

Making yogurt

To make *mast* (yogurt), follow these steps:

1. **In a nonreactive pot, add 4 cups of whole milk and bring to a boil over medium heat.**

   Dirty or greasy utensils won't produce the desired results, so make sure your pot is as clean as possible before you start.

WARNING

2. **Remove the milk from heat and let stand until cool but not completely cold.**

   The temperature of the milk is very important at this stage. It should not be too cold or too hot. If the milk is too cool, the culture will not grow; if it's too warm, the heat will kill the bacteria in the culture. If you're using a thermometer, the temperature should be 115 degrees. (With some experience, you can test by hand: Just put your little finger in the milk and count to ten. The temperature is correct if you can just tolerate the heat.)

3. **Pour the milk into a glass baking dish, large enough for 8 cups of milk.**

4. **Pull out the rack in the center shelf of the oven and place the dish on it.**

5. **Add ½ cup plain whole yogurt to the milk in the four corners of the dish.**

6. **Gently push the rack back inside the oven (avoid shaking the milk), close the oven door, and turn on the oven light. Do not heat the oven.**

7. **Allow to rest, uncovered and undisturbed, for at least 48 hours.**

TIP

   Yogurt must be stored in a draft-free, protected spot and must not be moved or touched during this period, and the oven is the ideal place for this. As an alternative, cover tightly with plastic wrap, wrap the entire the dish with a large towel or blanket, and let it rest undisturbed in a corner of your kitchen for at least 48 hours.

Store the yogurt in the refrigerator, covered with a layer of parchment paper and then plastic wrap, and use as needed.

Here are some variations on the preceding recipe:

>> **Creamy yogurt:** In Step 1, replace 1 cup of the milk with 1 cup heavy cream.

>> **Sweet yogurt:** Add 1 cup of sugar to the milk in Step 1.

Thickening store-bought yogurt

Ready-made, store-bought yogurt can be drained and thickened. To drain and thicken yogurt, which is what I use for all yogurt-based salads and spreads, follow these steps:

1. **Place 3 layers of cheesecloth on top of a sieve over a container.**

2. **Pour the yogurt onto the cheesecloth, pull the ends together, and then hang the bag for 2 to 3 hours over a large pot to catch the yogurt drips.**

Alternatively use a yogurt funnel. All the liquid will slowly drain out, leaving behind a thick and creamy yogurt.

TIP

Thick yogurt is available in supermarkets under the name *labneh*. Labneh, which is often mislabeled as cheese, is also available in Persian markets, where they have the Persian variety as well, called *mast-e mast-e khiky* or *chekideh*.

Making kashk

Kashk is cooked and dried fermented yogurt used in cooking as a liquid. Traditionally, for convenience of storage, it was formed into balls or patties and sun-dried; these balls or patties would then be diluted as needed and used for cooking (see Figure 4-8).

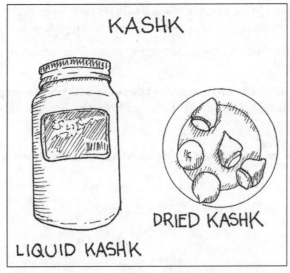

FIGURE 4-8:
Kashk.

Illustration by Elizabeth Kurtzman.

To use solid *kashk* balls, follow these steps:

1. **In a small bowl, place 1 cup solid *kashk* and ½ cup boiling water, cover, and allow to soak for at least 4 hours.**

2. **Transfer to a blender or food processor and mix until smooth and creamy.**

3. **Use immediately or transfer to an airtight glass container and store in the refrigerator for up to 3 days.**

These days, you can buy liquid *kashk* from Persian grocery stores, but you can also make it at home. To make *kashk*, follow these steps:

1. **In a blender, add 4 cups drained plain whole yogurt, 4 cups water, ¼ cup fresh lime juice, and ¼ cup fine sea salt. Blend on low for 5 minutes.**

2. **Transfer to a large saucepan and bring to a boil, stirring constantly, until foam rises to the surface, about 5 minutes.**

3. **Reduce the heat to medium and continue to boil, stirring frequently, until it thickens, about 1 to 1½ hours.**

4. **Remove from the heat and allow to cool.**

   At this stage, you have liquid *kashk,* which you can store in an airtight container in the refrigerator for up to 4 weeks.

5. **If you want solid *kashk,* place 4 layers of cheesecloth over a sieve in a bowl, pour in the *kashk,* and allow to drain for 20 minutes. Then bundle in the cheesecloth and squeeze out any extra liquid.**

   The *kashk* inside the cheesecloth should have the consistency of a soft dough that you can shape.

6. **Shape into balls, place on a sheet pan lined with parchment paper, and allow to dry in the sun or place in the oven with only the light on.**

   It takes about 3 days to dry completely.

7. **Store in an airtight glass container in the refrigerator for 4 to 8 weeks.**

Chapter 5

Using Staple Ingredients in Persian Dishes

I want you to personalize my recipes to your taste, while keeping in mind the philosophy behind the ingredients, to create a balanced, deeply flavored dish.

In this chapter, I cover the important role of adjusting the seasoning before serving a dish. I also introduce you to the five basic tastes that are used to balance the flavors of a dish. Finally, I offer a list of ingredients that you may not be familiar with but that are often used in Persian cooking.

Adjusting Seasoning to Taste

One of the philosophies behind Persian cooking is that food is classified as *garmi* (hot) and *sardi* (cold), but this has nothing to do with the temperature or spiciness of the food. *Garmi* ingredients are thought to "thicken" the blood and speed the metabolism; *sardi* ingredients "dilute" the blood and slow the metabolism. For example, walnut (which is *garmi*) and pomegranate (which is *sardi*) are a match made in heaven, which is why Chicken, Walnut, and Pomegranate Braise (Khoresh-e Fesenjoon; see Chapter 13) is one of the most cherished braises in Persian cooking.

Certain spices are combined with certain ingredients to help the digestion and balance the dish. For example, cumin (which is *garmi*) is always added to chickpeas (which are *sardi*) to help the digestion. With practice and experience, you'll get the hang of the properties of each ingredient and will be able to personalize your recipes while making a balanced dish.

REMEMBER

Be sure to measure spices and seasonings accurately according to the recipe, and go for scant measures rather than generous measures — you can always add more salt or spices, but you won't be able to take them away. This is especially true for the sea salt I use in this book. If you use another kind of salt (such as basic table salt), you'll need to use less of it.

TIP

Don't forget to taste your dish just before serving and adjust the seasoning to your taste.

Understanding the Five Basic Tastes

In Persian cooking, the five basic tastes are used to balance the flavors and nutrition properties of a dish. These are the five basic tastes:

>> **Saltiness:** I generally cook with fine sea salt. If you're using coarse salt, you may need to add more because there are fewer grains in a given measure; on the other hand, Morton Iodized Salt tends to be saltier, so you'll need less. Adding more or less salt is up to you, but rice dishes in particular need the minimum recommended amount for both taste and texture. For finishing a dish just before serving, or for adding texture (to kabobs, for example), I recommend a good-quality coarse sea salt, such as *fleur de sel* or Maldon Sea Salt Flakes.

>> **Sourness:** Ingredients with a sour taste profile appear in many recipes in this book, so you should know the distinct flavor that each of these ingredients give to your dish. Ingredients that add various sour notes to your dish include the following:

- Barberries
- Bitter oranges
- Grapes (unripe)
- Limes (fresh and dried)
- Pomegranate molasses
- Sumac powder

- Tamarind

- *Verjuice* (unripe grape juice)

- Vinegar

TIP

When combined with sweet notes from date molasses, grape molasses, honey, or sugar, you get the perfect sweet-and-sour flavor that's one of the most cherished signatures of Persian cooking.

» **Sweetness:** Ancient Persians used grape or date molasses, or honey, as a sweetener. In my recipes, I am doing the same whenever possible. Try them instead of sugar! They will add a subtle flavor and sweetness to your dishes.

» **Bitterness:** Our taste buds are very sensitive to bitterness, and a lot of it will be undesirable, but a little bit is pleasurable. A good example is the use of lime zest or orange peel.

» **Umami:** *Umami* is a Japanese word meaning "pleasant, savory taste." It's one of the characteristics of Persian cooking in soups, braises, and cooked meats.

Digging into Common Ingredients in Persian Cooking

This section covers ingredients that are often used in Persian cooking. You may not be familiar with some of them, but give them a try — I bet you'll love them! And before long, you'll find the "exotic" has become familiar.

Barberries

Barberries add a distinctive tart flavor to rice dishes, braises, fish, and chicken. As a garnish, they add a wonderful sparkle to any dish. I caramelize barberries to add another taste dimension.

TIP

Look for dried barberries that are red in color and not brown — the brown ones are probably from a previous season. Be sure to clean them by removing any sharp stems, soak in cold water, rinse, and dry thoroughly before using. For more information on cooking with barberries, including how to clean them, turn to Chapter 4.

Bitter oranges

Bitter oranges (also called sour oranges, wild oranges, or Seville oranges) are what oranges were like before they were first domesticated and cultivated in China thousands of years ago to become the sweet orange that we know today. Bitter oranges have a uniquely tart flavor, with undertones of bitterness. Squeeze some over your fish — you'll love it!

You can find bitter oranges in Persian markets from late autumn to spring.

Date molasses

Date molasses is made by boiling dates in water to the consistency of a syrup and then straining it to use as a sweetener. It's used instead of sugar in many Persian dishes. You can drizzle date molasses over rice pudding or ice cream like chocolate syrup, or spread it over bread like honey.

High-quality date molasses (sometimes called date syrup) is made in California and readily available not only in Persian markets but also in many supermarkets these days.

Dried fruits

Dried fruits and berries such as apricots, barberries, sour or tart cherries, dates, and prunes are used often in Persian cooking to enhance the flavor and add texture. You can find them in rice dishes, braises, and casseroles. They also help to create a perfect balance of sweet-and-sour flavors.

Garlic

Choose garlic bulbs that are whole, firm, and without blemishes. To prepare garlic you need to first break up the bulb into cloves and peel them by cutting off the top and bottom parts of the clove. Then dry them thoroughly with a dish towel and store them in a covered glass container in the fridge. That way, whenever the recipe calls for garlic, you can just grate, mince, or slice them.

Don't worry if there are some green shoots in your garlic — they're edible.

You can also peel and mince a batch of garlic and keep it, covered in olive oil, in an airtight glass container for in the refrigerator for up to three weeks.

Ginger

Choose firm ginger with a shiny skin — the wrinkled ones tend to be old. Use a paring knife or a teaspoon to scrape off the skin. Then place the peeled ginger in an airtight glass container and freeze them. When a recipe calls for ginger, you can take some out of the freezer and grate it while it's still frozen.

TIP

It's much easier to grate ginger while it's still frozen. Soft ginger doesn't grate well.

Grape molasses

Grape molasses is reduced grape juice. Reducing was an ancient way of preserving the juice as a sweetener. Having a bottle of grape molasses in your kitchen isn't essential, but it can give your dishes another dimension of flavor.

Grapes (unripe)

Baby, unripe grapes are in season from March to July and available from Iranian grocery stores in the United States (you can also find both frozen and jarred ones there or on the Internet). When they're combined with tomato, eggplant, and saffron in a braise, the combination creates a depth of flavor and umami.

Herbs (fresh or dried)

Use fresh herbs when in season. Sometimes, when a recipe calls for a lot of sautéed herbs — such as in the Lamb with Herbs and Dried Lime Braise (Khoresh-e Qormeh Sabzi; see Chapter 13) — which can be quite labor-intensive, you can use dried herbs. In Persian grocery stores, you can also find dried or frozen herbs specifically prepared for making this dish.

If you don't have fresh herbs, you can use dried herbs. Some dried herbs (such as mint or fenugreek leaves) are even better because they can be more potent and flavorful when dried. When making pickles, dried herbs are more convenient to use because there will be no trace of water in them, which can cause pickles to spoil.

REMEMBER

Except when using dried herbs for pickles (which are used dry), if a recipe calls for large amounts of herbs, and you want to use dried herbs, you have to soak them first (see Chapter 4).

Limes (fresh and dried)

In this book, I call for fresh limes, because I prefer them to the taste of lemons in cooking (limes are slightly more sour with a hint of bitterness). In addition, I use dried limes in many recipes — whole (pierced) or ground. If you can find them, the ground hearts of dried lime are best.

Onions

Onions are a major contributor to the flavor of Persian dishes. I like to use small yellow onions so when they're thinly sliced and cooked, they don't create long strands. In Persian cooking, onions are either caramelized over medium heat or deep fried. Caramelizing onions releases the sugars and gives an added depth of flavor and umami to your dish.

Adding deep-fried crispy onions gives another layer of texture and flavor to a dish. I make large amounts of crispy fried onions once a week and store them in an air-tight glass container in the refrigerator to use as needed. They're a wonderful garnish when added just before serving to rice dishes and braises, as well as to the fillings of your meatballs.

TIP

For tips on caramelizing onions, as well as deep-frying onions, turn to Chapter 4.

Pomegranate molasses

Pomegranate molasses is reduced pomegranate juice. Reducing is an ancient method of creating and preserving the juice as a souring agent. Pomegranate juice has a specific sourness that isn't too sour, and when mixed with some grape molasses, it balances the dish and gives it a fabulous flavor.

Sumac

Sumac has a distinctive lemony taste. The berries are crushed and used as a condiment, mostly on kabobs, but also on soups, meatballs, and especially as a rub combined with lime on fish.

Tamarind

Tamarind paste is a wonderful souring agent that gives a distinctive fruity flavor to your dish, especially when combined with fish, plenty of sautéed garlic (which is *garmi*), and cilantro (which is *sardi*). (See "Adjusting Seasoning to Taste," earlier in this chapter, for more on *garmi* and *sardi*.) I use the Golchin brand of tamarind paste, which is available in Persian markets.

Tomatoes (fresh, canned, or paste)

I prefer to use fresh tomatoes in season because they're tastier and more nutritious. If I can't find ripe fresh tomatoes, I like using good-quality canned tomatoes because they're canned at the height of their freshness. For tomato paste, I use the kind in tubes because they're easier to use and less wasteful.

TIP

Frying tomato paste in oil makes it bloom, giving a deep flavor to the dish.

Vinegar

I use mostly apple cider vinegar or wine vinegar when cooking. Many Persian dishes call for vinegar to create a sweet-and-sour balance. I also recommend using a splash of distilled vinegar in a container of water when soaking herbs. (Vinegar is also a great natural cleaner for your kitchen surfaces.)

Verjuice

Verjuice is unripe grape juice. It's a souring agent used in some Persian recipes. You can buy it in bottles at Persian or Middle Eastern markets and gourmet markets, as well as online.

» **Making Persian spice mix from scratch**

» **Using Persian hogweed in your cooking**

» **Preparing spices by grinding or toasting them**

Chapter 6

Delicately Spicing the Persian Way

I n most parts of Iran, dishes are spiced with a delicate touch to bring out the best of a dish's flavor and keep the integrity of the ingredients. In southern Iran, however, by the Persian Gulf, dishes tend to be more spiced and hotter, using plenty of red pepper flakes. I'm enjoying these dishes more and more these days!

In this chapter, I walk you through how to use spices — from saffron to *advieh* (Persian spice mix) and more. I also explain how to grind and toast spices.

Blooming Saffron

Saffron is made from the dried orange stigmas of the purple crocus. Iran produces the best saffron because of the climate and soil where it's grown.

I like to use saffron in my cooking, and many of the recipes in this book call for it. First things first: When you're shopping for saffron, buy saffron threads (see Figure 6-1), not powdered saffron. Powered saffron is often mixed with ground turmeric, and what you want is the pure stuff. I keep packaged saffron threads in the freezer; this helps it keep its aroma and quality for years.

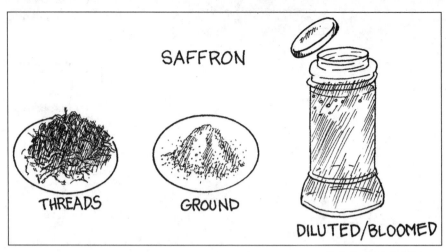

FIGURE 6-1:
Saffron.

SAFFRON

THREADS

GROUND

DILUTED/BLOOMED

Illustration by Elizabeth Kurtzman

When you're ready to use saffron in a recipe, you can't just throw saffron threads into the mixing bowl with the other ingredients. Saffron should be bloomed first. Blooming helps to create more color and aroma. I bloom my saffron by first grinding the saffron threads. Follow these steps:

1. **Using a mortar and pestle or a spice grinder, grind 4 or 5 grams of the threads into a powder with 1 sugar cube.**

   The sugar absorbs the moisture and helps create a fine powder.

   TIP

   In the recipes in this book, I tell you exactly how much powder to use and how much liquid to dissolve it in, so if you want to just stop here, you can store this saffron powder in an airtight glass jar in the fridge for at least a year, and use it when you're ready to cook with it.

2. **To bloom the saffron, in a small airtight glass container, dissolve 1 teaspoon of saffron powder in ½ cup of hot water or ice water.**

   For even more flavor, you can use rose water or orange blossom water instead.

3. **Cover tightly and store in the fridge for up to 3 weeks, using as needed.**

Making Your Own Advieh (Persian Spice Mix)

In Persian, *advieh* refers both to spice in general and to a spice mix that Iranians either make themselves or buy ready-made.

Most Persian soups, braises, and rices are seasoned with salt, pepper, and turmeric. Bloomed saffron is then often added to the finished dish. However, in every region of Iran, they have their own *advieh* and some families even have their own versions of the mix.

After 40 years of cooking Persian food, traveling throughout Iran, and cooking with cooks of various regions, I've come to the conclusion that spices such as cardamom, cinnamon, and cumin are the common denominator of the spice mixes of all the regions of Iran. As a result, I developed my own *advieh* made with five ingredients: cardamom, cinnamon, cumin, *golpar* (Persian hogweed), and rose petals. You can make your own *advieh* using the following recipe, or you can use a ready-made *advieh* — they're available at Persian markets, and my own *advieh* is available at `https://persianbasket.com/advieh-najmieh-batmanglij-s-persian-spice-mix.html`.

Adding 1 teaspoon of *advieh* to your dish creates balance and depth of flavor. When you gain confidence, you can adjust by adding more or less, to your taste.

Najmieh's Advieh

PREP TIME: ABOUT 5 MIN	COOK TIME: NONE	YIELD: ½ CUP

INGREDIENTS

2 tablespoons cardamom pods

2 tablespoons cumin seeds

Two 3-inch cinnamon sticks, crushed

1 tablespoon ground *golpar* (Persian hogweed)

2 tablespoons dried rose petals

DIRECTIONS

1 Using a spice grinder or mortar and pestle, grind each of the spices to a powder, separately, transferring them to a small mixing bowl after they're ground.

2 When all the spices have been ground and added to the bowl, mix well.

3 Store in an airtight glass container in a cool, dark place for up to 3 months to preserve freshness, and use as needed.

Cooking with Persian Hogweed

Golpar (Persian hogweed) is native to Iran and gives a delightful aroma and a zesty, earthy, tangy flavor, especially when added to dishes that have pomegranate in them. I also love to use *golpar,* mixed with salt, pepper, turmeric, and saffron, as a spice rub for fish.

TIP

The powdered seeds are sold at Iranian markets and online (including at Amazon), but they're often mislabeled *angelica* or *marjoram,* so it's best to search for *golpar* to make sure you get the right ingredient.

Figure 6-2 shows the plant, the dried seeds, and the ground powder for use in cooking.

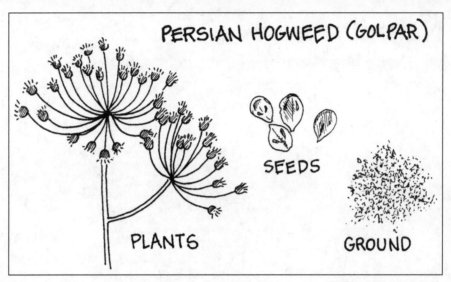

FIGURE 6-2:
Golpar.

Illustration by Elizabeth Kurtzman

Grinding and Toasting Spices

In Persian cooking, spices are generally ground and then sautéed with the rest of the ingredients in the pan (as opposed to toasting them before grinding them). Freshly grinding spices makes them more aromatic.

Whole spices such as coriander and cumin *are* toasted if they're being added to rice or pickles. If you need to toast whole spices, follow these steps:

1. **In a wide skillet, add the whole spice seeds.**

2. **Toast over medium-high heat, shaking the pan constantly, for 2 to 3 minutes, until the color slightly darkens and the aroma rises.**

3. **Remove from heat and set aside. Use right away or store in an airtight glass container in the fridge for up to 3 weeks.**

Chapter **7**

Bringing It All Together in a Persian Meal

I f you've only ever eaten Persian food in restaurants, you're probably thinking of one word: *kabobs.* But kabobs are only a small sample of what Persians eat at home. Most Persian dishes aren't actually prepared in restaurants because their menus have to be quite limited — they're trying to please as many customers as possible. Plus, restaurants make food in large quantities, which means they can't pay enough attention to the quality of the ingredients and the preparation of the food the way you can at home. Bottom line: If you want to experience the joys of Persian food, prepare it in your own kitchen!

In this chapter, I introduce you to the way Persians eat at home. I show you how to create a Persian meal full of color, texture, and flavor that will intrigue the palate. Taste is what your tongue tells you about saltiness, sourness, sweetness, bitterness, and umami (see Chapter 5). Flavor comes from aroma and texture. When taste and flavor are *combined,* they give your palate a great deal of pleasure! Creating this sensation is what Persian food is all about.

Sampling Several Persian Menus, for Every Occasion

Whether you're just trying to figure out what to make for dinner on a weeknight or you're preparing a meal for guests, you can find sample menus in this section.

TIP

When you're planning a Persian menu, keep in mind that each dish can be served at different temperatures. For example, a soup, braise, rice, or kabob must always be served hot. On the other hand, meatballs, egg *kukus*, patties, and stuffed vegetables can be served warm or at room temperature, so they can be made in advance.

TIP

When you cook a Persian meal at home, keep in mind the color palate of your menu. Use a platter of herbs for its fresh and green brightness; a rice dish for its white pearl color with flashes of saffron yellow; a parti-colored diced tomato and cucumber salad for its fresh reds and greens; and a yogurt and beet salad for its brightness.

Finally, when you're planning a Persian meal, keep in mind that there is no order of courses. You'll display your various dishes on the table, and everyone will help themselves according to their fancy.

A weeknight dinner

Home-cooked food is something you can eat every day and personalize to your own taste. When you make food at home, do it with love and pass on the good energy through the food. For Persian mothers, cooking a meal for the family is a way to convey their love.

PERSIAN HOSPITALITY

Persian hospitality is famous, and Iranians consider guests to be sacred and dear to God, or God's friend.

Whatever the food, the rules of hospitality says it must be the best the hosts can provide — and it must be given without asking. Generosity and appreciation form a bond between guest and host, and it's the breaking of bread together that seals the bond.

Keep in mind: Good thoughts, good deeds, and good words while you're eating.

When you know the key techniques, you can use the recipes in this book to personalize them according to your family's taste. When you use fresh, high-quality ingredients for making a Persian meal at home, and use the knowledge and confidence that you gain in this book, you'll be able to create a feast every time!

A weeknight Persian menu should include a main course, such as a braise served with plain rice, as well as a platter of fresh herbs, cheese, and bread; salads; and condiments. A Persian meal does not usually have a lettuce salad, but there is always a platter of fresh green herbs.

Side dishes, such as yogurt and Persian shallots and a spicy eggplant and vegetable pickle, not only add color and flavor, but also help the digestion of the meal. Adding a few leaves of basil and a little pickle will enhance the flavor of each bite and make the meal memorable.

REMEMBER

No Persian table is complete without a *sabzi khordan* (fresh herb platter) with good Persian flatbread beside it. A fresh herb platter is not only a great accompaniment to the meal, but also represents *barekat* (blessings). The ingredients vary from region to region and depend on the season. It can include the following:

>> **Fresh herbs:** Basil (ideally Persian basil, which is most suitable for eating raw), cilantro, dill, mint, summer savory, tarragon, and/or watercress

>> **Raw vegetables:** Persian cucumbers, radishes, and/or spring onions

>> **White cheese (sheep or goat)**

>> **Toasted nuts**

>> **Fruit:** Dates, figs, grapes, and/or watermelon

>> **Fresh edible flowers**

TIP

Here's are two sample menus for a weeknight meal for your family:

>> Meal 1

• **Braise:** Green Beans, Tomato, and Chicken Braise (Khoresh-e Lubia Sabz; Chapter 13)

• **Rice:** Plain Rice (Kateh; Chapter 12)

• **Accompaniments:** Fresh herb platter with bread and cheese, Cucumber and Tomato Salad (Salad-e Gojeh Khiar; Chapter 8)

» Meal 2:

- **Soup:** Pomegranate Soup (Osh-e Anar; Chapter 11)

- **Patties:** Meat Patties (Kotlet-e Gusht; Chapter 15)

- **Accompaniment:** Onion, Cucumber, and Coriander Quick Pickle (Torshi Hazeri-e Piaz; Chapter 17)

A party for guests

The key to entertaining the Persian way is preparation and more preparation in advance.

Many Persian dishes can be cooked in advance, which makes them great for entertaining. As the host, you can be calm and spend more time with your guests. Dishes that can be made in advance and served at room temperatures include patties, egg *kukus*, and stuffed vegetables, as well as all the yogurt-based salads. Soups and braises can be cooked in advance and reheated an hour before serving. Even your rice can be prepared in a pot in advance, kept in the refrigerator, and steamed before serving. The fresh herb platter should be assembled the same day as your party. I wash and dry my herbs up to 24 hours before the party and keep them wrapped in paper towels in a resealable plastic bag in the fridge.

TIP

If you're planning a menu to entertain many people, your mind may go to kabobs. But I would avoid making kabobs, unless you have an outdoor grill or you're planning a day of barbecue because kabobs should be served hot off the grill. Plus, I prefer to serve kabobs and rice with all its trimmings on its own; I don't like mixing it with any other main dishes.

CULTURAL
WISDOM

In Iran, there are restaurants called *chelow-kababi* (house of rice and kabob) that do exactly this. These are the most popular restaurants in Iran, where the whole family goes on weekends. I have delicious memories of these occasions. Interestingly, these types of restaurants are also still the most common ones outside Iran.

TIP

An ever-steaming *samovar* (tea urn) is part of entertaining the Persian way. Prepare your tea setting, including teapot, tea glasses, kettle or samovar, and any sweets (such as dates, jujubes, or crystal rock candy that will be served with the tea) so you're ready to serve the tea immediately after the main meal is finished.

TIP

Here's a sample menu for a party, but you can choose any recipes you prefer from these categories (just look in the chapters where these recipes are located, and you'll find similar options). Many people are vegetarian these days, so be sure to have some options for them (or inquire about your guests' dietary restrictions before planning your menu):

>> **Soup:** Barley and Leek Soup (Osh-e Jow; see Chapter 11)

>> **Meatball:** Fava Bean and Dill Meatballs (Kufteh Baqali; see Chapter 15)

>> **Braise:** Chicken, Walnut and Pomegranate Braise (Khoresh-e Fesenjoon; see Chapter 13)

>> **Fish:** Sumac Grilled Fish (Mahi-e Kababi ba Somaq; see Chapter 16)

>> **Rice:** Jeweled Rice (Javaher Polow; see Chapter 12)

>> **Accompaniments:**

  ● Fresh herb platter with bread and cheese

  ● Yogurt and Persian Shallot Salad (Mast-o Musir; see Chapter 8)

  ● Onion, Cucumber and Coriander Quick Pickle (Torshi Hazeri-e Piaz; see Chapter 17)

SETTING THE TABLE

When I'm entertaining, I like to make a few small bouquets from branches of fresh basil, mint, and rosemary, combined with a few stems of small garden flowers, and place them in vases on my table. Lit candles are also a wonderful addition.

Just make sure that flowers or centerpieces aren't so large that people across from each other have to dodge the flowers to see each other.

Set up your table the day before. If possible, I prefer for everyone to be able to sit around one or more tables next to each other.

I like to display all the dishes buffet-style on my kitchen counter and ask everyone to take a plate, serve themselves, and eat around the dining table. I don't like guests to eat their meal sitting on various couches and chairs around the room. Having spent three days preparing and cooking, it's a crying shame not to be able to sit together to enjoy each other's company and the meal! I also like the wonderful tradition of giving thanks before you start to eat, and that's easier to do gathered around a table together.

Jazzing Up the Look of Your Dishes

Imaginative decorations will make any dish more appetizing. In Persian cooking, feasting the eyes is as important as filling the stomach. It's especially important with braises, which often have a brownish color and need a garnish to give them color and a fresh look. A little mint garnish, crispy fried onions, and a dollop of *kashk* (fermented sun-dried yogurt) will not only make the dish look good, but also add umami (see Chapter 5).

TIP

Here are some ways to make your dishes more appealing:

» **To add a fresh, festive look (as well as mouthwatering flavor):**

- Pomegranate *arils* (seeds) and caramelized barberries (see Chapter 4)

- Edible flowers, such as rose petals or blossoms and orange blossoms

- Leaves of fresh herbs, such as basil, cilantro, and mint

- Radish slices

- A slice of lime or roasted tomato

» **To add crunch (as well as flavor):**

- Toasted slivered almonds, pistachios, or walnuts

- Dried fruits, such as dates, caramelized orange peel, or raisins

» **To add color, flavor, and aroma:** Bloomed saffron and a drizzle of brown butter over rice

3

Appetizers and First Courses

Chapter 8

Healthy Yogurt Vegetable Dishes, Salads, and Sides

Hospitality is the soul of Persian cooking, and its symbol is appetizers. Iranian homes always have many of them, so whoever drops in will feel welcomed by abundance. A Persian first course — like its descendants, the *mezze* of Turkey, the *mezedes* of Greece, or the *tapas* of Spain — consists of a variety of little dishes that people help themselves to, according to their fancy. In traditional houses, these dishes are arranged on a *sofreh* (a cotton cloth embroidered with poems or prayers), which is spread over the carpet or table. There is no particular order when it comes to what you might eat or when. The general idea is to make the presentation inviting, pretty, and refreshing to the palate. Appetizers balance the dishes that make up the rest of a meal.

This chapter has a number of refreshing yogurt-based dishes, as well as spreads and various vegan and vegetarian salads made from a range of ingredients — from chickpeas, carrots, and spinach, to eggplants, beets, and even butternut squash.

TIP

Later chapters in this book cover egg-based *kukus* (see Chapter 9), stuffed vegetables (Chapter 10), and meatballs (Chapter 15), all of which can also be served as side dishes.

Yogurt, Cucumber, and Rose Petal Salad (Mast-o Khiar)

PREP TIME: 15 MIN	COOK TIME: NONE	YIELD: 6 SERVINGS

INGREDIENTS

3 Persian cucumbers or 1 long seedless cucumber, peeled and grated

3 cups thick, plain whole yogurt or labneh

2 spring onions, chopped (white and green parts)

2 tablespoons chopped fresh mint or 1 teaspoon dried mint

2 tablespoons chopped fresh dill weed

2 tablespoons chopped fresh tarragon or 2 teaspoons dried tarragon

1 clove garlic, peeled and grated

1 teaspoon fine sea salt

1 teaspoon freshly ground black pepper

3 tablespoons coarsely chopped walnuts

¼ cup seedless raisins, for garnish

Sprigs of fresh dill weed, for garnish

1 tablespoon dried rose petals, for garnish

1 radish, diced, for garnish

DIRECTIONS

1 In a large bowl, combine the cucumber, yogurt or labneh, onions, mint, dill weed, tarragon, garlic, salt, pepper, and walnuts. Mix thoroughly, and adjust the seasoning to taste.

2 Just before serving, mix in the raisins, dill weed, rose petals, and radish. Serve with toasted bread or as a side dish. *Nush-e joon!*

PER SERVING: *Calories 131 (From Fat 66); Fat 7g (Saturated 3g); Cholesterol 16mg; Sodium 371mg; Carbohydrate 12g (Dietary Fiber 1g); Protein 5g.*

VARY IT! In the summer, this yogurt salad can be transformed into a wonderfully refreshing cold soup by adding 1 cup cold water and 2 or 3 ice cubes. Add more salt and pepper to taste. You can also crumble toasted bread or croutons into the soup just before serving. My husband increases the amount of raisins and adds more ice and water to make a very thin but delicious version of this cold soup.

Yogurt and Spinach Salad (Borani-e Esfenaj)

PREP TIME: 10 MIN	COOK TIME: 30 MIN	YIELD: 4 SERVINGS

INGREDIENTS

2 tablespoons olive oil

2 medium onions, peeled and ¼-inch diced

4 cloves garlic, peeled and chopped

1 pound fresh spinach, chopped, or 1½ cups frozen chopped spinach, thawed (with any juice squeezed out)

2 tablespoons chopped fresh cilantro

2 tablespoons chopped fresh mint or 2 teaspoons dried mint

1½ cups thick, plain whole yogurt or labneh

1 teaspoon fine sea salt

¼ teaspoon freshly ground black pepper

⅛ teaspoon ground saffron threads dissolved in 1 tablespoon hot water, for garnish (optional)

A few of your favorite edible fresh flowers, such as marigolds or pansies, for garnish (optional)

DIRECTIONS

1 In a wide skillet, add the oil and warm over medium heat. Add the onions and garlic, and sauté, stirring occasionally to prevent burning, until the onions are golden brown, about 10 minutes.

2 Add the spinach, cilantro, and mint; cover; and steam until the spinach is wilted, about 3 to 5 minutes. Uncover and allow to cook for a few minutes longer, until all the liquid has been absorbed or evaporated.

3 Remove from the heat and allow to cool for 10 to 15 minutes before transferring to a serving bowl.

4 Add the yogurt or labneh, salt, and pepper, and mix well. Adjust the seasoning to taste and garnish with saffron and/or flowers, according to your fancy.

5 Serve as an appetizer with lavash bread or as an accompaniment to other dishes. *Nush-e joon!*

PER SERVING: *Calories 164 (From Fat 3); Fat 10g (Saturated 3g); Cholesterol 12mg; Sodium 603mg; Carbohydrate 14g (Dietary Fiber 3g); Protein 7g.*

Yogurt and Persian Shallot Salad (Mast-o Musir)

PREP TIME: 30 MIN PLUS 4–24 HR FOR SOAKING	COOK TIME: NONE	YIELD: 5 SERVINGS

INGREDIENTS

1½ cups dried *musir* (Persian shallots)

1½ cups thick, plain whole yogurt or labneh

1 teaspoon fine sea salt

½ teaspoon freshly ground black pepper

2 tablespoons chopped fresh mint or 1 teaspoon dried mint

1 tablespoon chopped fresh tarragon or 1 teaspoon dried tarragon

1 teaspoon crushed dried rose petals, for garnish (optional)

½ teaspoon dried mint leaves, for garnish (optional)

DIRECTIONS

1 Place the *musir* in a bowl, cover with water, and soak in the refrigerator, covered, for 4 to 24 hours. Drain, rinse in cold water, and pat dry. Inspect the soaked *musir*, cutting out any stems that remain hard after soaking, and mince (you can use a food processor).

2 In a large bowl, combine the chopped *musir* with the yogurt or labneh, salt, pepper, mint, and tarragon. Mix well, cover, and refrigerate for at least 30 minutes before serving.

3 Garnish with the rose petals and/or mint leaves if you like, and serve as an appetizer with bread or as an accompaniment to other dishes. *Nush-e joon!*

PER SERVING: *Calories 60 (From Fat 22); Fat 2g (Saturated 2g); Cholesterol 10mg; Sodium 411mg; Carbohydrate 7g (Dietary Fiber 0g); Protein 3g.*

Yogurt and Beet Salad (Borani-e Labu)

PREP TIME: 5 MIN	COOK TIME: 2 HR	YIELD: 4 SERVINGS

INGREDIENTS

2 pounds raw large beets or one 16-ounce can cooked beets, drained, rinsed, and patted dry

2 tablespoons sugar dissolved in 5 cups water (if using raw beets)

1½ cups thick, plain whole yogurt or labneh

2 tablespoons chopped fresh mint or 1 teaspoon dried mint, for garnish

½ teaspoon toasted black sesame seeds, for garnish

DIRECTIONS

1 If you're using raw beets, place the oven rack in the center of the oven and preheat the oven to 350 degrees. Place the beets on a quarter-size rimmed sheet pan. Add the water and sugar to the pan. Bake in the oven until the beets are tender and all the liquid has been absorbed, about 1 to 2 hours (depending on the size of the beets). Peel and cut the beets (into slices or cubes, according to your fancy).

2 In a serving bowl, mix the beets with the yogurt or labneh and garnish with mint and sesame seeds. Serve as an appetizer with bread or as an accompaniment to other dishes. *Nush-e joon!*

PER SERVING: *Calories 181 (From Fat 32); Fat 4g (Saturated 2g); Cholesterol 12mg; Sodium 220mg; Carbohydrate 33g (Dietary Fiber 7g); Protein 7g.*

NOTE: The beets can also be cooked on the stovetop. Place them in a large saucepan, cover with water, add 2 tablespoons of sugar, and bring to a boil. Reduce the heat to medium, cover, and cook for 30 to 60 minutes (depending on the size of the beets).

Cucumber and Pomegranate Salad (Salad-e Khiar-o Anar)

PREP TIME: 25 MIN	COOK TIME: NONE	YIELD: 4 SERVINGS

INGREDIENTS

2 tablespoons fresh lime juice (juice of 1 lime)

¼ cup olive oil

1 teaspoon fine sea salt

¼ teaspoon freshly ground black pepper

1 teaspoon ground *golpar* (Persian hogweed; optional)

½ cup peeled and diced red onions

3 tablespoons fresh mint leaves or 1 tablespoon dried mint

6 Persian cucumbers or 2 long seedless cucumbers, peeled and diced

Arils of 1 or 2 pomegranates (about 1 cup, depending on the size; see Chapter 4)

DIRECTIONS

1 In a serving bowl, whisk together the lime juice, olive oil, salt, pepper, and *golpar* to make the dressing.

2 Just before serving, add to the bowl the onions, mint, cucumbers, and pomegranate arils, and toss lightly. Season to taste with extra salt and lime juice. *Nush-e joon!*

PER SERVING: *Calories 181 (From Fat 129); Fat 14g (Saturated 2g); Cholesterol 0mg; Sodium 475mg; Carbohydrate 13g (Dietary Fiber 3g); Protein 2g.*

Cucumber and Tomato Salad (Salad-e Gojeh Khiar)

PREP TIME: 25 MIN	COOK TIME: NONE	YIELD: 4 SERVINGS

INGREDIENTS

1 tablespoon olive oil

1 tablespoon fresh lime juice

2 tablespoons rice vinegar

1 clove garlic, peeled and grated

1 teaspoon fine sea salt

¼ teaspoon freshly ground black pepper

2 firm ripe tomatoes, peeled and diced

6 Persian cucumbers or 2 long seedless cucumbers, peeled and diced

2 spring onions, chopped (white and green parts)

3 radishes, sliced

2 tablespoons chopped fresh parsley

2 tablespoons chopped fresh mint or 1 teaspoon dried mint

2 tablespoons chopped fresh cilantro

DIRECTIONS

1 In a salad bowl, whisk together the olive oil, lime juice, vinegar, garlic, salt, and pepper to make the dressing.

2 Just before serving, add to the bowl the tomatoes, cucumbers, onions, radishes, parsley, mint, and cilantro. Toss well and season to taste. Serve immediately. *Nush-e joon!*

PER SERVING: *Calories 76 (From Fat 35); Fat 4g (Saturated 1g); Cholesterol 0mg; Sodium 484mg; Carbohydrate 9g (Dietary Fiber 3g); Protein 2g.*

TIP: Be sure to add the dressing and toss the salad just before serving to prevent the salad from becoming soggy.

Smoked Eggplant and Pomegranate Spread (Nazkhatun)

PREP TIME: 15 MIN	COOK TIME: 2 HR	YIELD: 4 SERVINGS

INGREDIENTS

2½ pounds large eggplants (2 to 3 eggplants)

3 tablespoons olive oil

2 medium onions, peeled and chopped

5 cloves garlic, peeled and chopped

1 medium tomato, peeled and finely chopped

1 tablespoon pomegranate molasses

1 teaspoon grape molasses

1 teaspoon fine sea salt

½ teaspoon freshly ground black pepper

¼ teaspoon turmeric

1 teaspoon ground *golpar* (Persian hogweed)

2 teaspoons ground cumin

2 tablespoons chopped fresh mint or 2 teaspoons dried mint

DIRECTIONS

1 On a grill or, one at a time, over the flame of a gas cooktop, smoke and burn the eggplant skins on all sides, turning frequently, until the skin is burned and completely blackened, about 3 to 5 minutes. Place the eggplant on a rack in a rimmed sheet pan.

2 Use a knife to cut a lengthwise slit in the eggplant so any juice left can drain into the sheet pan. When cool enough to handle, remove and discard the skins; then transfer the flesh to a cutting board and chop finely. Set aside.

3 In a wide skillet, add the oil and warm over medium heat. Add the onions and garlic, and sauté, stirring occasionally, until golden, about 10 to 15 minutes. Add the tomatoes, pomegranate molasses, and grape molasses, and sauté another 10 minutes.

4 Add the eggplant, salt, pepper, turmeric, *golpar*, cumin, and mint. Simmer over low heat, stirring occasionally, until the mixture is thick and the eggplant is tender, about 45 to 55 minutes. Adjust the seasoning to taste.

5 Transfer to a serving dish and serve hot or at room temperature as an appetizer with lavash bread or as an accompaniment to other dishes. *Nush-e joon!*

PER SERVING: *Calories 205 (From Fat 97); Fat 11g (Saturated 2g); Cholesterol 0mg; Sodium 480mg; Carbohydrate 27g (Dietary Fiber 11g); Protein 4g.*

TIP: You can cook the eggplants in the oven instead of on a grill, if you prefer. Preheat the oven to 450 degrees, prick the eggplants in several places with a fork to prevent them from bursting during cooking, place them on a rack in a rimmed sheet pan, and roast in the oven for 1 hour.

Smoked Butternut Squash and Kashk Spread (Kashk-o Kadu)

PREP TIME: 10 MIN	COOK TIME: 1 HR	YIELD: 6 SERVINGS

INGREDIENTS

1 large butternut squash (about 3 pounds)

2 tablespoons olive oil

2 medium onions, peeled and thinly sliced

6 cloves garlic, peeled and sliced

1½ teaspoons fine sea salt

½ teaspoon freshly ground black pepper

1 teaspoon turmeric

1 tablespoon dried mint

1 cup walnuts, ground

¾ cup liquid *kashk*

1 cup fresh mint leaves, for garnish

1 cup fresh basil leaves, for garnish

2 tablespoons liquid *kashk*, for garnish

DIRECTIONS

1 Preheat the oven to 450 degrees. Cut the butternut squash in half lengthwise and remove the seeds using a spoon.

2 Place an oiled rack in a rimmed sheet pan. Arrange the butternut squash halves, face side up, on the rack. Bake in the oven for 1 hour. Remove the squash from the oven and leave until cool enough to handle.

3 Meanwhile, in a large, deep skillet, add the oil and warm over medium heat. Add the onions and garlic, and sauté until golden brown, about 15 minutes. Add the salt, pepper, turmeric, and mint, and stir-fry for 20 seconds.

4 Use a spoon to remove the flesh of the butternut squash and add it to the onion mixture in the skillet. Add the walnuts and ¾ cup of *kashk*, mashing and mixing together until you have a smooth texture. Adjust the seasoning to taste.

5 Transfer the spread to a serving dish and garnish with the mint leaves, the basil leaves, and 2 tablespoons of *kashk*. Serve warm or at room temperature with bread or a tortilla (as a taco), with fresh basil and mint, or as an accompaniment to other dishes. *Nush-e joon!*

PER SERVING: *Calories 270 (From Fat 132); Fat 15g (Saturated 2g); Cholesterol 3mg; Sodium 573mg; Carbohydrate 34g (Dietary Fiber 6g); Protein 5g.*

Smoked Eggplant, Mint, Kashk, and Walnut Spread (Kashk-e Bademjan)

PREP TIME: 15 MIN	COOK TIME: 1 HR	YIELD: 4 SERVINGS

INGREDIENTS

2½ pounds large eggplants (2 to 3 eggplants)

¼ cup olive oil

2 medium onions, peeled and thinly sliced

6 cloves garlic, peeled and sliced

1½ teaspoons fine sea salt

½ teaspoon freshly ground black pepper

1 teaspoon turmeric

1 cup walnuts, ground

½ cup water

1 tablespoon dried mint

⅔ cup liquid *kashk* (or 1 cup yogurt, beaten with 1 tablespoon fresh lime juice for 5 minutes)

⅛ teaspoon ground saffron dissolved in 1 teaspoon hot water, for garnish

1 tablespoon plain liquid *kashk,* for garnish

1 cup fresh mint leaves, for garnish

DIRECTIONS

1 On a grill or, one at a time, over the flame of a gas cooktop, smoke and burn the eggplant skins on all sides, turning frequently, until the skin is burned and completely blackened, about 3 to 5 minutes. Place them on a rack in a rimmed sheet pan.

2 Use a knife to cut a lengthwise slit in the eggplant so any juice left can drain into the sheet pan. When cool enough to handle, remove and discard the skins; then transfer the flesh to a cutting board and chop. Set aside.

3 In a wide, deep skillet, add the oil and warm over medium heat. Add the onions and garlic, and sauté, stirring occasionally, until golden brown, about 15 minutes. Add the salt, pepper, turmeric, eggplant, walnuts, and water; stir well. Cover and cook over medium heat, stirring occasionally, until all the juices have been absorbed, about 10 to 12 minutes.

4 Mix-in the mint and ⅔ cup of *kashk* and adjust the seasoning to taste. Remove from the heat and transfer to a serving dish. Garnish with saffron, 1 tablespoon of *kashk*, and mint leaves, and serve warm or at room temperature with bread, fresh basil, and mint, or serve as an accompaniment to other dishes. *Nush-e joon!*

PER SERVING: *Calories 382 (From Fat 259); Fat 29g (Saturated 3g); Cholesterol 4mg; Sodium 838mg; Carbohydrate 29g (Dietary Fiber 14g); Protein 8g.*

TIP: You can cook the eggplants in the oven instead of on a grill, if you prefer. Preheat the oven to 450 degrees, prick the eggplants in several places with a fork to prevent them from bursting during cooking, place them on a rack in a rimmed sheet pan, and roast in the oven for 1 hour.

Smoked Eggplant Tapenade (Kaleh Kabab)

PREP TIME: 30 MIN	COOK TIME: 5 MIN	YIELD: 4 SERVINGS

INGREDIENTS

2½ pounds large eggplants (2 to 3 eggplants)

3 cloves garlic, peeled

2 cups walnuts

1¼ teaspoons fine sea salt

¼ teaspoon freshly ground black pepper

½ teaspoon ground coriander

½ teaspoon ground *golpar* (Persian hogweed)

1 teaspoon finely chopped fresh basil leaves

½ cup fresh mint leaves or 2 tablespoons dried mint

½ cup fresh cilantro leaves

2 tablespoons oil

Sprigs of mint, for garnish

1 tablespoon fresh pomegranate arils, for garnish

DIRECTIONS

1 On a grill or, one at a time, over the flame of a gas cooktop, smoke and burn the eggplant skins on all sides, turning frequently, until the skin is burned and completely blackened, about 3 to 5 minutes. Place them on a rack in a rimmed sheet pan.

2 Use a knife to cut a lengthwise slit in the eggplant so any juice left can drain into the sheet pan. When cool enough to handle, remove and discard the skins; then transfer the flesh to a cutting board and chop. Set aside.

3 In a food processor, puree the garlic and walnuts. Add the eggplant, salt, pepper, coriander, *golpar*, basil, mint, cilantro, and oil, and pulse until you have a grainy paste. Adjust the seasoning to taste.

4 Transfer to a serving bowl and garnish with the mint and pomegranate arils. Serve as an appetizer with bread or as an accompaniment to other dishes. *Nush-e joon!*

PER SERVING: *Calories 552 (From Fat 419); Fat 47g (Saturated 5g); Cholesterol 0mg; Sodium 595mg; Carbohydrate 32g (Dietary Fiber 15g); Protein 13g.*

TIP: You can cook the eggplants in the oven instead of on a grill, if you prefer. Preheat the oven to 450 degrees, prick the eggplants in several places with a fork to prevent them from bursting during cooking, place them on a rack in a rimmed sheet pan, and roast in the oven for 1 hour.

Sweet–and–Savory Lamb Turnovers (Sanbuseh)

PREP TIME: 30 MINUTES	COOK TIME: 35 MINUTES	YIELD: 36 SERVINGS

INGREDIENTS

2 tablespoons olive oil

1 onion, peeled and ¼-inch diced

2 cloves garlic, peeled and chopped

2 tablespoons water

1 pound ground lamb or ground chicken

1 teaspoon cayenne

2 teaspoons fine sea salt

1 teaspoon freshly ground black pepper

½ teaspoon turmeric

1 teaspoon cinnamon

2 teaspoons ground cumin

1¼ cup ground pistachio kernels

1 cup chopped fresh mint leaves or 1 tablespoon dried mint

2 cups chopped fresh parsley

3 tablespoons chopped fresh tarragon leaves or 1 tablespoon dried tarragon

6 sheets ready-made frozen puff pastry, thawed for 1 hour

2 egg yolks, lightly beaten with 2 tablespoons milk

½ cup confectioners' sugar

2 tablespoons dried crushed rose petals

DIRECTIONS

1   In a wide skillet, place the oil, onion, garlic, water, and lamb or chicken. Cover and cook over low heat for 20 minutes. Remove the cover and mash the ground meat mixture in the skillet to avoid any lumping. Add the cayenne, salt, pepper, turmeric, cinnamon, cumin, 1 cup of the ground pistachios, mint, parsley, and tarragon. Increase the heat to medium-high, stir, and sauté until all the juices have been absorbed, about 10 to 15 minutes. Remove from the heat and allow to cool. Set aside.

2   Line 2 sheet pans with parchment paper.

3   On a cool, floured surface, unfold 1 package of the dough. Cut the dough into 3-inch circles, using a cookie cutter or the open end of a glass dipped in flour. Fill each circle with 2 heaping teaspoons of the filling from Step 1. Fold each circle into a crescent shape and seal. Fold over the edges using your fingers and pinch to double seal. Carefully transfer to the sheet pans 1 inch apart (do not crowd). Cover with a layer of parchment paper and plastic wrap and keep chilled in the refrigerator until ready to bake.

4 Place the oven rack in the middle and preheat the oven to 350 degrees.

5 Just before baking, paint the turnovers with the egg wash and bake until golden brown, about 30 to 35 minutes. Remove the sheet pan from the oven and immediately dust the turnovers with the confectioners' sugar, rose petals, and the remaining ¼ cup of ground pistachios. Gently transfer to a serving platter and serve warm. *Nush-e joon!*

PER SERVING: *Calories 311 (From Fat 198); Fat 22g (Saturated 4g); Cholesterol 21mg; Sodium 220mg; Carbohydrate 23g (Dietary Fiber 1g); Protein 6g.*

TIP: Pick over the shelled pistachios carefully to remove any bits of shell that may have remained.

Olive Walnut and Pomegranate Tapenade (Zaytun Parvardeh)

PREP TIME: 30 MIN	COOK TIME: NONE	YIELD: 8 SERVINGS

INGREDIENTS

1 cup walnuts

7 cloves garlic, peeled

½ cup fresh basil leaves

2 tablespoons fresh cilantro leaves

½ cup fresh mint leaves or 1¼ tablespoons dried mint

1 teaspoon ground *golpar* (Persian hogweed)

½ teaspoon fine sea salt

½ teaspoon freshly ground black pepper

1 cup pitted olives (your favorite type), divided

½ cup freshly squeezed pomegranate juice or store-bought pure pomegranate juice

2 tablespoons fresh lime juice (optional)

1 cup pomegranate arils

DIRECTIONS

1   In a food processor, add the walnuts, garlic, basil, cilantro, mint, *golpar*, salt, pepper, and ½ cup of the olives. Pulse until you have a grainy paste. Transfer to a serving bowl.

2   Add the remaining ½ cup of olives, the pomegranate juice, the lime juice (if you prefer it extra sour), and the pomegranate arils. Mix well.

3   Adjust the seasoning to taste, and serve as an appetizer with bread or as an accompaniment with other dishes. *Nush-e joon!*

PER SERVING: *Calories 156 (From Fat 116); Fat 13g (Saturated 1g); Cholesterol 0mg; Sodium 405mg; Carbohydrate 10g (Dietary Fiber 3g); Protein 3g.*

TIP: If you don't plan to use this tapenade immediately, store in an airtight container in the refrigerator for up to 3 days.

Chapter 9
Egg-xotic Egg Dishes

Eggs and egg dishes are popular throughout the Middle East. Iranians are especially fond of *kukus,* a type of open-faced omelet similar to the Italian frittata and the Arab *eggah.* Filled with vegetables and herbs, a good *kuku* should be thick and rather fluffy.

Frittata pans consisting of two interlinking pans that fit one on top of the other are perfect for *kukus.* They make flipping a stovetop-cooked *kuku* easy as one, two, three. But these days, I prefer to cook my *kukus* in the oven.

Kukus are served as appetizers, side dishes, or main dishes with bread. They may be enjoyed hot or at room temperature, and they keep well in the refrigerator for two or three days. Most Iranian households keep *kukus* on hand for snacks or to serve to unexpected guests. They're ideal for picnics as well.

Fried Eggs with Fresh Ginger, Dates, and Saffron (Khagineh-ye Khorma)

PREP TIME: 10 MIN	COOK TIME: 15 MIN	YIELD: 2 SERVINGS

INGREDIENTS

12 dates, any remaining hard stalk parts removed, pitted and sliced

¼ cup water

½ teaspoon ground cinnamon

½ inch fresh ginger, peeled and grated, or ¼ teaspoon ground dried ginger

4 tablespoons olive oil, butter, or ghee

4 eggs

½ teaspoon fine sea salt

½ teaspoon freshly ground black pepper

⅛ teaspoon ground saffron threads dissolved in 1 teaspoon orange blossom water

1 cup fresh Persian basil leaves, for garnish (optional)

DIRECTIONS

1 In a wide skillet, place the dates, water, cinnamon, and ginger. Cook over medium heat until the dates are soft, about 3 to 4 minutes.

2 Spread the date mixture evenly in the skillet and, using a wooden spoon, make 4 openings. Then drizzle a little oil, butter, or ghee on top. Break each egg into a small bowl, one by one, and drop one egg into each opening; then sprinkle with salt and pepper. Cover and cook over medium heat until the egg yolks are cooked to your liking, about 5 to 10 minutes — I like mine neither too hard nor too runny.

3 Drizzle the saffron on top, garnish with fresh basil (if using), and serve hot with bread. *Nush-e joon!*

PER SERVING: *Calories 672 (From Fat 247); Fat 27g (Saturated 4g); Cholesterol 0mg; Sodium 580mg; Carbohydrate 109g (Dietary Fiber 10g); Protein 10g.*

Tomato, Egg, and Garlic Omelet (Pomodor Cheghertemeh)

PREP TIME: 20 MIN | COOK TIME: 1 HR 25 MIN | YIELD: 4 SERVINGS

INGREDIENTS

Tomato Sauce

2 medium onions, peeled and quartered

8 cloves garlic, peeled

3 cups peeled fresh tomato puree (about 3 large tomatoes) or canned peeled tomatoes

6 tablespoons olive oil, butter, or ghee, divided

2 teaspoons fine sea salt

1 teaspoon freshly ground black pepper

½ teaspoon dried thyme

1 teaspoon turmeric

6 eggs

2 cups fresh basil leaves, for garnish

DIRECTIONS

1 In a food processor, place the onions and garlic, and pulse into small pieces. Remove from the food processor; set aside.

2 In a wide skillet, place ¼ cup of the oil, butter, or ghee and warm over medium-low heat. Add the onion and garlic mixture and sauté until golden brown, about 10 to 15 minutes,. Add the salt, pepper, thyme, and turmeric, and sauté for 1 minute. Add the pureed tomatoes and cook until all the juices have been absorbed and you have a thick sauce, about 40 to 50 minutes.

3 Spread the tomato sauce evenly in the skillet. With the handle of a wooden spoon, make 6 holes. In each hole, drizzle 1 teaspoon of the remaining oil, butter, or ghee; add an egg; and sprinkle salt and pepper on top. Cook over low heat until the eggs are softly set, about 20 to 25 minutes.

4 Garnish with basil and serve with rice or your favorite toasted bread. *Nush-e joon!*

PER SERVING: *Calories 261 (From Fat 187); Fat 21g (Saturated 3g); Cholesterol 0mg; Sodium 1,029mg; Carbohydrate 13g (Dietary Fiber 3g); Protein 8g.*

Eggs and Fava Beans (Baqala Qataq)

PREP TIME: 25 MIN | COOK TIME: 30 MIN | YIELD: 6 SERVINGS

INGREDIENTS

6 tablespoons olive oil, butter, or ghee

10 cloves garlic, peeled and grated

3 pounds fresh fava beans in the pod, or 1 pound fresh or frozen fava beans second skins removed, rinsed

1½ teaspoons fine sea salt

½ teaspoon freshly ground black pepper

1 teaspoon turmeric

1½ cups chopped fresh dill weed or ½ cup dried dill weed

1 tablespoon rice flour diluted in 1½ cups water

5 eggs

Juice of ½ sour orange

½ teaspoon red pepper flakes, for garnish

DIRECTIONS

1 In a medium braiser, add the oil, butter, or ghee, and warm over medium-low heat. Add the garlic and sauté until the aroma arises, about 1 minute.

2 Add the fava beans, salt, pepper, and turmeric, and sauté for 1 minute.

3 Add the dill and sauté for 2 minutes, stirring gently in order not to crush the fava beans.

4 Add the diluted rice flour mixture, and bring to a boil. Reduce the heat to low, cover, and cook until the beans are tender, about 10 to 15 minutes.

5 Break each egg into a small bowl and drop them, one by one, on top of the sauce. Simmer over low heat until the eggs are set, about 10 to 15 minutes.

6 Squeeze the sour orange juice over the braise, sprinkle the red pepper flakes on top, and give the mixture a gentle stir. Serve warm over rice with smoked fish, olive tapenade, or bread. *Nush-e joon!*

PER SERVING: *Calories 355 (From Fat 138); Fat 15g (Saturated 2g); Cholesterol 0mg; Sodium 573mg; Carbohydrate 45g (Dietary Fiber 0g); Protein 22g.*

TIP: The fava beans are available at Persian markets. Turn to Chapter 3 for more information on this ingredient.

Smoked Eggplant and Egg Spread (Mirza Qasemi)

PREP TIME: 10 MIN	COOK TIME: 30 MIN	YIELD: 4 SERVINGS

INGREDIENTS

2½ pounds large eggplants (2 to 3 eggplants)

6 tablespoons olive oil, butter, or ghee

5 cloves garlic, peeled and thinly sliced

2 teaspoons fine sea salt

½ teaspoon freshly ground black pepper

1 teaspoon turmeric

4 eggs

1 cup fresh basil leaves, for garnish

½ cup plain thick yogurt or labneh, for garnish

DIRECTIONS

1 On a grill or, one at a time, over the flame of a gas cooktop, smoke and burn the eggplant skins on all sides, turning frequently, until the skin is burned and completely blackened, about 3 to 5 minutes. Place the eggplant on a rack in a rimmed sheet pan.

2 Use a knife to cut a lengthwise slit in the eggplants so any juice left in them can drain into the sheet pan. When cool enough to handle, remove and discard the skins; then transfer the flesh to a cutting board and chop finely.

3 In a wide, deep skillet, add ¼ cup of the oil, butter, or ghee and warm over medium heat. Add the garlic and sauté until golden, about 1 to 2 minutes. Add the salt, pepper, turmeric, and chopped eggplants, and sauté until all the juices have been absorbed, about 5 to 10 minutes.

4 Reduce the heat to low and spread out the eggplant mixture evenly in the skillet. Make 4 holes in the mixture using a wooden spoon, drizzle 1½ teaspoons of the remaining oil into each of them, and break the eggs on top. Cook over low heat until the eggs are softly set, about 15 to 20 minutes.

5 With a wooden spoon, stir the eggs and eggplant gently together. Season to taste, and transfer to a serving platter. Garnish with fresh basil and yogurt, and serve with toasted bread. *Nush-e joon!*

PER SERVING: *Calories 288 (From Fat 197); Fat 22g (Saturated 4g); Cholesterol 4mg; Sodium 1,012mg; Carbohydrate 19g (Dietary Fiber 10g); Protein 8g.*

TIP: You can cook the eggplants in the oven instead of on a grill, if you prefer. Preheat the oven to 450 degrees, prick the eggplants in several places with a fork to prevent them from bursting during cooking, place them on a rack in a rimmed sheet pan, and roast in the oven for 1 hour.

Fresh Herb Kuku (Kuku Sabzi)

PREP TIME: 45 MIN	COOK TIME: 15 MIN	YIELD: 6 SERVINGS

INGREDIENTS

5 tablespoons olive oil, butter, or ghee, divided

2 medium yellow onions, peeled and diced

½ cup dried barberries, soaked in cold water for 15 minutes, rinsed, and drained

1 teaspoon grape molasses or sugar

2 tablespoons water

7 eggs

1 teaspoon baking powder

1 tablespoon *advieh* (Persian spice mix)

1½ teaspoons fine sea salt

1 teaspoon freshly ground black pepper

½ teaspoon turmeric

1 tablespoon rice flour

2 cloves garlic, peeled and finely chopped

½ cup finely chopped romaine lettuce

½ cup finely chopped spring onions (white and green parts)

1 cup finely chopped fresh parsley

1 cup finely chopped fresh cilantro

DIRECTIONS

1 In a wide skillet, add ¼ cup of the oil, butter, or ghee, and warm over medium heat. Add the onions and sauté until golden brown, about 10 to 15 minutes. Remove the onion, set aside, and allow to cool.

2 Wipe the skillet and place the remaining 1 tablespoon of oil, butter, or ghee; the barberries; the grape molasses or sugar; and the water. Stir-fry over medium heat for 4 minutes (taking care not to burn the barberries).

3 Preheat the oven to 400 degrees and line a quarter-sized (9½-x-13-inch) rimmed sheet pan with parchment paper. Paint the lined sheet pan with oil.

4 In a large bowl, break the eggs and beat lightly with a fork. Add the caramelized onions, baking powder, *advieh*, salt, pepper, turmeric, rice flour, garlic, lettuce, onions, parsley, cilantro, dill weed, fenugreek, walnuts, and olive oil. Fold in using a rubber spatula (do not overmix).

5 Pour the batter into the sheet pan, and gently shake the pan to even out the batter. Bake until a tester inserted in the center comes out clean, about 15 to 20 minutes.

1 cup finely chopped fresh dill weed

1 tablespoon dried fenugreek leaves (not seeds)

½ cup coarsely chopped walnuts (optional)

2 tablespoons olive oil

6 Remove from the oven and place on a cooling rack. Cut into squares, garnish, and serve hot or at room temperature, with lavash bread and Yogurt and Persian Shallot Salad (Mast-o Musir; see Chapter 8). *Nush-e joon!*

PER SERVING: *Calories 281 (From Fat 197); Fat 22g (Saturated 4g); Cholesterol 247mg; Sodium 592mg; Carbohydrate 13g (Dietary Fiber 3g); Protein 10g.*

Zucchini Kuku (Kuku-ye Kadu Sabz)

INGREDIENTS

1½ pounds fresh zucchini (about 3 to 5, depending on size)

½ cup oil, butter, or ghee, divided

2 medium onions, peeled and thinly sliced

4 cloves garlic, peeled and thinly sliced

4 eggs

1 cup chopped fresh parsley or ⅓ cup dried parsley

Zest of 1 lime

1 teaspoon baking powder

1 tablespoon all-purpose flour

1 tablespoon plain breadcrumbs

1 teaspoon fine sea salt

½ teaspoon freshly ground black pepper

1 teaspoon turmeric

½ teaspoon red pepper flakes

1 cup plain, thick yogurt or labneh, for garnish

1 cup fresh basil leaves, for garnish

DIRECTIONS

1 Thinly slice the zucchini into rings.

2 In a wide skillet, add 6 tablespoons of the oil, butter, or ghee and warm over medium heat. Add the onions, garlic, and zucchini, and sauté until lightly brown, about 10 to 15 minutes. Allow to cool.

3 Preheat the oven to 400 degrees. Line a quarter-sized (9½-x-13-inch) rimmed sheet pan with parchment paper, and paint the entire surface of the parchment paper with 1 tablespoon of the oil.

4 In a large bowl, break the eggs and beat lightly with a fork. Add the parsley, lime zest, baking powder, flour, breadcrumbs, salt, pepper, turmeric, red pepper flakes, and the zucchini mixture, and fold using a rubber spatula.

5 Pour the batter into the prepared sheet pan, and gently shake the pan to even out the batter. Bake uncovered until lightly golden on top, about 30 to 35 minutes,.

6 Remove from the oven and cut into 4-inch squares. Garnish each square with small dollops of yogurt and basil and serve with bread. *Nush-e joon!*

PER SERVING: *Calories 433 (From Fat 315); Fat 35g (Saturated 7g); Cholesterol 219mg; Sodium 624mg; Carbohydrate 21g (Dietary Fiber 4g); Protein 13g.*

Chicken and Egg Salad (Salad-e Olivier)

PREP TIME: 30 MIN PLUS 30 MIN FOR CHILLING	COOK TIME: 45 MIN	YIELD: 6 SERVINGS

INGREDIENTS

1 pound skinless boneless chicken thighs and/or breasts, cut into ½-inch cubes

1 medium onion, peeled and diced (½ inch)

1 teaspoon fine sea salt

½ teaspoon freshly ground black pepper

2 carrots, peeled and chopped

1 cup fresh shelled or frozen green peas

3 pounds russet potatoes (about 4 large)

4 spring onions, chopped (white and green parts)

2 celery stalks, strings removed and chopped

½ cup chopped pickled cucumbers or cornichons

½ cup chopped fresh parsley or 3 tablespoons dried parsley

2 tablespoons chopped fresh tarragon or 2 teaspoons dried tarragon

⅔ cup olives, pitted and chopped

3 hard-boiled eggs, peeled and chopped

DIRECTIONS

1 In a medium pot, place the chicken cubes, onion, 1 teaspoon of the salt, and ½ teaspoon of the pepper. Give the mixture a stir, cover, and cook over low heat for 30 minutes (no need to add any water). Add the carrots and peas, cover again, and cook 10 more minutes, checking to be sure the chicken is done. Remove from the heat and allow to cool.

2 Meanwhile, in a medium saucepan, place the potatoes and cover with water. Bring to a boil, reduce the heat to medium, and cook, covered, until the potatoes are tender, about 20 to 30 minutes (there should be no resistance when you push the tip of a paring knife through a potato). Peel, dice, and set aside.

1½ cups mayonnaise

2 tablespoons Dijon mustard

¼ cup olive oil

¼ cup rice vinegar

2 tablespoons fresh lime juice

2 teaspoons fine sea salt

2 teaspoons freshly ground
black pepper

3 In a large glass bowl whisk together the mayonnaise, mustard, olive oil, vinegar, lime juice, the remaining 2 teaspoons of salt, and the remaining 2 teaspoons of pepper to make the dressing. Add the chicken mixture to the bowl, with all the juices. Tip in the potatoes, onions, celery, cucumbers or cornichons, parsley, tarragon, olives, and eggs. Toss well, adjusting the seasoning to taste. Cover and chill in the refrigerator for 30 minutes or up to 24 hours. Serve on a platter with your favorite toasted bread and and/or with a stack of green leaf or butter lettuce to use as a wrap. *Nush-e joon!*

PER SERVING: *Calories 788 (From Fat 519); Fat 58g (Saturated 7g); Cholesterol 146mg; Sodium 1,623mg; Carbohydrate 58g (Dietary Fiber 7g); Protein 14g.*

Potato Kuku with Saffron-Rosewater Glaze (Kuku-ye Sib Zamini)

PREP TIME: 35 MIN	COOK TIME: 40 MIN	YIELD: 4 SERVINGS

INGREDIENTS

4½ cups water, divided

2 pounds russet potatoes (about 2 medium)

2 eggs

2 tablespoons thick plain yogurt or labneh

1 teaspoon baking powder

1 tablespoon potato starch or cornstarch

1 teaspoon fine sea salt

½ teaspoon freshly ground black pepper

½ teaspoon turmeric

1 cup finely chopped spring onions (white and green parts)

¼ cup oil, butter, or ghee

½ cup sugar

¼ teaspoon ground saffron threads dissolved in 2 tablespoons rose water

1 tablespoon slivered pistachios, for garnish

1 tablespoon slivered almonds, for garnish

2 tablespoons barberries, rinsed thoroughly and drained, for garnish

DIRECTIONS

1 In a medium saucepan, add 4 cups of the water and bring to a boil. Score around the middle of each of the potatoes, add them to the boiling water, and cook, uncovered, until they're almost tender, about 15 to 20 minutes. Drain and allow to cool; then peel and grate on the coarse side of the grater. Set aside.

2 In a large bowl, break the eggs. Add the yogurt or labneh, baking powder, potato starch or cornstarch, salt, pepper, turmeric, and onions. Beat lightly with a fork until smooth. Add the grated potatoes and use a rubber spatula to fold them in until you have a thick batter.

3 In a wide nonstick skillet, add the oil, butter, or ghee, and warm over medium-low heat until hot. Scoop ¼ cup of the potato batter onto the skillet, until you have 8 *kukus* that are 3 inches each in diameter. Cook on each side until golden brown, about 5 minutes (cook in batches to avoid overcrowding your skillet). Transfer to a serving platter.

4 In a small saucepan, mix together the sugar, the remaining ½ cup of water, and the saffron and bring to a boil. Reduce the heat to low and allow to simmer for 2 to 5 minutes until you have a light syrup (taking care to not overcook it). Remove from the heat, drizzle over the *kukus*, and garnish with pistachios, almonds, and barberries. Serve with bread and a fresh herb platter (see Chapter 7) on the side. *Nush-e joon!*

PER SERVING: *Calories 474 (From Fat 166); Fat 18g (Saturated 3g); Cholesterol 107mg; Sodium 536mg; Carbohydrate 71g (Dietary Fiber 4g); Protein 10g.*

Chapter **10**

Fill 'er Up! Stuffed Vegetables

Rarely do Iranians eat cooked vegetables on the side of other dishes. Instead, vegetables are usually combined with yogurt as a salad, or stuffed with fruits, rice, meats, and aromatic herbs — these stuffed vegetables are called *dolmeh*. Generally speaking, *dolmeh* may be served at room temperature as an appetizer or hot as a main dish accompanied with bread and yogurt.

Use fresh vegetables in season whenever possible. You can be assured they're at their height of flavor and nutritional value — they give superior results in every way.

In this chapter, I offer some favorite stuffed vegetables: grape leaves, cabbage leaves, eggplants, and onions. Fruits such as quinces and apples are also popular for stuffing.

CULTURAL WISDOM

A basic *dolmeh* stuffing is made of onion, ground meat, rice, split peas, and aromatic herbs (such as parsley, savory, and tarragon). The flavors vary depending on the regions. For example, by the Caspian coast, citrus or pomegranate juice gives the sauce its distinctive northern flavor; in central Iran, they use vinegar and grape molasses; and in southern Iran, tamarind and red pepper flavor the sauce.

Grape Leaves with Sweet-and-Sour Stuffing (Dolmeh-ye Barg-e Mo)

PREP TIME: 1 HR	COOK TIME: 2 HR	YIELD: 8 SERVINGS

INGREDIENTS

50 fresh grape leaves (in season) or canned leaves

⅔ cup rice

¼ cup yellow split peas

3 cups water

2½ teaspoons fine sea salt, divided

½ cup olive oil, butter, or ghee, divided

1 medium onion, peeled and thinly sliced

2 cloves garlic, peeled and sliced

½ pound ground lamb, ground beef, chicken thighs, or fish fillets

1 cup chopped spring onions

½ cup fresh savory or 2½ tablespoons dried savory

½ cup chopped fresh dill or 2½ tablespoons dried dill

¼ cup chopped fresh tarragon or 1½ tablespoons dried tarragon

¼ cup chopped fresh mint or 1½ tablespoons dried mint

3 cups chopped fresh parsley or 1 cup dried parsley

½ teaspoon freshly ground black pepper

DIRECTIONS

1 Preheat the oven to 350 degrees. If using fresh grape leaves, pick small and tender ones, tie them together in batches, and blanch them in boiling water for 2 minutes; then drain in a colander and rinse. If using canned grape leaves, drain in a colander and rinse.

2 In a saucepan, place the rice and split peas, add the water and ½ teaspoon of the salt, and bring to a boil over high heat. Reduce the heat to medium and cook, covered, until the split peas are almost tender, about 15 to 20 minutes. Drain in a colander (but don't rinse).

3 In a wide skillet, add 3 tablespoons of the olive oil, butter, or ghee and warm over medium heat. Add the onion, garlic, and meat or fish. Add 1½ teaspoons of the salt, the rice and split pea mixture, the spring onion, savory, dill, tarragon, mint, parsley, pepper, red pepper, cinnamon, and 2 tablespoons of the fresh lime juice. Mix thoroughly. Set aside.

4 On the bottom of a well-oiled 9-x-9-inch ovenproof dish or a medium pot with a cover, place 3 layers of grape leaves.

5 Place a grape leaf on top of a wooden cutting board with the vein side up, and nip off the little stem. Top with 1 tablespoon of the filling. Fold in both side ends of the leaf, to prevent the filling from leaking out while cooking; then roll up the leaf. Place in the prepared baking dish and repeat, filling all the leaves and placing them in the dish, side-by-side (see Figure 10-1).

½ teaspoon red pepper flakes

1 teaspoon ground cinnamon

2 tablespoons plus ⅓ cup fresh lime juice, divided

1 cup broth

⅔ cup grape molasses or brown sugar

⅓ cup wine vinegar

6 Pour the broth and the remaining 5 tablespoons of oil into the dish. Set a small ovenproof plate on top of the stuffed grape leaves to keep them rolled up. Cover and bake in the oven for 1 hour. (If your baking dish doesn't have a cover, use a layer of parchment paper and a layer of aluminum foil to cover tightly.)

7 In a bowl, add the grape molasses or brown sugar, vinegar, the remaining ½ teaspoon of salt, and the remaining ⅓ cup of lime juice. Mix thoroughly to make the glaze. Pull out the oven rack, uncover, and baste with the glaze. Cover again and push back into the oven. Bake until the leaves are tender, about 1 more hour. Adjust the seasoning to taste. The sauce should be quite reduced. Serve in the same baking dish or on a platter, while hot, with bread and yogurt, or Yogurt and Persian Shallot Salad (Mast-o Musir; Chapter 8), or use at room temperature as an appetizer. *Nush-e joon!*

PER SERVING: *Calories 409 (From Fat 190); Fat 21g (Saturated 5g); Cholesterol 21mg; Sodium 718mg; Carbohydrate 47g (Dietary Fiber 6g); Protein 10g.*

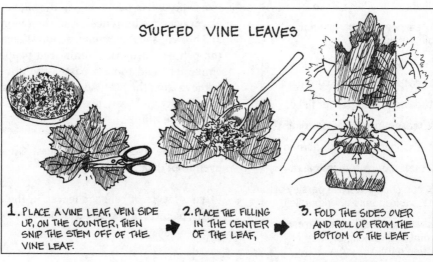

STUFFED VINE LEAVES

1. PLACE A VINE LEAF, VEIN SIDE UP, ON THE COUNTER, THEN SNIP THE STEM OFF OF THE VINE LEAF.

2. PLACE THE FILLING IN THE CENTER OF THE LEAF,

3. FOLD THE SIDES OVER AND ROLL UP FROM THE BOTTOM OF THE LEAF.

FIGURE 10-1: How to stuff vine leaves.

Illustration by Elizabeth Kurtzman

Cabbage Leaves with Rice and Split Pea Stuffing (Dolmeh-ye Kalam)

PREP TIME: 1 HR	COOK TIME: 2 HR	YIELD: 6 SERVINGS

INGREDIENTS

3 cups water plus enough to fill the large pot for boiling the cabbage, divided

2 large heads of green or savory cabbage

2 tablespoons plus 1½ teaspoons fine sea salt, divided

¼ cup rice

¼ cup split peas or mung beans

½ cup olive oil, butter, or ghee, divided

1 medium onion, peeled and thinly sliced

1 pound ground lamb, ground beef, chicken thighs, or fish fillets

1 teaspoon freshly ground black pepper

½ teaspoon turmeric

2 teaspoons ground cumin

1 teaspoon red pepper flakes

½ teaspoon smoked paprika

1 teaspoon ground cinnamon

2 tablespoons tomato paste

¼ cup chopped fresh parsley or 1½ tablespoons dried parsley

3 tablespoons chopped fresh mint or 1 tablespoon dried mint

DIRECTIONS

1 Line a sheet pan with parchment paper.

2 Fill a large pot with water, add 2 tablespoons of the salt, and bring to a boil. Core the cabbage and plunge it into the boiling water. Cover and boil for 5 minutes, drain in a colander, and rinse under cold water. Remove the individual leaves using your hands (if too hot, use tongs). Place on the sheet pan; set aside.

3 In a saucepan, place the rice and split peas or mung beans. Add the remaining 3 cups of water and ½ teaspoon of the salt, and bring to a boil. Reduce the heat to medium, cover, and cook until the split peas or mung beans are almost tender, about 15 to 20 minutes. Drain and set aside (but don't rinse).

4 In a wide skillet, add ¼ cup of the oil, butter, and ghee, and warm over medium heat. Add the onion and meat or fish and brown, about 20 minutes. Add 1½ teaspoons of the salt, the pepper, turmeric, cumin, red pepper flakes, paprika, cinnamon, and tomato paste, and stir-fry for 1 minute. Remove from the heat. Add the parsley, mint, dill, tarragon, and the rice and bean mixture; mix thoroughly and set aside (this is the filling).

5 Preheat the oven to 350 degrees. Grease a 9-x-13-inch ovenproof dish.

6 Place 2 layers of cabbage leaves in the dish (use any that might be torn, and save the good ones for the filling).

2 tablespoons chopped fresh dill or 2 teaspoons dried dill

3 tablespoons chopped fresh tarragon or 1 tablespoon dried tarragon

1½ cups fresh tomatoes (2 medium), peeled and pureed (or canned)

½ cup grape molasses or brown sugar

⅓ cup wine vinegar or fresh lime juice

7 To stuff the cabbage leaves, place 1 leaf, vein side up, on the counter and shave off any thick veins using a sharp knife. Place 1 tablespoon of filling on the leaf and roll tightly, folding in the sides of the leaf to prevent the filling from leaking out while cooking. Arrange the stuffed cabbage leaves side-by-side in the prepared dish.

8 To make the sauce, combine the tomatoes, the remaining ½ teaspoon of salt, and the remaining ¼ cup of oil, butter, or ghee; drizzle on top of each stuffed cabbage. Cover (if you don't have a cover, use a layer of oiled parchment paper and a layer of aluminum foil, and seal tightly). Bake for 1½ hours.

9 To make the glaze, in a mixing bowl, combine the grape molasses or brown sugar and the vinegar or lime juice. Pour this mixture over the cabbage. Cover and return to the oven, and bake for another 30 minutes.

10 When the stuffed cabbage leaves are done, taste the sauce and adjust the seasoning by adding more vinegar/lime juice or grape molasses/brown sugar. Serve hot or at room temperature, in the same baking dish, with bread, Yogurt and Persian Shallot Salad (Mast-o Musir; see Chapter 8), and fresh herbs. *Nush-e joon!*

PER SERVING: *Calories 650 (From Fat 329); Fat 37g (Saturated 10g); Cholesterol 55mg; Sodium 770mg; Carbohydrate 65g (Dietary Fiber 14g); Protein 22g.*

Eggplant with Lamb and Pomegranate Stuffing (Bademjan-e Shekam Por)

PREP TIME: 30 MIN PLUS 20 MIN FOR SOAKING	COOK TIME: 2 HR	YIELD: 6 SERVINGS

INGREDIENTS

6 Italian eggplants, peeled (stems left intact)

2 tablespoons fine sea salt, plus a pinch for sprinkling, divided

½ cup plus 3 tablespoons oil, plus extra for oiling the baking dish

2 medium onions, peeled and thinly sliced

6 cloves garlic, peeled and sliced

1 pound ground lamb

½ teaspoon freshly ground black pepper

½ teaspoon red pepper flakes

1 teaspoon turmeric

1 tablespoon ground cumin

2 tablespoons pomegranate molasses, divided

1 teaspoon grape molasses

2 fresh tomatoes, peeled and pureed

3 tablespoons fresh chopped mint or 1 tablespoon dried mint

DIRECTIONS

1   Make a slit, lengthwise, in each eggplant without opening the ends. Soak the in a container of cold water with 1 tablespoon of the salt for 20 minutes. Drain, rinse, blot dry, and set aside (this removes any bitterness in the eggplants).

2   Preheat the oven to 350 degrees. Oil a baking dish large enough for 6 eggplants.

3   In a large skillet, heat ½ cup of the oil over medium heat and sauté the eggplants, in batches, until golden brown on all sides, about 20 minutes. Arrange the eggplant side-by-side on the baking dish.

4   To make the filling, in the same skillet, add 2 more tablespoons of the oil and warm over medium heat; add the onions, garlic, and lamb and brown, about 20 minutes. Add 2 teaspoons of the salt, the pepper, red pepper flakes, turmeric, cumin, 1 tablespoon of the pomegranate molasses, tomatoes, mint, parsley, cilantro, and fenugreek; stir-fry for 1 minute longer. Remove from the heat and set aside.

5   Open the slits in the eggplants with your hands, sprinkle a pinch of sea salt on each eggplant, and stuff each eggplant with the filling.

½ cup fresh chopped parsley or 2½ tablespoons dried parsley

¼ cup fresh chopped cilantro or 1¼ tablespoons dried cilantro

1 teaspoon dried fenugreek leaves

1 cup broth or water

1 tablespoon grape molasses

6 In a small bowl, combine the broth or water, grape molasses, the remaining 1 tablespoon of pomegranate molasses, and the remaining 1 teaspoon of salt; pour it around the eggplants. Drizzle the remaining 1 tablespoon of oil over the eggplants. Cover (if your baking dish does not have a cover, use a layer of oiled parchment paper and aluminum foil, and seal the baking dish thoroughly so that no steam can escape). Bake for 1½ hours. Uncover and continue to bake for 30 minutes.

7 Serve hot or at room temperature with bread and Yogurt and Persian Shallot Salad (Mast-o Musir; Chapter 8). *Nush-e joon!*

PER SERVING: *Calories 470 (From Fat 306); Fat 34g (Saturated 10g); Cholesterol 55mg; Sodium 936mg; Carbohydrate 28g (Dietary Fiber 7g); Protein 16g.*

VARY IT! You can use ground beef, chicken thighs, or fish fillets in place of the ground lamb, if you prefer.

Onions with Rice and Herb Stuffing (Dolmeh-ye Piaz)

PREP TIME: 45 MIN	COOK TIME: 2 HR	YIELD: 4 SERVINGS

INGREDIENTS

4 equally sized large yellow or white onions

½ cup olive oil, butter, or ghee

½ pound ground lamb, ground beef, chicken thighs, or fish fillets

2 teaspoons fine sea salt, divided

1 teaspoon freshly ground black pepper

1 teaspoon red pepper flakes

1 teaspoon *advieh* (Persian spice mix)

1 tablespoon tomato paste

½ cup chopped fresh parsley or 2½ tablespoons dried parsley

¼ cup chopped fresh mint or 1½ tablespoons dried mint

¼ cup chopped fresh savory or 1½ tablespoons dried savory

⅓ cup rice, rinsed and drained

1 cup water

1 cup water or stock

1 cup tomato juice

1 teaspoon turmeric

2 tablespoons grape molasses

¼ cup fresh lime juice

¼ cup chopped fresh tarragon or 1½ tablespoons dried tarragon, for garnish

DIRECTIONS

1 Remove the 2 outer onion layers and cut off the tops ½ inch from the crown (set aside the crowns to use later). Slice off the bottoms of the onions so they can sit flat in the dish. Hollow out the onions using the tip of a knife or a melon baller to scoop out the pulp, leaving a shell about 1 inch thick (save the pulp and chop to use later in the filling). Place the onion shells in a large pot of water, bring to a boil, reduce the heat to low, and simmer for 10 minutes. Drain in a colander and set aside.

2 To make the filling, in a medium saucepan, add the oil, butter, or ghee and warm over medium heat; add the reserved onion pulp and the meat or fish and brown, about 20 minutes. Add 1 teaspoon of the salt, the pepper, red pepper flakes, *advieh*, tomato paste, parsley, mint, savory, and rice, and stir-fry for 1 minute. Add 1 cup of water, stir well, cover, and cook over medium heat until all the liquid has been absorbed, about 15 to 20 minutes. Remove from the heat and set aside.

3 Preheat the oven to 350 degrees. Grease an enameled cast-iron pot or a baking dish large enough for the onions to sit side-by-side.

4 Place the onion shells in the pot or baking dish and stuff them with the filling. Pack down the filling and replace the crowns of the onions.

5 In a small bowl, combine 1 cup of water or broth, tomato juice, the remaining 1 teaspoon of salt, and the turmeric; mix well. Pour the mixture into the pot around the onions (adding any leftover filling). Cover tightly and bake for 1 hour.

6 In a small bowl, combine the grape molasses and lime juice, and stir well. Remove the crowns from the onions and drizzle the glaze over the onions; then baste with the sauce. Replace the crowns, cover the pot, and return to the oven. Bake until the onions are tender, about 30 to 35 minutes.

7 Adjust the seasoning to taste, and garnish with the tarragon. Serve 1 onion per person with some of the sauce, and some bread, Yogurt and Persian Shallot Salad (Mast-o Musir; Chapter 8), and a fresh herb platter. *Nush-e joon!*

PER SERVING: *Calories 606 (From Fat 366); Fat 41g (Saturated 10g); Cholesterol 41mg; Sodium 1,164mg; Carbohydrate 49g (Dietary Fiber 4g); Protein 14g.*

Chapter **11**

Warm and Hearty Soups and Porridge

M ost soups in Persian cooking are substantial enough to serve as a main course. Persian soup called *osh* (rhymes with squash), is usually a hearty dish — slow-cooked in one pot with beans, fresh herbs, vegetables of the season, and sometimes including noodles, bulgur, or nuts. An *osh* can be made a day in advance to give the flavors a chance to meld, and then reheated just before serving. These soups can also be frozen with good results, for later reheating and garnishing. What's more, these soups are hearty, healthy, and economical.

There is a good reason why in Persian, the cook is the *osh paz* (soup maker), and the kitchen is the *osh paz khaneh* (soup maker's house). Soup plays an important role in Iranian life, with a special soup for each occasion. Some of my happiest childhood memories revolve around the noodle soup lunches held at our house on Fridays (the equivalent of Sundays in the West). The ritual would start the day before, with my mother and her helpers making the noodles. Everything was prepared from scratch — beans were soaked and armfuls of herbs were meticulously washed and chopped. Everyone lent a hand, cheerfully singing and reciting poetry as they worked. The next day, family and friends would gather together, all seated around the table, young and old alike, each with a bowl of warm, delicious, noodle soup in front of them. I remember those times like yesterday, and I still crave that wonderful sense of togetherness. Nothing can replace the power of a bowl of hot soup on a cold day. In Persian culture, sharing a bowl of soup is believed to forge the bonds of friendship. Sometimes, in an act symbolizing great intimacy, friends or lovers sip from the same spoon to seal their devotion.

Onion, Egg, and Spinach Soup (Eshkeneh)

PREP TIME: 20 MIN	COOK TIME:1½ HR	YIELD: 6 SERVINGS

INGREDIENTS

¼ cup olive oil, butter, or ghee

4 medium onions, peeled and thinly sliced

1 tablespoon fine sea salt

½ teaspoon freshly ground black pepper

1 teaspoon turmeric

2 tablespoons wheat or rice flour

2 tablespoons fenugreek leaves

2 cups chopped fresh or frozen spinach

8 cups water

1 cup pitted dried tart cherries or 2 tablespoons fresh lime juice

3 pounds russet potatoes (about 3 potatoes), peeled and diced to 8 pieces

2 eggs, beaten

Drained yogurt or labneh, for garnish

Persian flatbread, for garnish

DIRECTIONS

1 In a heavy-bottomed pot, add the oil, butter, or ghee, and warm over medium heat. Add the onions and sauté until golden brown, about 7 to 15 minutes. Add the salt, pepper, turmeric, flour, fenugreek, and spinach, and sauté for 1 minute.

2 Add the water, cherries or lime juice, and potatoes and bring to a boil. Reduce the heat to medium-low, cover, and allow to simmer until the potatoes are tender, about 35 to 45 minutes (add more warm water if the soup is too thick).

3 Add the eggs in a thin stream, stirring gently and constantly, and return to a boil. Adjust the seasoning to taste.

4 Pour the soup into individual bowls and serve with yogurt or labneh and bread. *Nush-e joon!*

PER SERVING: *Calories 368 (From Fat 100); Fat 11g (Saturated 2g); Cholesterol 70mg; Sodium 997mg; Carbohydrate 61g (Dietary Fiber 5g); Protein 9g.*

VARY IT! You can replace the tart cherries with 1 tablespoon pomegranate molasses if you like. You can also poach the eggs in the soup instead of mixing them in.

Pomegranate Soup (Osh-e Anar)

PREP TIME: 50 MIN | **COOK TIME: 1 HR 50 MIN** | **YIELD: 8 SERVINGS**

INGREDIENTS

½ cup dried mung beans

¼ cup barley

¼ cup lentils

8 cups water, plus extra for soaking the legumes and barley, divided

¼ cup olive oil, butter, or ghee

4 medium onions, peeled and thinly sliced

8 cloves garlic, peeled and sliced

1 large beet, peeled and chopped

2 teaspoons fine sea salt

1 teaspoon freshly ground black pepper

2 teaspoons turmeric

1 teaspoon ground cinnamon

1 tablespoon *advieh* (Persian spice mix)

One 32-ounce bottle pomegranate juice

¼ cup rice

2 cups chopped fresh parsley or ⅔ cup dried parsley

DIRECTIONS

1 In a bowl, place the mung beans, barley, and lentils. Cover with water 2 inches above the legumes, and soak for 30 minutes. Drain, rinse, and set aside.

2 In a large, heavy-bottomed pan, add the oil, butter, or ghee, and warm over medium heat. Add the onions and garlic and sauté, stirring occasionally, until lightly golden brown, about 7 to 15 minutes.

3 Add the legumes and barley, the beets, salt, pepper, turmeric, cinnamon, and *advieh*, and sauté for 1 minute. Pour in the remaining 8 cups of water and bring to a boil. Reduce the heat to medium-low, cover, and simmer, stirring occasionally to prevent sticking, for 40 minutes.

4 Add the pomegranate juice and rice, and bring back to a boil. Reduce the heat to low, cover, and continue to simmer until the beans are tender, about 45 minutes.

2 cups chopped fresh cilantro or ⅔ cup dried cilantro

2 cups chopped fresh mint or ⅔ cup dried mint

2 cups chopped spring onions (white and green parts)

2 tablespoons ground *golpar* (Persian hogweed)

2 tablespoons chopped fresh dill weed, for garnish

1 cup pomegranate arils, for garnish

Mint garnish (see Chapter 4)

5 Use a handheld mixer to partially puree the soup. Add the parsley, cilantro, mint, spring onions, and *golpar*, and give it a stir. Cook, uncovered, over medium heat, stirring occasionally, for 10 minutes. Adjust the seasoning to taste (the flavor should be sweet and sour — if too sweet, add a squeeze of lime). Cover and keep warm until ready to serve.

6 Pour the soup into individual bowls and garnish with dill weed, pomegranate arils, and mint garnish. *Nush-e joon!*

PER SERVING: *Calories 347 (From Fat 73); Fat 8g (Saturated 1g); Cholesterol 0mg; Sodium 529mg; Carbohydrate 62g (Dietary Fiber 10g); Protein 10g.*

TIP: If using dried herbs, increase the cooking time in Step 5 to 20 minutes.

Barley and Leek Soup (Osh-e Jow)

PREP TIME: 20 MIN | COOK TIME: 1 HR 20 MIN | YIELD: 8 SERVINGS

INGREDIENTS

½ cup olive oil, butter, or ghee

1 medium onion, peeled and thinly sliced

2 cloves garlic, peeled and thinly sliced

1 carrot, peeled and roughly chopped

3 leeks, washed thoroughly and finely diced (white and green parts)

1 kohlrabi or turnip (about ½ pound), peeled and roughly chopped

1 teaspoon sea salt

½ teaspoon freshly ground black pepper

1 cup barley

¼ cup mung beans

10 cups water

1 cup *kashk* or sour cream or 2 cups buttermilk

2 tablespoons fresh lime juice

1 teaspoon grape molasses or honey

½ cup chopped fresh parsley or 2½ tablespoons dried parsley, for garnish

½ cup chopped fresh cilantro or 2½ tablespoons dried cilantro, for garnish

½ cup chopped fresh dill weed or 2½ tablespoons dried dill weed, for garnish

½ cup chopped fresh tarragon or 2½ tablespoons dried tarragon, for garnish

DIRECTIONS

1 In a large, heavy-bottomed pot, add the oil, butter, or ghee, and warm over medium heat. Add the onion, garlic, carrot, leeks, kohlrabi or turnip, salt, and pepper, and sauté until lightly golden, about 10 to 15 minutes. Add the barley and mung beans and stir-fry for 1 minute. Add the water and bring to a boil. Reduce the heat to medium-low, cover, and simmer, stirring occasionally, until the beans are tender, about 45 minutes.

2 Add the *kashk*, sour cream, or buttermilk; lime juice; and grape molasses or honey. Use a handheld mixer to partially puree the soup. Cover and continue to simmer over medium-low heat for 10 minutes.

3 Add the parsley, cilantro, dill weed, and tarragon 5 minutes before serving, stir well, and continue to cook, uncovered, for another 5 minutes. Adjust the seasoning to taste.

4 Pour into individual bowls and serve with flatbread. *Nush-e joon!*

PER SERVING: *Calories 340 (From Fat 179); Fat 20g (Saturated 5g); Cholesterol 15mg; Sodium 291mg; Carbohydrate 37g (Dietary Fiber 8g); Protein 7g.*

TIP: Adding the fresh herbs at the end, and cooking uncovered, helps to keep them bright.

Spinach and Beet Soup (Osh-e Shuly)

INGREDIENTS

1 cup brown lentils

7 cups water, plus extra for soaking the lentils, divided

2 tablespoons olive oil, butter, or ghee

2 medium onions, peeled and diced

4 teaspoons fine sea salt

1 teaspoon freshly ground black pepper

2 teaspoons turmeric

2 teaspoons nigella seeds

1 pound red or white beets, peeled and diced

½ cup unbleached all-purpose wheat flour or rice flour

1 pound chopped fresh or frozen spinach

1 cup chopped spring onions

1 cup chopped fresh beet leaves

1 cup chopped fresh dill weed or ⅓ cup dried dill weed

1 cup chopped fresh parsley leaves

1 teaspoon dried fenugreek leaves

⅔ cup apple cider vinegar

1 tablespoon date sugar or granulated sugar

Mint garnish (see Chapter 4)

DIRECTIONS

1 In a bowl, place the lentils. Cover with water, and soak for 30 minutes. Drain, rinse, and set aside.

2 To make the broth, in a large pot place the oil, butter, or ghee, and warm over medium heat. Add the onions and sauté until golden brown, about 10 to 15 minutes. Add the salt, pepper, turmeric, nigella seeds, and lentils, and stir-fry for 1 minute. Add 5 cups of the water and the beets, and bring to a boil. Reduce the heat to medium-low, cover, and simmer until the lentils and beets are tender, about 40 to 45 minutes.

3 In a bowl, add the flour with the remaining 2 cups of water and whisk together until smooth. Add it to the broth, gradually while stirring until the flour has been completely absorbed and you have a smooth broth, about 2 minutes. Then cover and simmer for 15 minutes.

4 Add the spinach, spring onions, beet leaves, dill weed, parsley, and fenugreek, and simmer, uncovered, stirring occasionally, for 5 minutes. Add the vinegar and sugar and give it a stir; then cover and simmer for another 10 minutes. Adjust the seasoning to taste and keep warm.

5 Pour into individual bowls and add the mint garnish. Stir in the garnish just before serving. *Nush-e joon!*

PER SERVING: *Calories 341 (From Fat 56); Fat 6g (Saturated 1g); Cholesterol 0mg; Sodium 1,466mg; Carbohydrate 58g (Dietary Fiber 18g); Protein 16g.*

Noodle and Chickpea Soup (Osh-e Reshteh)

PREP TIME: 12 HR | COOK TIME: 2 HR | YIELD: 10 SERVINGS

INGREDIENTS

¼ cup dried chickpeas

¼ cup dried black-eyed peas

1½ cups green lentils

12 cups water, plus extra for soaking, divided

¼ cup olive oil, butter, or ghee

4 large onions, peeled and thinly sliced

10 cloves garlic, peeled and sliced

1 tablespoon sea salt

1 teaspoon freshly ground black pepper

2 teaspoons turmeric

3 tablespoons ground cumin

1 tablespoon ground coriander

2 tablespoons ground ginger

12 cups water

2 cups liquid *kashk* or 3 cups buttermilk

1 tablespoon grape molasses

12 ounces dried Persian noodles or fettuccine

3 tablespoons dried mint

1 cup coarsely chopped spring onions (white and green parts)

DIRECTIONS

1   In a bowl, place the chickpeas, black-eyed peas, and green lentils. Cover with water 2 inches above the legumes, and soak overnight. Then drain, rinse, and set aside.

2   In a large heavy-bottomed stock pot, add the oil, butter, or ghee and warm over medium heat. Add the onions and garlic, and sauté until golden brown, 7 to 15 minutes. Add the salt, pepper, turmeric, cumin, coriander, ginger, and the soaked legumes, and sauté for 1 minute.

3   Add the remaining 12 cups of water and bring to a boil. Reduce the heat to medium-low, cover, and simmer for 1½ hours.

4   Add the *kashk* or buttermilk and the grape molasses. Use a handheld mixer to partially puree the ingredients (to add body while showing some of the ingredients in the soup).

5   Add the noodles and cook for 5 minutes, stirring occasionally.

1 cup chopped fresh dill weed or ⅓ cup dried dill weed

2 cups chopped fresh parsley or ⅔ cup dried parsley

2 pounds chopped fresh spinach or 1 pound frozen chopped spinach

Mint garnish (see Chapter 4)

6 Add the mint, spring onions, dill weed, parsley, and spinach and continue to cook, stirring occasionally, for another 10 minutes. Adjust the seasoning to taste. Pour the soup into individual serving bowls, and add the mint garnish. *Nush-e joon!*

PER SERVING: *Calories 350 (From Fat 77); Fat 9g (Saturated 1g); Cholesterol 5mg; Sodium 789mg; Carbohydrate 56g (Dietary Fiber 9g); Protein 13g.*

TIP: To save time, you can use canned chickpeas, black-eyed peas, and green lentils instead of the dried ones (which require overnight soaking). Just rinse and drain them before using and reduce the cooking time in Step 3 to 10 minutes.

Yogurt and Chickpea Soup (Osh-e Mast)

PREP TIME: 20 MIN PLUS OVERNIGHT SOAKING	COOK TIME: 2 HR	YIELD: 10 SERVINGS

INGREDIENTS

½ cup chickpeas

9 cups water, plus extra for soaking, divided

¼ cup olive oil, butter, or ghee

2 large onions, peeled and thinly sliced

1 tablespoon fine sea salt

½ teaspoon freshly ground black pepper

1 teaspoon ground coriander

½ cup rice, soaked 30 minutes and drained

4 cups plain yogurt

1 egg

2 tablespoons unbleached all-purpose flour

½ cup chopped fresh parsley

1 cup chopped fresh beet leaves

½ cup chopped fresh dill weed

5 cloves garlic, peeled and grated

½ cup fresh tarragon or 3 tablespoons dried tarragon

1 teaspoons red pepper flakes, for garnish

1 teaspoon dried thyme, for garnish

DIRECTIONS

1 In a bowl, place the chickpeas, cover with water, and soak overnight. Then drain, rinse, and set aside.

2 To make the broth, in a large heavy-bottomed stock pot, place the oil, butter, or ghee, and warm over medium heat until hot. Add the onions and sauté until golden brown, about 10 to 15 minutes. Add the chickpeas, salt, pepper, and coriander, and sauté for 1 minute. Pour in 5 cups of the water and bring to a boil. Reduce the heat to medium-low, cover, and simmer for 55 minutes. Add the rice, cover, and simmer for another 15 minutes.

3 To make the yogurt mixture, in a large bowl, place the yogurt, egg, and flour and whisk for 5 minutes (beating the yogurt prevents it from curdling). Then add the remaining 4 cups of water and continue to whisk until smooth.

4 Add the yogurt mixture to the pot, stirring constantly for 1 minute. Reduce the heat to low, cover, and simmer until the beans are tender, about 25 to 30 minutes.

5 Add the parsley, beet leaves, dill weed, and garlic, and give the pot a stir. Simmer over low heat until the chickpeas are tender, about 15 minutes. Adjust the seasoning to taste. Pour the soup into individual bowls. Sprinkle a pinch of red pepper flakes and thyme on top. *Nush-e joon!*

PER SERVING: *Calories 221 (From Fat 90); Fat 10g (Saturated 3g); Cholesterol 34mg; Sodium 631mg; Carbohydrate 26g (Dietary Fiber 3g); Protein 8g.*

Walnut and Kashk Soup (Kaleh Jush)

PREP TIME: 15 MIN	COOK TIME: 35 MIN	YIELD: 4 SERVINGS

INGREDIENTS

2 cups walnuts

1 tablespoon fennel seeds

2 tablespoons olive oil, butter, or ghee

2 large onions, peeled and thinly sliced

4 cloves garlic, peeled and finely sliced

1 tablespoon flour

1 teaspoon fine sea salt

½ teaspoon freshly ground black pepper

1 teaspoon ground turmeric

1 teaspoon ground anise seeds

3 cups water

2 cups liquid *kashk*

2 tablespoons pepitas (shelled pumpkin seeds), toasted

Mint garnish (see Chapter 4)

1 flatbread, cut into ½-inch squares and toasted (see Tip)

DIRECTIONS

1 In a food processor, place the walnuts and fennel seeds, and pulse until coarsely chopped. Set aside.

2 In a medium heavy-bottomed pot, place the oil, butter, or ghee, and warm over medium heat. Add the onions and garlic, and sauté until the onions are golden brown, about 10 to 15 minutes.

3 Add the walnut mixture and stir-fry for 2 minutes (taking care, as the walnuts will burn quickly). Add the flour, salt, pepper, turmeric, and anise seeds, and stir for 1 minute.

4 Add the water and bring to a boil. Reduce the heat to low, cover, and simmer for 10 minutes. Add the *kashk*, and stir for 5 to 10 minutes over low heat. As soon as it begins to boil, remove it from the heat. Adjust the seasoning to taste.

5 Pour the soup into individual bowls, add the pepitas and mint garnish. Add the croutons to a bowl and place on the side for everyone to add to the soup as they please. *Nush-e joon!*

PER SERVING: *Calories 683 (From Fat 457); Fat 51g (Saturated 7g); Cholesterol 25mg; Sodium 947mg; Carbohydrate 46g (Dietary Fiber 6g); Protein 14g.*

TIP: To toast bread to make croutons, preheat the oven to 350 degrees. Place pieces of bread on a rimmed sheet pan lined with parchment paper and toast in the oven for 5 to 7 minutes until lightly toasted.

Pistachio Soup (Sup-e Pesteh)

INGREDIENTS

1 cup raw, unsalted pistachios kernels

2 tablespoons olive oil, butter, or ghee

1 shallot, peeled and thinly chopped

1 leek, washed thoroughly and finely chopped (white and green parts)

1 clove garlic, peeled and grated

½ inch fresh ginger, peeled and grated

1 tablespoon ground cumin

1 teaspoon ground coriander

½ teaspoon cayenne

1 tablespoon rice flour

8 cups homemade chicken broth

1 teaspoon sea salt

¼ teaspoon freshly ground black pepper

1 teaspoon grape molasses

½ cup sour orange juice or a mixture of 2 tablespoons fresh lime juice and ¼ cup orange juice

2 tablespoons barberries, picked over and rinsed thoroughly with cold water, for garnish

DIRECTIONS

1 In a food processor, place the pistachios and grind until very smooth. Set aside.

2 In a heavy, medium pot, add the oil, butter, or ghee, and warm over medium heat. Add the shallots, leeks, garlic, ginger, cumin, coriander, and cayenne, and sauté for 5 minutes. Add the rice flour and sauté for 1 minute. Add the broth, stirring constantly, until it comes to a boil, about 10 minutes.

3 Reduce the heat to low. Add the pistachios, salt, pepper, and grape molasses, and stir well. Cover and simmer over low heat, stirring occasionally, for 55 minutes.

4 Add the juice. Adjust the seasoning to taste. Pour the soup into individual bowls and garnish with barberries. Serve with hot flatbread. *Nush-e joon!*

PER SERVING: *Calories 384 (From Fat 220); Fat 24g (Saturated 4g); Cholesterol 0mg; Sodium 2,110mg; Carbohydrate 26g (Dietary Fiber 5g); Protein 18g.*

TIP: Pick over the shelled pistachios to be sure there are no broken shells or particles in them.

Wheat and Turkey Porridge (Halim-e Gandom)

PREP TIME: 15 MIN PLUS OVERNIGHT SOAKING	COOK TIME: 4 HR	YIELD: 6 SERVINGS

INGREDIENTS

3 pounds turkey, bone in

14 cups water, divided

2 medium onions, peeled and thinly sliced

2 cloves garlic, peeled and grated

1 tablespoon fine sea salt

1 teaspoon freshly ground black pepper

1 teaspoon turmeric

2 bay leaves

Wheat

2½ cups whole-wheat berries, soaked overnight and drained

¼ cup butter, melted, for garnish

1 teaspoon ground cinnamon, for garnish

2 tablespoons confectioners sugar, for garnish

DIRECTIONS

1 In a large saucepan, place the turkey and 6 cups of the water. Bring to a boil, skimming away any froth until it stops foaming. Add the onions, garlic, salt, pepper, turmeric, and bay leaves. Return to a boil, and then reduce the heat to low, cover, and simmer until the turkey is tender and falling off the bone, about 2½ to 3 hours.

2 Meanwhile, in a large, heavy-bottomed stock pot, place the wheat and the remaining 8 cups of water. Bring to a boil, reduce the heat to low, cover, and simmer until the wheat is tender, about 3 hours.

3 Place a large sieve over the pot containing the wheat. Drain the turkey broth through the sieve. Separate the meat from the bones and add it to the pot. Discard the bones and bay leaves. Cover the pot and cook over low heat, stirring occasionally, for 20 minutes.

4 Use a handheld mixer to puree the turkey and wheat, while still on the stove, until you have a homogenized, slightly elastic porridge. Adjust the seasoning to taste and keep warm until ready to serve.

5 Spoon the porridge into individual bowls and garnish to taste with the butter, cinnamon, and sugar. *Nush-e joon!*

PER SERVING: *Calories 674 (From Fat 161); Fat 18g (Saturated 7g); Cholesterol 150mg; Sodium 2,694mg; Carbohydrate 73g (Dietary Fiber 16g); Protein 63g.*

TIP: A good *halim* needs a patient cook. If you have time, you can use a long-handled wooden spoon instead of a mixer, stirring constantly, while still on the stove, until you have a stringy porridge, about 20 to 30 minutes.

VARY IT! You can use shoulder of lamb (bone in) in place of the turkey, if you like.

Main Courses

4

Chapter **12**

Rice Is a Very Nice Dish

ranians love rice and make the most delicious dishes by cooking it in multiple ways for different occasions and needs. In this chapter, I walk you through the different methods of cooking rice, show you how to make a delicious golden crust, and give you a variety of rice recipes so you can find exactly the one you need for any occasion.

Choosing the Right Type of Rice

I use aged basmati rice grown in the Himalayas (Khazana and Empire brands are my favorites). Basmati rice is very similar to Persian rice, which is slender and long-grained.

Washing the Rice

Basmati is an old rice that has matured under controlled conditions and benefits from being washed thoroughly, resulting in a more flavorful, aromatic rice. Soaking the rice helps remove any dirt, dust or debris. It also removes the surface starch from the rice grains, which allows them to absorb water, shortening the amount of cooking time needed. When properly washed, aged rice is cooked, it gives off a delightful perfume that unwashed rice doesn't have.

The first method for washing rice (and the one I recommend) is as follows (see Figure 12-1):

1. **Place the unwashed rice in a fine-mesh sieve and immerse it in a large container filled with cold water.**

TIP

   A fine-mesh, free-standing colander is required so the water can drain from the rice. If you use an ordinary colander to drain your rice, you may lose some rice through the holes.

2. **Allow to soak for 30 minutes.**

3. **Lift the sieve out of the water, and rinse thoroughly with cold water before using.**

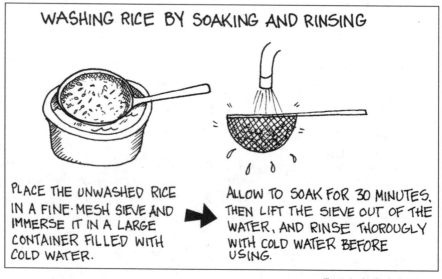

FIGURE 12-1:
Washing rice by soaking and rinsing it.

WASHING RICE BY SOAKING AND RINSING

PLACE THE UNWASHED RICE IN A FINE-MESH SIEVE AND IMMERSE IT IN A LARGE CONTAINER FILLED WITH COLD WATER.

ALLOW TO SOAK FOR 30 MINUTES. THEN LIFT THE SIEVE OUT OF THE WATER, AND RINSE THOROUGLY WITH COLD WATER BEFORE USING.

Illustration by Elizabeth Kurtzman

If you don't have a sieve, you can follow these steps instead:

1. **Place the rice in a large pot and cover with water.**

2. **Agitate gently with your hand without breaking the rice and then pour off the water.**

3. **Repeat Step 2 at least five more times, until the drained water is completely clear.**

Choosing the Right Pot

Use a deep, nonstick pot with a lid to allow the rice grains to swell properly and for a good crust to form without sticking. I use a 5-quart pot (measuring 11¼ inches in diameter and 3¼ inches deep).

Cooking the Rice

There are four main methods of cooking rice, Persian-style:

>> *Kateh* **(plain rice):** This method is the fastest way to make Persian-style rice. To make rice this way, check out the Plain Rice (Kateh) recipe in this chapter.

>> *Dami* **(smothered rice):** This method is the *easiest* way to make Persian-style rice. To make rice this way, check out the Smothered Rice, Rice Cooker–Style (Dami) recipe in this chapter.

>> *Chelow* **(saffron-steamed rice):** This method is the most sophisticated and elaborate way of making Persian rice. It needs more care in the cooking process, including parboiling, rinsing, preparing the crust base, and steaming. This process results in a fluffy rice, with each grain separated; the bottom of the pot has a layer of crunchy, crisp golden crust. To make rice this way, check out the Saffron Steamed Rice (Chelow) recipe in this chapter.

>> *Polow* **(rice with herbs, vegetables, fruit, and meat):** This method of cooking rice makes a complete dish on its own. It's initially cooked in the same way as *chelow*. Then meat, fruit, herbs, spices, and/or vegetables are combined, sautéed together, and arranged in alternating layers with the rice. It's all then steamed together. The result is a delicious, satisfying dish — a complete meal. This chapter has a variety of *polow* recipes.

SAVORING THAT GOLDEN CRUST

Iranians love *tahdig,* the golden crust of the rice. When I was growing up in Iran, at the dinner table, my sisters, brothers, and I would keep a polite but competitive eye on who would get the last piece. *Tahdig,* literally meaning "bottom of the pot" in Persian, is the crunchy, crispy layer that forms in the bottom of the pot when making Persian-style rice.

TIP

Keep in mind when making any kind of rice that the ratio of rice, water, and salt is very important for making a delicious rice that has separated grains.

REMEMBER

Always use a wooden spoon or silicone spatula to stir or for transferring the rice from the pot to the serving platter to avoid scratching your nonstick pot.

Plain Rice (Kateh)

INGREDIENTS

3 cups basmati rice, soaked for 30 minutes, rinsed, and drained

2 teaspoons fine sea salt

6 cups water

½ cup olive oil, butter, or ghee

DIRECTIONS

1   In a medium nonstick pot, place the rice and salt. Add the water and bring to a boil over high heat, gently stirring the rice with a wooden spoon for a few times as it comes to a boil.

2   Reduce the heat to medium and cook, uncovered, until all the water has been absorbed, about 10 to 15 minutes.

3   Swirl the oil, butter, or ghee over the rice. Reduce the heat to medium-low, wrap the lid with a clean dish towel, cover firmly to prevent any steam from escaping, and cook for 15 minutes.

4   Remove from the heat and use a wooden spoon to serve the rice. *Nush-e joon!*

PER SERVING: *Calories 262 (From Fat 164); Fat 18g (Saturated 3g); Cholesterol 0mg; Sodium 625mg; Carbohydrate 22g (Dietary Fiber 0g); Protein 2g.*

TIP: For brown basmati rice, use 7 cups of water and increase the cooking time in Step 2 to 20 to 25 minutes.

TIP: If you want the *kateh* to have a *tahdig,* in Step 3 cover and cook the rice for 45 minutes. Use a wooden spoon to serve the rice and then unmold the crust to serve on the side.

Saffron Steamed Rice (Chelow)

INGREDIENTS

11½ cups plus 2 tablespoons water, divided

3 tablespoons fine sea salt

1 tablespoon cardamom seeds (not whole pods; optional)

2 tablespoons rose water (optional)

3 cups basmati rice, soaked 30 minutes, drained, and rinsed

¾ cup olive oil, butter, or ghee, divided

2 tablespoons plain whole yogurt

½ teaspoon ground saffron threads dissolved in 2 tablespoons rose water or hot water, divided

DIRECTIONS

1 In a large nonstick pot, add 8 cups of the water and bring to a boil. Add the salt, cardamom, rose water (if using), and rice. Boil briskly for 6 to 10 minutes, gently stirring twice with a wooden spoon to loosen any grains that stick to the bottom. When all the rice has risen to the surface, bite a few grains; if the rice feels soft, it's ready to be drained.

2 Drain the rice in a large fine-mesh strainer and rinse with 3 cups of the water.

3 In the same pot, combine 2 spatulas of the parboiled rice (about 2 heaped cups) with ½ cup of the oil, butter, or ghee; the yogurt; 2 tablespoons of the water, and 1 tablespoon of the saffron water. Mix well, using a rubber spatula, until the mixture is smooth and no longer lumpy; then spread out evenly in the pot (this will form the *tahdig*).

4 Gently heap the remaining rice, one spatula at a time, onto the *tahdig* layer. Shape the rice into a pyramid to allow it to expand. Sprinkle the remaining 1 tablespoon of saffron water on top. Cover the pot and cook over medium heat until steam rises, about 10 to 12 minutes.

5 Mix ½ cup water with the remaining ¼ cup of oil, butter, or ghee and pour over the rice. Wrap the lid in a clean dish towel and then place on the pot to absorb condensation and prevent any steam from escaping. Reduce the heat to low and cook for 1 hour 10 minutes.

6 Remove the pot from the heat and leave it to cool, still covered, on a damp surface (a damp dish towel on a rimmed sheet pan) for 5 minutes to loosen the crust.

7 To serve, use a wooden spatula to gently loosen the crust around edges. Then hold a serving platter (larger than the opening of the pot) tightly over the uncovered pot and invert the two together, unmolding the entire mound onto the platter; the rice will emerge as a golden-crusted cake. Or, if you prefer the traditional approach, transfer the rice to a serving platter, without disturbing the *tahdig* and serve the *tahdig* on the side. *Nush-e joon!*

PER SERVING: *Calories 344 (From Fat 246); Fat 27g (Saturated 4g); Cholesterol 1mg; Sodium 627mg; Carbohydrate 23g (Dietary Fiber 0g); Protein 2g.*

Smothered Rice, Rice Cooker–Style (Dami)

INGREDIENTS

3 cups white basmati rice, soaked for 30 minutes, rinsed, and drained

4 cups water

2 teaspoons fine sea salt

½ cup olive oil, butter, or ghee

¼ teaspoon ground saffron threads dissolved in 1 tablespoon hot water or rose water

DIRECTIONS

1 In a rice cooker, place the rice, water, salt, and oil, butter, or ghee. Gently stir with a wooden spoon for 1 minute to ensure the salt is dissolved. Then start the rice cooker.

2 After 1 hour, uncover and pour the saffron water over the top of the rice. Then unplug the rice cooker.

3 Allow to cool for 5 minutes without uncovering the pot.

4 Remove the lid and take out the inner pot. Place a round serving dish, larger than the opening of the pot, over it. Hold the dish and the pot tightly together and turn them over to unmold the rice. The rice will be like a cake, crispy on the top with separated grains of rice inside. Cut into wedges and serve. *Nush-e joon!*

PER SERVING: *Calories 262 (From Fat 164); Fat 18g (Saturated 3g); Cholesterol 0mg; Sodium 625mg; Carbohydrate 22g (Dietary Fiber 0g); Protein 2g.*

TIP: Don't have a rice cooker? No problem. Just use a medium nonstick pot, combine all the ingredients, stir well, wrap the lid with a clean dish towel (to prevent steam from escaping and to absorb any condensation), cover tightly, and steam over medium heat for 1 hour. Continue with Step 3.

NOTE: For this recipe, be sure to use a standard measuring cup, not the smaller cup that sometimes comes with rice cookers.

TIP: If you're using American long-grain rice, reduce the water to 3 cups. No need to soak the rice, just rinse it in a sieve.

Chelow kabob is the national dish of Iran; it consists of Saffron Steamed Rice (Chelow; Chapter 12) and kabobs (Chapter 14).

Onions with Rice and Herb Stuffing (Dolmeh-ye Piaz; Chapter 10)

Fish Cooked in a Tamarind, Cilantro, and Garlic Broth (Qaliyeh-ye Mahi; Chapter 16)

Noodle and Chickpea Soup (Osh-e Reshteh; Chapter 11)

Butternut Squash and Prune Braise (Khoresh-e Kadu Halvai-o Alu; Chapter 13)

Sweet-and-Sour Kabob (Kabab-e Torsh; Chapter 14)

Pomegranate-Infused Leg of Lamb (Barreh-ye Berivan; Chapter 15)

Chicken Kabob (Jujeh Kabab; Chapter 14)

Fish with Fresh Herb and Barberry Stuffing (Mahi-e Tu Por ba Sabzi; Chapter 16)

Pistachio and Pomegranate Meatballs (Kufteh-ye Pesteh-o Anar; Chapter 15)

Raisin Cookies (Nan-e Keshmeshy; Chapter 18)

NAJMIEH BATMANGLIJ

A typical Persian table setting with various dishes from the book

Saffroned Persian-Style Quinoa (Quinoa)

PREP TIME: 10 MIN | COOK TIME: 45 MIN | YIELD: 6 SERVINGS

INGREDIENTS

3 cups quinoa

4 cups water

2 teaspoons fine sea salt

¼ cup olive oil

¼ teaspoon ground saffron threads

1 teaspoon ground cardamom

DIRECTIONS

1 Wash the quinoa by placing it in a fine-mesh colander and rinsing thoroughly.

2 In a large nonstick pot, place the quinoa, water, salt, olive oil, saffron, and cardamom; stir gently with a long-handled wooden spoon for 1 minute to dissolve the salt. Bring to a boil, reduce the heat to low, cover, and cook for 30 minutes, without stirring.

3 Fluff the cooked quinoa with a fork and serve as you would rice. *Nush-e joon!*

PER SERVING: *Calories 392 (From Fat 127); Fat 14g (Saturated 2g); Cholesterol 0mg; Sodium 628mg; Carbohydrate 55g (Dietary Fiber 6g); Protein 12g.*

Oven–Baked Rice with Lamb, Eggplant, and Barberries (Tachin)

PREP TIME: 1 HR 40 MIN PLUS 30 MIN FOR SOAKING	COOK TIME: 2½ HR	YIELD: 6 SERVINGS

INGREDIENTS

2 pounds boneless leg of lamb, cut into 1-inch cubes

6 small onions, peeled and thinly sliced, divided

2 cloves garlic, peeled and sliced

3 tablespoons fine sea salt, divided

2 teaspoons freshly ground black pepper, divided

1 teaspoon turmeric

2 tablespoons fresh lime juice

11 cups water, divided

3 cups basmati rice, soaked for 30 minutes, drained, and rinsed

1 cup olive oil, butter, or ghee, divided

3 pounds Chinese eggplants, peeled and cut into 3-inch rounds

2 teaspoons cumin seeds, toasted

DIRECTIONS

1 In a deep, wide skillet, place the lamb, 2 of the sliced onions, garlic, 2 teaspoons of the salt, 1 teaspoon of the pepper, the turmeric, and the lime juice. Cover tightly and cook over low heat for 1 hour. Uncover, give it a stir, raise the heat to medium, and continue to cook, uncovered, until all the juices have been absorbed, about 5 minutes. Set aside.

2 In a large nonstick pot, place 8 cups of the water and 2 tablespoons of the fine sea salt and bring to a boil. Add the rice and boil briskly for 6 minutes, gently stirring once (for this recipe, at this stage, the rice should be al dente — neither hard nor soft). Drain the rice in a large fine-mesh colander and rinse with 3 cups of the water. Set aside.

3 In a wide nonstick skillet, add 1 tablespoon of the oil, butter, or ghee and warm over medium heat. Add the eggplant slices and brown on both sides, about 3 minutes per side; remove from the skillet and set aside. Add 2 tablespoons of the oil, butter, or ghee to the same skillet along with the remaining 4 sliced onions and sauté over medium heat until golden brown, about 7 to 15 minutes. Remove from the skillet and set aside.

4 Wipe the skillet, and add 1 tablespoon of the oil, butter, or ghee; 1 tablespoon water; the cumin; the sugar; and the barberries; stir-fry over medium-high heat for 4 minutes. Set aside.

5 In a large bowl, add the eggs; yogurt or labneh; saffron water; ¼ cup of oil, butter, or ghee; the remaining 1 teaspoon of salt; the remaining 1 teaspoon of pepper; the cinnamon; and the caramelized orange peel. Whisk together until smooth; then add the rice and fold in.

1 tablespoon sugar

1 cup dried barberries, cleaned (see Chapter 4)

3 eggs

2 cups thick plain whole yogurt or labneh

1 teaspoon ground saffron threads dissolved in ¼ cup orange blossom water

1 teaspoon ground cinnamon

2 tablespoon caramelized orange peel (see Chapter 4)

6 Brush the remaining ½ cup of oil, butter, or ghee evenly and thoroughly all over the base and sides of a 4-quart ovenproof Pyrex dish and place it in the oven. Then heat the oven to 375 degrees.

7 When the oven reaches 375 degrees, remove the hot baking dish from the oven and place it on the counter. Spread half the rice mixture evenly in the baking dish and arrange the lamb pieces on top. Spread the barberry mixture over the lamb and arrange the eggplants and onions on top. Cover with the remaining rice. Place a layer of oiled parchment paper and a layer of aluminum foil on top. Press down evenly with the palms of your hands, compacting the rice (this will help with the unmolding process later). Seal tightly around the rim and pierce several holes on top using the tip of a knife so steam can escape.

8 Return to the oven and bake until the crust is golden brown, about 2 to 2¼ hours (an ovenproof glass dish allows you to see through). Spread a wet dish towel on the counter or on a rimmed sheet pan.

9 Remove the dish from the oven (without uncovering) and allow to cool for 15 minutes on the wet dish towel. Uncover and, with an offset spatula, loosen the rice around the edges of the dish. Place a serving platter (larger than the baking dish) on top. Hold the dish and platter firmly together and turn over in a single motion to unmold the rice. Allow to rest for a moment; then gently lift off the dish. Serve hot. *Nush-e joon!*

PER SERVING: *Calories 792 (From Fat 424); Fat 47g (Saturated 9g); Cholesterol 185mg; Sodium 1,112mg; Carbohydrate 61g (Dietary Fiber 11g); Protein 35g.*

VARY IT! If you prefer, you can use skinless, boneless chicken thighs instead of lamb.

VARY IT! For vegetarians, replace the meat with 1 pound of cremini mushrooms, cleaned and sliced. In Step 1, sauté all the ingredients together over medium heat until golden brown, about 10 to 15 minutes; then continue with Step 2.

Rice with Lentils (Adas Polow)

PREP TIME: 35 MIN PLUS 30 MIN FOR SOAKING	COOK TIME: 1 HR 20 MIN	YIELD: 6 SERVINGS

INGREDIENTS

2 cups lentils, rinsed

15 cups water, divided

2 tablespoons plus 1½ teaspoons fine sea salt, divided

1 cup olive oil, butter, or ghee, divided

2 medium onions, peeled and thinly sliced

2 cups raisins

2 cups dates, pitted and any hard stem parts removed

½ cup caramelized orange peel, finely chopped (see Chapter 4)

½ teaspoon freshly ground black pepper

2 teaspoons *advieh* (Persian spice mix)

1 teaspoon ground saffron dissolved in ¼ cup orange blossom water, divided

2 cups basmati rice, soaked for 30 minutes, drained, and rinsed

Sangak or lavash flatbread

1 cup crispy fried onions (see Chapter 4), for garnish

DIRECTIONS

1 In a medium saucepan, place the lentils, 6 cups water, and 1 teaspoon of the salt, and bring to a boil. Reduce the heat to medium and cook, uncovered, for 10 minutes. Drain and set aside (don't rinse).

2 In a wide skillet, add 3 tablespoons of the oil, butter or ghee and warm over medium heat. Add the onions and sauté until golden brown, about 7 to 15 minutes. Add the raisins, dates, caramelized orange peel, the remaining ½ teaspoon of salt, pepper, *advieh*, and 1 tablespoon of the saffron water. Stir-fry for 20 seconds and set aside.

3 In a large nonstick pot, add 6 cups of the water and bring to a boil. Add the remaining 2 tablespoons of salt. Pour in the rice and boil briskly for 6 to 10 minutes, gently stirring with a wooden spoon to loosen any grains that may have stuck to the bottom. Bite a few grains; if the rice feels soft and all of it has risen to the surface, it is ready to be drained. Drain the rice in a large, fine-mesh colander and rinse with 2 cups of the water.

4 In the same pot, use a rubber spatula to mix ½ cup of the oil, ½ cup of the water, and 1 tablespoon of the saffron water over the bottom of the pot. Spread a layer of *sangak* to cover the bottom of the pot.

5 Place 2 spatulas full of rice in the pot. Add 1 spatula full of lentils and 1 spatula of the onion, raisin, and date mixture. Repeat, mounding in the shape of a pyramid.

6 Cover and cook the rice over medium heat for 10 minutes. Pour the remaining 5 tablespoons oil, the remaining ½ cup of water, and the remaining 3 tablespoons of saffron water over the rice. Wrap the lid of the pot with a clean dish towel and cover the pot firmly to prevent steam from escaping. Cook over low heat for 50 minutes. Remove from the heat and allow to cool for 5 minutes, without uncovering, on a damp dish towel (this will help with unmolding the rice).

7 Uncover the rice and add the crispy fried onions; then place a round serving dish, larger than the pot, over it. Hold the dish and the pot tightly together and turn them over to unmold the rice. It will have a crispy layer of bread on the top with separated grains of rice inside. Cut the crust into wedges and use an offset spatula to transfer the rice crust and the rice under it to individual plates. Serve with roast lamb or chicken (see Chapter 15 for recipes) on the side with *torshi* (Persian pickles) and fresh herbs. *Nush-e joon!*

PER SERVING: *Calories 963 (From Fat 386); Fat 43g (Saturated 8g); Cholesterol 9mg; Sodium 616mg; Carbohydrate 128g (Dietary Fiber 25g); Protein 23g.*

Rice with Fava Beans and Dill (Baqala Polow)

| PREP TIME: 20 MIN | COOK TIME: 1 HR 10 MIN | YIELD: 4 SERVINGS |

INGREDIENTS

8¾ cups water, divided

2 tablespoons fine sea salt

2 cups basmati rice, soaked for 30 minutes, drained, and rinsed

2 pounds fresh or 1 pound frozen fava beans, second skins removed

¼ teaspoon turmeric

2 tablespoons rose water

¾ cup olive oil, butter, or ghee, divided

1 teaspoon ground saffron dissolved in ¼ cup rose water, divided

Sangak, lavash, or flatbread

10 baby green garlic, trimmed, or 4 cloves of garlic, peeled and finely chopped

1 tablespoon ground cardamom

1½ teaspoons ground cinnamon

4 cups chopped fresh dill weed

DIRECTIONS

1 In a large nonstick pot, add 6 cups of the water and bring to a boil. Add the salt, rice, fava beans, turmeric, and rose water while the water is boiling. Boil briskly for 6 to 10 minutes, gently stirring twice with a wooden spoon to loosen any grains that may have stuck to the bottom. Bite a few grains; when the rice feels soft, drain in a large, fine-mesh colander and rinse with 2 cups of the water (cold is best) to stop the cooking.

2 In the same pot, use a rubber spatula to mix together ½ cup of the oil, butter, or ghee; ½ cup of the water; and 1 tablespoon of the saffron water. Spread a layer of *sangak,* lavash, or flatbread to fit the bottom of the pot.

3 Taking a spatula full of rice and beans, begin to form a pyramid by alternating layers of rice with the garlic, cardamom, and cinnamon. Cover and cook over medium heat for 10 minutes.

4 Mix ¼ cup of the oil with ¼ cup of the water and pour over the rice. Pour the remaining 3 tablespoons of saffron water over the top. Wrap the lid of the pot with a clean dish towel and cover firmly to prevent steam from escaping. Cook for another 40 minutes over low heat. Uncover, add the dill, and gently fluff using 2 forks. Cover and cook for another 10 minutes.

5 Remove the pot from the heat and allow to cool for 5 minutes on a damp surface without uncovering. Uncover and hold a serving platter, larger than the pot, tightly over the pot and invert the two together, unmolding the entire mound onto the platter. Serve with fish, lamb, or chicken and your favorite pickle. *Nush-e joon!*

PER SERVING: *Calories 856 (From Fat 422); Fat 47g (Saturated 9g); Cholesterol 13mg; Sodium 697mg; Carbohydrate 88g (Dietary Fiber 14g); Protein 24g.*

TIP: If you want to use dry dill instead of fresh, use 1½ cups and add it in Step 1 with the fava beans.

NOTE: Turmeric helps to keep the fava beans green.

Barberry Rice (Zereshk Polow)

PREP TIME: 15 MIN PLUS 30 MIN FOR SOAKING	COOK TIME: 1 HR 35 MIN	YIELD: 6 SERVINGS

INGREDIENTS

11¾ cups water, divided

3 tablespoons fine sea salt

3 cups basmati rice, soaked for 30 minutes, drained, and rinsed

3 tablespoons cumin seeds

¾ cup plus 2 tablespoons olive oil, butter, or ghee, divided

2 tablespoons whole plain yogurt

½ teaspoon ground saffron dissolved in 2 tablespoons rose water, divided

2 cups dried barberries, cleaned (see Chapter 4)

2 tablespoons sugar

¼ cup slivered almonds, toasted

¼ cup slivered pistachio kernels, toasted

DIRECTIONS

1 In a large nonstick pot, add 8 cups of the water and bring to a boil. Add the salt, the rice, and the cumin, and boil briskly for 6 to 10 minutes, gently stirring twice with a wooden spoon to loosen any grains that may have stuck to the bottom. Bite a few grains; when the rice feels soft, drain in a large fine-mesh colander and rinse with 3 cups of the water (cold is best).

2 In the same pot, use a rubber spatula to mix together ½ cup of the oil, butter, or ghee; 2 tablespoons of the water, the yogurt, 1 tablespoon of the saffron water, and 2 spatulas of the rice. Spread it evenly over the bottom of the pot. Transfer the remaining rice to the pot, mound it in the shape of a pyramid, cover, and cook over medium heat for 10 minutes.

3 Mix ¼ cup of oil, butter, or ghee with ½ cup of the water and pour over the rice. Wrap the lid of the pot with a clean dish towel and cover firmly to prevent steam from escaping. Cook over low heat for 1 hour 10 minutes.

4 Meanwhile, in a wide skillet, add the barberries; the remaining 2 tablespoons of oil, butter, or ghee; the sugar; the remaining 2 tablespoons of water; and the remaining 1 tablespoon of saffron water. Stir-fry over medium-high heat for 4 minutes (be careful — barberries burn very easily). Add the almonds and pistachios, give the mixture a stir, and set aside.

5 Remove the pot from the heat and allow to cool, covered, for 5 minutes on a damp dish towel to free the crust from the bottom of the pot.

6 Carefully transfer the rice, without disturbing the crust, onto a serving platter in alternating layers with the barberry mixture. Detach the crust with a wooden spoon and serve it on the side. Serve with roast chicken (see Chapter 15 for recipes) and a fresh herb platter (see Chapter 7). *Nush-e joon!*

PER SERVING: *Calories 857 (From Fat 502); Fat 56g (Saturated 8g); Cholesterol 1mg; Sodium 169mg; Carbohydrate 82g (Dietary Fiber 9g); Protein 13g.*

Rice with Potatoes and Cumin (Dami-e Zireh)

PREP TIME: 15 MIN PLUS 30 MINUTES FOR SOAKING	COOK TIME: 1 HR	YIELD: 6 SERVINGS

INGREDIENTS

½ cup olive oil, butter, or ghee, divided

2 medium onions, peeled and thinly sliced

1 pound yellow potatoes, peeled and diced into 1-inch cubes

¼ cup cumin seeds

1 tablespoon fine sea salt

2 teaspoons turmeric

2 cups basmati rice, soaked for 30 minutes, drained, and rinsed

4 cups water or chicken stock

DIRECTIONS

1 In a large nonstick pot, add ¼ cup of the oil, butter, or ghee and warm over medium heat. Add the onions and sauté until lightly golden brown, about 10 to 15 minutes. Add the potatoes, cumin, salt, and turmeric, and sauté for 5 minutes. Add the rice and sauté for 1 minute.

2 Add the water or chicken stock and bring to a boil over high heat, *gently* stirring the mixture with a wooden spoon a few times while it comes to a boil. Reduce the heat to medium, cover, and cook for 20 minutes.

3 When the rice has absorbed all the water, swirl the remaining ¼ cup of oil, butter, or ghee over the rice. Reduce the heat to low, wrap the lid of the pot with a clean dish towel, and cover firmly to prevent steam from escaping. Cook for 25 minutes.

4 Remove the pot from the heat and allow to cool for 5 minutes on a damp dish towel without uncovering it.

5 Using a wooden spoon, carefully transfer the rice mixture, one spoonful at a time, to a serving platter without disturbing the crust. Mound the rice mixture in the shape of a pyramid, detach the crust, and serve it on the side. Serve with fried eggs, a fresh herb platter (see Chapter 7), and the Onion, Cucumber and Coriander Quick Pickle (Torshi Hazeri-e Piaz; see Chapter 17). *Nush-e joon!*

PER SERVING: *Calories 336 (From Fat 173); Fat 19g (Saturated 3g); Cholesterol 0mg; Sodium 957mg; Carbohydrate 38g (Dietary Fiber 3g); Protein 5g.*

VARY IT! Replace the potatoes for this rice with peeled and diced butternut squash if you like.

Jeweled Rice (Javaher Polow)

PREP TIME: 40 MIN	COOK TIME: 1 HR 35 MIN	YIELD: 6 SERVINGS

INGREDIENTS

1 cup dried barberries, cleaned (see Chapter 4)

¾ cup plus 3 tablespoons olive oil, butter, or ghee, divided

1 cup plus 1 teaspoon sugar, divided

11¾ cups water, plus extra for boiling the carrots, divided

1 cup slivered orange peel (about 3 large oranges)

1 pound carrots, peeled and cut into 3-x-¼-inch strips (about 2 cups), or ready-made julienned carrots

½ teaspoon ground saffron dissolved in 2 tablespoons orange blossom water

One 4-inch cinnamon stick

2 teaspoons ground cardamom

½ cup sliced raw almonds, toasted (see Chapter 4)

¼ cup sliced raw pistachios kernels

2 tablespoons fine sea salt

3 cups basmati rice, soaked for 30 minutes, drained, and rinsed

DIRECTIONS

1 In a wide skillet, add the barberries; 1 tablespoon of the oil, butter, or ghee; 1 teaspoon of the sugar; and 2 tablespoons of water. Stir-fry over medium-high heat for 4 minutes (be careful — barberries burn easily!). Set aside.

2 Fill a small saucepan with water, and bring to a boil. Drop the orange peel in the pan, and return to a boil. Drain and rinse with cold water. In a wide skillet, place the remaining 2 tablespoons of oil, butter, or ghee, and warm over medium heat. Add the carrots and the orange peel, and stir-fry for 2 minutes. Add the remaining 1 cup of sugar, 1 tablespoon of the saffron water, the cinnamon, cardamom, and the remaining 1 cup water; bring to a boil. Reduce the heat to medium and simmer for 10 minutes. Drain, reserving the syrup. Add the almonds and pistachios to the carrot mixture; set aside.

3 In a large nonstick pot, place 8 cups of water and bring to a boil. Add the salt and rice. Boil briskly for 6 to 10 minutes, gently stirring twice with a wooden spoon to loosen any grains that may have stuck to the bottom. Bite a few grains; when the rice feels soft, drain in a large, fine-mesh colander and rinse with 2 cups of water.

4 In the same pot, use a rubber spatula to mix ½ cup of the oil, butter, or ghee; 2 tablespoons of the water; the remaining 1 tablespoon of the saffron water; and 2 spatulas of rice. Spread the mixture over the bottom of the pot.

5 Gently heap the remaining rice on top. Cover and cook over medium heat for 10 minutes. Swirl the remaining ½ cup of water; the remaining ¼ cup of oil, butter, or ghee; and the reserved syrup over the rice. Wrap the lid of the pot with a clean dish towel and cover firmly. Cook over low heat for 50 minutes. Remove the pot from the heat and allow to cool on a damp surface for 5 minutes without uncovering.

6 Using a wooden spatula, gently take 1 spatula full of rice at a time (trying not to disturb the crust), and mound it on a platter in alternating layers with the carrot mixture and the barberries. Detach the crust to serve on the side. Serve with Chicken Kabob (Jujeh Kabab; see Chapter 14) or Chicken, Walnut and Pomegranate Braise (Khoresh-e Fesenjoon; see Chapter 13). *Nush-e joon!*

PER SERVING: *Calories 706 (From Fat 368); Fat 41g (Saturated 5g); Cholesterol 0mg; Sodium 177mg; Carbohydrate 82g (Dietary Fiber 8g); Protein 8g.*

Rice with Green Beans (Lubia Polow)

PREP TIME: 45 MIN	COOK TIME: 1 HR 45 MIN	YIELD: 6 SERVINGS

INGREDIENTS

3 tablespoons olive oil, butter, or ghee

2 medium onions, peeled and thinly sliced

2 cloves garlic, peeled and sliced

1 pound fresh or frozen green beans, trimmed and cut into 1½-inch lengths

3 tablespoons fine sea salt

1 teaspoon freshly ground black pepper

1 teaspoon turmeric

¼ teaspoon cayenne

1 tablespoon *advieh* (Persian spice mix)

1 teaspoon ground cinnamon

1 tablespoon *limu omani* (ground dried Persian lime)

Zest of 1 fresh lime

2 tablespoons fresh lime juice

2 large fresh tomatoes, peeled and pureed, or 2 cups canned peeled pureed tomatoes

8 cups water, divided

2 cups basmati rice, soaked for 30 minutes, drained, and rinsed

¾ cup oil, melted butter, or ghee

¼ teaspoon ground saffron dissolved in 1 tablespoon rose water

2 russet potatoes, peeled and cut into ¼-inch slices

DIRECTIONS

1 In a medium saucepan, add the 3 tablespoons of oil, butter, or ghee, and warm over medium heat. Add the onions and garlic and brown, about 10 minutes. Add the green beans, 1 tablespoon of the salt, pepper, turmeric, cayenne, *advieh*, cinnamon, *limu omani*, and lime zest, and sauté for 4 minutes. Add the lime juice and tomatoes, and bring to a boil. Reduce the heat to low, give the pot a gentle stir, cover, and simmer for 40 minutes.

2 In a large nonstick pot, place 6 cups of the water and bring to a boil. Add the remaining 2 tablespoons of salt and the rice. Boil briskly for 6 minutes (for this recipe, at this stage, the rice should be al dente — neither hard nor soft), gently stirring twice with a wooden spoon to loosen any grains that may have stuck to the bottom. Drain the rice in a large, fine-mesh colander and rinse with the remaining 2 cups of water.

3 In the same pot, use a rubber spatula to mix together ½ cup of the oil, melted butter, or ghee, and the saffron water. Arrange the potato slices side-by-side to fit the bottom of the pot.

4 Place 2 spatulas full of rice over the potatoes in the pot; then add a layer of the green bean mixture (use a slotted spatula to avoid bringing in the sauce). Reserve the sauce to use later. Repeat, alternating layers of rice and beans to form a pyramid. Cover and cook over medium heat for 10 minutes.

5 Reduce the heat to low, pour the remaining ¼ cup of oil, melted butter, or ghee and the reserved sauce over the rice. Wrap the lid with a clean dish towel, cover the pot firmly, and cook for 50 minutes. Remove from the heat and allow to cool for 5 minutes on a damp dish towel without uncovering.

6 Uncover and hold a serving platter, larger than the pot, tightly over the pot and invert the two together, unmolding the entire mound onto the platter. The rice will emerge as a golden-crusted cake. Serve with a fresh herb platter (see Chapter 7), cucumber and tomato salad, and Persian pickles. *Nush-e joon!*

PER SERVING: *Calories 517 (From Fat 309); Fat 34g (Saturated 5g); Cholesterol 0mg; Sodium 953mg; Carbohydrate 49g (Dietary Fiber 5g); Protein 6g.*

Rice with Sour Cherries (Albalu Polow)

PREP TIME: 1 HR 30 MIN	COOK TIME: 1 HR	YIELD: 6 SERVINGS

INGREDIENTS

3 pounds fresh sour cherries, stemmed and pitted, or 1 pound frozen, pitted sour cherries

1 cup sugar

¾ cup plus 2 tablespoons olive oil, butter, or ghee, divided

½ teaspoon cinnamon

½ teaspoon freshly ground black pepper

1 tablespoon cardamom

1 teaspoon ground saffron dissolved in ¼ cup rose water, divided

10½ cups water, divided

2 tablespoons fine sea salt

3 cups basmati rice, soaked for 30 minutes, drained, and rinsed

Sangak, lavash, or pita bread

2 tablespoons slivered almonds, toasted, for garnish

2 tablespoons slivered pistachios, toasted, for garnish

1 cup crispy fried onions (see Chapter 4), for garnish

DIRECTIONS

1 In a medium saucepan, place the cherries and sugar and bring to a boil. Reduce the heat to medium and cook for 20 minutes. Drain using a fine-mesh colander over a bowl, and reserve the syrup to use later. Return the cherries to the saucepan and add 2 tablespoons of the oil, butter, or ghee; the cinnamon; pepper; cardamom; and 1 tablespoon of the saffron water. Stir gently and set aside.

2 In a large nonstick pot, place 8 cups of the water and bring to a boil. Add the salt and rice. Boil briskly for 6 minutes, gently stirring twice with a wooden spoon to loosen any grains that may have stuck to the bottom (for this recipe, at this stage, the rice should be al dente — neither hard nor soft). Drain the rice in a large, fine-mesh colander, and rinse with 2 cups of the water.

3 In the same pot, use a rubber spatula to mix together ½ cup of the oil, butter, or ghee; the remaining ½ cup of water; and 1 tablespoon of the saffron water. Place a layer of *sangak*, lavash, or pita bread on top to fit the bottom of the pot.

4 Place 2 spatulas of rice over the bread in the pot; then add 1 slotted spatula of cherries. Do not add any of the syrup. Repeat, alternating layers of rice and cherries to mound the rice.

5 Cover and cook over medium heat for 10 minutes. Reduce the heat to low and pour the remaining 2 tablespoons of saffron water over the rice. Wrap the lid of the pot with a clean dish towel and cover firmly to prevent steam from escaping. Cook for 40 minutes. Remove the lid and pour 1 cup of the reserved cherry syrup and the remaining ¼ cup of oil, butter, or ghee over the rice. Cover and cook for 10 minutes.

6 Remove the pot from the heat and allow to cool on a damp dish towel for 5 minutes without uncovering. Uncover and garnish with almonds, pistachios, and fried onions. Hold a large serving platter tightly over the pot and invert the two together, unmolding the entire mound onto the platter. Serve with Lime and Turmeric Roast Chicken (Morgh-e Beriyan; Chapter 15). *Nush-e joon!*

PER SERVING: *Calories 725 (From Fat 380); Fat 42g (Saturated 9g); Cholesterol 9mg; Sodium 257mg; Carbohydrate 83g (Dietary Fiber 3g); Protein 6g.*

Spicy Fish-Crusted Rice (Havari-e Mahi)

PREP TIME: 50 MIN PLUS 30 MIN FOR SOAKING	COOK TIME: 1 HR 30 MIN	YIELD: 6 SERVINGS

INGREDIENTS

2 tablespoons plus 2½ teaspoons fine sea salt, divided

1 teaspoon freshly ground black pepper, divided

2 teaspoons turmeric, divided

2 pounds thick, fatty fish fillets (such as salmon), cut into 3-x-3-inch pieces

8 cups water, divided

2 cups basmati rice, soaked for 30 minutes, drained, and rinsed

¾ cup olive oil, butter, or ghee, divided

1 teaspoon ground saffron threads dissolved in ¼ cup rose water, divided

2 medium onions, peeled and thinly sliced

6 cloves garlic, peeled and grated

1 teaspoon red pepper flakes

1 teaspoon ground cardamom

1 teaspoon ground cinnamon

1 tablespoon ground cumin

DIRECTIONS

1 In a small bowl, add 1 teaspoon of the salt, ½ teaspoon of the pepper, and ½ teaspoon of the turmeric and mix together. Dust the fish on both sides with this mixture. Cover and refrigerate.

2 In a large nonstick pot, add 6 cups of the water and 2 tablespoons of the salt and bring to a boil. Add the rice and boil briskly for 6 minutes, stirring gently with a wooden spoon to loosen any grains stuck to the bottom of the pot (for this recipe, at this stage, the rice should be al dente — neither hard nor soft). Drain the rice in a large fine-mesh colander, rinse with the remaining 2 cups of cold tap water, and set aside.

3 In a wide skillet, add ¼ cup of the oil, butter, or ghee and warm over medium heat. Add the onions and sauté until golden brown, about 10 to 15 minutes. Add the garlic, 1½ teaspoons of the salt, ½ teaspoon of the pepper, the red pepper flakes, 1½ teaspoons of the turmeric, the cardamom, cinnamon, cumin, and dried Persian limes, and sauté for 1 minute.

4 Add the cilantro and fenugreek and sauté for 1 minute. Add the diluted tamarind paste and bring to a boil. Remove from the heat; set aside.

2 tablespoons ground hearts of dried Persian limes

2 cups chopped fresh cilantro

2 tablespoons dried fenugreek leaves

3 tablespoons tamarind paste, diluted with 1½ cups water

1 cup chopped fresh dill weed, for garnish

1 green jalapeño pepper, thinly sliced, for garnish

5   In the nonstick pot, add ¼ cup of the oil, butter, or ghee, and 1 tablespoon of the saffron water. Arrange the fish fillets, side-by-side, to fit the bottom of the pot. Mound the rice in alternating layers with the cilantro mixture over the fish to form a pyramid.

6   Pour the remaining ¼ cup of oil, butter, or ghee over the rice. Drizzle the remaining 3 tablespoons of saffron water on top. Wrap the lid of the pot with a clean dish towel and cover firmly to prevent steam from escaping. Cook the rice for 50 minutes over medium-low heat.

7   Remove the pot from the heat and allow to cool on a damp dish towel for 5 minutes without uncovering. Uncover, and add the fresh dill and jalapeño on top. Hold a large serving platter tightly over the pot and invert the two together, unmolding the entire mound onto the platter. The result will be crispy crusted fish on top with separated grains of rice underneath. Serve with Spicy Lime Pickle (Torshi-e Limu; Chapter 17). *Nush-e joon!*

PER SERVING: *Calories 551 (From Fat 325); Fat 36g (Saturated 5g); Cholesterol 77mg; Sodium 1,157mg; Carbohydrate 24g (Dietary Fiber 1g); Protein 32g.*

VARY IT! If you like, you can replace the fish with deveined shrimp, rinsed and patted dry.

Chapter **13**

Practicing Patience for Braises

Few dishes are so evocative of the Persian love of fragrance as the delicate braise known as *khoresh*.

Khoresh is a more delicate, refined version of a stew, with less liquid. Ideally, a *khoresh* should be made with fresh, seasonal herbs and vegetables. They're usually served on a bed of plain rice and called *chelow khoresh*. I suggest serving in individual bowls of rice with a little *khoresh* spooned over each one and garnishing with fresh herbs — a traditional style of eating in Iran. This way, you'll experience the taste and aroma of Persian cooking in a single plate. If you don't want to use rice, check out my recipe for Saffroned Persian-Style Quinoa (Quinoa; Chapter 12) for cooking quinoa, like a Persian-style rice.

I like to use a shallow medium, heavy-bottomed pot, such as the Le Creuset medium enameled cast-iron braiser (see Chapter 2). Natural clay pots — traditionally used in Iran but also produced by many potters in the United States today — are excellent, too.

FIXING COMMON *KHORESH* MISTAKES

TIP

Here are some remedies if you think you've messed up:

- **If your braise has too much liquid,** uncover the pan and continue to cook, still over low heat, until any excess liquid has evaporated.

- **If your braise is too thick,** add a little warm water or stock, cover, and continue to simmer over low heat for a few minutes longer.

- **If your braise is too spicy,** add ½ teaspoon of grape molasses and a squeeze of lime juice to reduce the spiciness.

- **If your braise is too sour,** add 1 tablespoon of chopped sweet, dried fruit (such as raisins or dates) or 1 teaspoon of honey, and a pinch of salt.

- **If your braise is too sweet,** add a squeeze of lime juice.

- **If your braise is too bitter,** usually from overfrying the onions, add 1 teaspoon of honey, grape molasses, or yogurt.

- **If your braise is too salty,** add a squeeze of lime juice and 1 teaspoon of grape molasses.

TIP

A good braise needs each ingredient to be cooked for a specific time and temperature to create layers of flavor. To develop a depth of flavor in a braise, you need to create a balance between, salt, sweet, sour, and bitter.

The green color and wonderful aroma of some Persian braises comes from plenty of sautéed, chopped herbs (such as parsley, cilantro, mint, spinach, and fenugreek). You can see an example of this in the renowned Lamb with Herbs and Dried Lime Braise (Khoresh-e Qormeh Sabzi) in this chapter.

TIP

A *khoresh* can be made a day in advance and reheated just before serving.

Butternut Squash and Prune Braise (Khoresh-e Kadu Halvai-o Alu)

PREP TIME: 35 MIN	COOK TIME: 2 HR	YIELD: 6 SERVINGS

INGREDIENTS

5 tablespoons olive oil, butter, or ghee, divided

2 medium onions, peeled and ½-inch diced

2 cloves garlic, peeled and sliced

1 pound boneless leg of lamb or chicken thighs, cut into 2-inch cubes

1 teaspoon fine sea salt

½ teaspoon freshly ground black pepper

½ teaspoon turmeric

1 teaspoon ground cinnamon

2 cups water

1 butternut squash (about 2 pounds), peeled and cut into 1½-inch cubes

1 pound carrots, peeled and ½-inch sliced

2 tablespoons grape molasses

¼ cup fresh lime juice

¼ teaspoon ground saffron dissolved in 2 tablespoons rose water

1½ cups pitted prunes

½ teaspoon cayenne

Zest of 1 orange

1 cup crispy fried onions (see Chapter 4), for garnish

DIRECTIONS

1 In a medium braiser, add 3 tablespoons of the oil, butter, or ghee and warm over medium heat. Add the onions and garlic and sauté until lightly golden, about 5 minutes. Add the lamb or chicken and sauté until browned on all sides, about 10 minutes. Add the salt, pepper, turmeric, and cinnamon, and sauté for 1 minute. Add the water, bring to a boil, reduce the heat to low, cover, and simmer for 1¼ hours, stirring occasionally.

2 Meanwhile, in a wide skillet, add the remaining 2 tablespoons of oil, butter or ghee and warm over medium heat. Add the butternut squash and carrots and brown on all sides, about 15 to 20 minutes.

3 To the braiser, add the grape molasses, lime juice, saffron water, prunes, cayenne, orange zest, and butternut squash and carrot mixture. Gently stir, cover, and simmer over low heat until the butternut squash and carrots are tender, about 35 to 45 minutes. Check the seasoning — it should be sweet and sour. Add more lime juice or grape molasses to taste. Garnish with crispy onions and serve with Plain Rice (Kateh; Chapter 12). *Nush-e joon!*

PER SERVING: *Calories 485 (From Fat 184); Fat 20g (Saturated 4g); Cholesterol 30mg; Sodium 720mg; Carbohydrate 70g (Dietary Fiber 9g); Protein 12g.*

VARY IT! For vegetarians, replace the lamb or chicken with 1 pound firm tofu, diced into 2-inch cubes, and reduce the cooking time in Step 1 to 30 minutes.

Celery Braise (Khoresh-e Karafs)

INGREDIENTS

6 tablespoons olive oil, butter, or ghee, divided

2 medium onions, peeled and ½-inch diced

2 cloves garlic, peeled and sliced

1 pound boneless leg of lamb or chicken thighs, cut into 2-inch cubes

1½ teaspoons fine sea salt

½ teaspoon freshly ground black pepper

½ teaspoon red pepper flakes

1 teaspoon turmeric

2½ cups water

1 bunch or 8 stalks celery, washed, strings removed, and cut into 1-inch lengths

3 cups chopped fresh parsley or 1 cup dried parsley

½ cup chopped fresh mint or 3 tablespoons dried mint

1 tablespoon dried fenugreek leaves

2 tablespoons tomato paste

½ cup freshly squeezed lime juice

¼ teaspoon ground saffron threads dissolved in 2 tablespoons rose water

DIRECTIONS

1 In a medium braiser, add the oil, butter, or ghee, and warm over medium heat. Add the onion and garlic and sauté until lightly golden, about 5 minutes. Add the lamb or chicken and sauté on all sides until browned, about 10 minutes. Add the salt, pepper, red pepper flakes, and turmeric, and sauté for 1 minute. Add the water, bring to a boil, reduce the heat to low, cover, and simmer for 45 minutes.

2 Meanwhile, in a wide skillet, add the remaining 3 tablespoons of oil, butter, and ghee and warm over medium heat. Add the celery and sauté, stirring occasionally, for 15 minutes. Add the parsley, mint, and fenugreek, and sauté for 10 minutes. Add the tomato paste, and sauté for 1 minute.

3 To the braiser, add the celery and herb mixture, lime juice, and saffron water. Cover and simmer over low heat for 1 to 1¼ hours, until the lamb and celery are tender. Adjust the seasoning to taste by adding more salt or lime juice. Cover and keep warm until ready to serve. Serve with Plain Rice (Kateh; Chapter 12). *Nush-e joon!*

PER SERVING: *Calories 253 (From Fat 157); Fat 17g (Saturated 3g); Cholesterol 30mg; Sodium 699mg; Carbohydrate 15g (Dietary Fiber 4g); Protein 11g.*

VARY IT! For vegetarians, replace the lamb or chicken with 2 cups cooked canned cannellini beans and reduce the cooking time in Step 1 to 15 minutes.

Green Beans, Tomato, and Chicken Braise (Khoresh-e Lubia Sabz)

PREP TIME: 15 MIN	COOK TIME: 2 HR	YIELD: 4 SERVINGS

INGREDIENTS

6 tablespoons olive oil, butter, or ghee, divided

2 medium onions, peeled and ½-inch diced

2 cloves garlic, peeled and sliced

1 pound boneless, skinless chicken thighs, cut into 2-inch cubes

2 teaspoons fine sea salt

½ teaspoon freshly ground black pepper

½ teaspoon turmeric

¼ teaspoon cayenne

½ teaspoon ground cinnamon

1 cup water

1 pound fresh, trimmed or frozen green beans, cut into 1½-inch lengths

3 tablespoons tomato paste

1 medium fresh tomato, peeled and pureed, or 1 cup canned pureed tomatoes

2 tablespoons fresh lime juice

¼ teaspoon ground saffron dissolved in 2 tablespoons rose water

½ cup crispy fried onions (see Chapter 4), for garnish

DIRECTIONS

1 In a medium braiser, add 3 tablespoons of the oil, butter, or ghee, and warm over medium heat. Add the onions and garlic and sauté until lightly golden, about 5 minutes. Add the chicken and sauté until browned on all sides, about 10 minutes. Add the salt, pepper, turmeric, cayenne, and cinnamon, and sauté for 1 minute. Add the water, bring to a boil, reduce the heat to low, cover, and cook, stirring occasionally, for 15 minutes.

2 Meanwhile, in a wide skillet, add the remaining 3 tablespoons of oil, butter, or ghee and warm over medium heat. Add the green beans and sauté for 2 minutes (longer if using frozen beans). Add the tomato paste and sauté for 1 minute.

3 To the braiser, add the green bean mixture, tomato, lime juice, and saffron water. Cover and simmer over low heat until the chicken and beans are tender, about 1¼ hours. Adjust the seasoning to taste, garnish with the fried onions, and serve with Plain Rice (Kateh; Chapter 12), Cucumber and Tomato Salad (Salad-e Gojeh Khiar; Chapter 8), and a fresh herb platter (see Chapter 7). *Nush-e joon!*

PER SERVING: *Calories 410 (From Fat 249); Fat 28g (Saturated 5g); Cholesterol 45mg; Sodium 1,194mg; Carbohydrate 27g (Dietary Fiber 6g); Protein 17g.*

VARY IT! For vegetarians, replace the chicken with 1 pound firm tofu, diced into 2-inch cubes.

Spinach, Prune, and Lamb Braise (Khoresh-e Esfenaj-o Alu)

PREP TIME: 30 MIN | COOK TIME: 2 HR | YIELD: 6 SERVINGS

INGREDIENTS

6 tablespoons olive oil, butter, or ghee, divided

3 medium onions, ½-inch diced, divided

2 cloves garlic, peeled and sliced

1 pound boneless leg of lamb, cut into 2-inch cubes

1½ teaspoons fine sea salt

½ teaspoon freshly ground black pepper

½ teaspoon red pepper flakes

½ teaspoon turmeric

2 cups water

2 tablespoons tomato paste

2 pounds fresh spinach, coarsely chopped, or 1 pound frozen chopped spinach

1½ cups pitted prunes

1 tablespoon grape molasses

¼ cup *ab-ghureh* (verjuice) or 2 tablespoons fresh lime juice

DIRECTIONS

1 In a medium braiser, add 3 tablespoons of the oil, butter, or ghee, and warm over medium heat. Add 1 of the diced onions and the garlic and sauté until lightly golden, about 5 minutes. Add the lamb and sauté until browned on all sides, about 10 minutes. Add the salt, pepper, red pepper flakes, and turmeric, and sauté for 1 minute. Add the water, bring to a boil, reduce the heat to low, cover, and simmer for 45 minutes.

2 Meanwhile, in a wide skillet, add the remaining 3 tablespoons of oil, butter, or ghee, and warm over medium heat. Add the remaining 2 diced onions and sauté until golden brown, about 12 minutes. Add the tomato paste and sauté for 1 minute. Add the spinach, cover, and cook for 5 minutes. Stir and transfer the mixture to the braiser. Add the prunes, grape molasses, and verjuice or lime juice. Cover and simmer 1¼ hours over low heat.

3 Check to see that the lamb is tender. Adjust the seasoning to taste by adding more grape molasses or verjuice (or lime juice). Cover and keep warm until ready to serve. Serve with Plain Rice (Kateh; Chapter 12). *Nush-e joon!*

PER SERVING: *Calories 393 (From Fat 171); Fat 19g (Saturated 3g); Cholesterol 30mg; Sodium 755mg; Carbohydrate 47g (Dietary Fiber 8g); Protein 15g.*

VARY IT! You can use chicken thighs instead of the lamb, if you prefer. For vegetarians, replace the lamb with 1 pound firm tofu, diced into 2-inch cubes, and reduce the cooking time in Step 1 to 15 minutes.

Chicken, Walnut and Pomegranate Braise (Khoresh-e Fesenjoon)

PREP TIME: 30 MIN	COOK TIME: 1 HR 30 MIN	YIELD: 5 SERVINGS

INGREDIENTS

¼ cup olive oil, butter, or ghee, divided

1 medium onion, peeled and ½-inch diced

2 cloves garlic, sliced

1 cup butternut squash, peeled and ½-inch diced

2 cups (½ pound) walnuts

½ cup pomegranate molasses diluted in 2 cups water

2 tablespoons grape molasses

1 pound boneless, skinless chicken thighs, cut into 2-inch cubes

1 teaspoon fine sea salt

½ teaspoon freshly ground black pepper

½ teaspoon turmeric

½ teaspoon ground cinnamon

½ teaspoon ground cumin

½ teaspoon ground cardamom

¼ teaspoon ground saffron threads dissolved in 2 tablespoons rose water

½ cup pomegranate arils (1 small pomegranate), for garnish

DIRECTIONS

1 In a medium braiser, add 2 tablespoons of the oil, butter, or ghee, and warm over medium heat until hot. Add the onions and garlic, and sauté until lightly golden, about 10 to 15 minutes. Add the butternut squash and walnuts, and sauté for 3 minutes. Transfer the mixture to a food processor, add the diluted pomegranate molasses and grape molasses, and mix well to create a smooth, creamy sauce. Set aside.

2 Wipe the braiser and add the remaining 2 tablespoons of oil, butter, or ghee. Warm over medium heat until hot. Add the chicken and sauté until browned on all sides, about 10 to 15 minutes. Add the salt, pepper, turmeric, cinnamon, cumin, cardamon, and saffron water, and sauté for 1 minute.

3 Transfer the sauce to the braiser, bring to a boil, reduce the heat to low, cover, and simmer for 1 hour, stirring occasionally with a wooden spoon to prevent the walnut sauce from burning. The sauce should be sweet and sour with the consistency of heavy cream. Adjust the seasoning to taste by adding more pomegranate molasses for sourness or grape molasses for sweetness. Garnish with pomegranate arils and serve over Plain Rice (Kateh; Chapter 12) or Jeweled Rice (Javaher Polow; Chapter 12). *Nush-e joon!*

PER SERVING: *Calories 531 (From Fat 372); Fat 41g (Saturated 5g); Cholesterol 36mg; Sodium 548mg; Carbohydrate 28g (Dietary Fiber 5g); Protein 18g.*

VARY IT! For vegetarians, eliminate the chicken and increase the butternut squash to 3 cups.

Rhubarb and Lamb Braise (Khoresh-e Rivas)

PREP TIME: 30 MIN | COOK TIME: 2 HR 30 MIN | YIELD: 6 SERVINGS

INGREDIENTS

6 tablespoons olive oil, butter, or ghee, divided

2 medium onions, peeled and ½-inch diced

1 pound boneless leg of lamb, cut into 2-inch cubes

1½ teaspoons fine sea salt

½ teaspoon freshly ground black pepper

½ teaspoon turmeric

2½ cups water

3 cups chopped fresh parsley or 1 cup dried parsley

½ cup chopped fresh mint or 2½ tablespoons dried mint

1 tablespoon tomato paste

¼ teaspoon ground saffron dissolved in 2 tablespoons rose water

2 tablespoons fresh lime juice

1 pound fresh or frozen rhubarb, cut into 2-inch pieces

1 tablespoon grape molasses (optional)

DIRECTIONS

1 In a medium braiser, add 3 tablespoons of the oil, butter, or ghee and warm over medium heat. Add the onions and sauté until lightly golden, about 5 minutes. Add the lamb and sauté until browned on all sides. Add the salt, pepper, and turmeric, and sauté for 1 minute. Pour in the water, bring to a boil, reduce the heat to low, cover, and simmer, stirring occasionally, for 45 minutes.

2 Meanwhile, in a wide skillet, add the remaining 3 tablespoons of oil, butter, or ghee and warm over medium heat. Add the parsley and mint and sauté until its fragrance rises, stirring frequently to avoid burning, about 10 to 15 minutes. Add the tomato paste and stir-fry for 2 minutes.

3 To the braiser, add the herb mixture, the saffron water, and lime juice. Cover and simmer over low heat for 55 minutes.

4 Preheat the oven to 350 degrees. Arrange the rhubarb on top of the braise; cover with a layer of parchment paper and a layer of aluminum foil. Pierce several holes in the foil and parchment paper. Bake until the rhubarb is tender, about 35 to 40 minutes. Rhubarb is fragile — the pieces must be cooked but not to the point of dissolving or falling apart. Adjust the seasoning to taste: If the braise is too sour, drizzle 1 tablespoon grape molasses over it (you don't want to break up the rhubarb by stirring). Serve with Plain Rice (Kateh; Chapter 12). *Nush-e joon!*

PER SERVING: *Calories 277 (From Fat 157); Fat 17g (Saturated 3g); Cholesterol 37mg; Sodium 534mg; Carbohydrate 18g (Dietary Fiber 4g); Protein 14g.*

VARY IT! You can use chicken thighs instead of the lamb, if you prefer. For vegetarians, replace the lamb with 2 cups cooked canned cannellini beans and reduce the cooking time in Step 1 to 15 minutes.

Saffroned Chicken and Barberry Braise (Qeymeh Zereshk)

PREP TIME: 30 MIN	COOK TIME: 1 HR 25 MIN	YIELD: 6 SERVINGS

INGREDIENTS

3 tablespoons olive oil, butter, or ghee plus 2 tablespoons oil, divided

2 medium onions, peeled and ½-inch diced

1½ pound boneless, skinless chicken thighs, cut into 1-inch cubes

2 teaspoons fine sea salt

½ teaspoon freshly ground black pepper

1 teaspoon turmeric

One 4-inch cinnamon stick

1 tablespoon ground cumin

1 teaspoon ground cardamom

3 tablespoons tomato paste

¾ teaspoon ground saffron threads dissolved in 6 tablespoons rose water, divided

2 cups water

2 cups dried barberries, soaked in cold water for 20 minutes, drained and rinsed thoroughly

3 tablespoons grape molasses or sugar

3 tablespoons blanched slivered almonds, toasted, for garnish

3 tablespoons raw pistachio kernels, toasted, for garnish

2 tablespoons rose petals, crushed, for garnish

½ cup crispy fried onions (see Chapter 4), for garnish

DIRECTIONS

1 In a medium braiser, add the oil, butter, or ghee and warm over medium heat. Add the onions and sauté until lightly golden, about 5 minutes. Add the chicken and sauté until browned on all sides, about 10 minutes. Add the salt, pepper, turmeric, cinnamon, cumin, cardamom, tomato paste, and ½ cup of the saffron water, and sauté for 2 minutes. Add the water, bring to a boil, reduce the heat to low, cover, and simmer until the chicken is cooked and tender, about 1 hour.

2 Meanwhile, in a wide skillet, add the barberries, the remaining 2 tablespoons of oil, the grape molasses or sugar, and the remaining 2 tablespoons of saffron water, and stir-fry over medium-high heat for 4 minutes. (Beware! Barberries burn easily.)

3 Transfer the barberries to the braiser, cover, and cook over low heat for 10 minutes. Adjust the seasoning to taste and garnish with the almonds, pistachios, rose petals, and fried onions. Serve with Plain Rice (Kateh; Chapter 12) and Onion, Cucumber, and Coriander Quick Pickle (Torshi Hazeri-e Piaz; Chapter 17). *Nush-e joon!*

PER SERVING: *Calories 435 (From Fat 194); Fat 22g (Saturated 4g); Cholesterol 45mg; Sodium 960mg; Carbohydrate 44g (Dietary Fiber 6g); Protein 19g.*

VARY IT! For vegetarians, replace the chicken with 1 pound firm tofu, diced into 1-inch cubes and reduce the cooking time in Step 1 to 15 minutes.

Chicken and Peach Braise (Khoresh-e Hulu)

PREP TIME: 30 MIN	COOK TIME: 1 HR 40 MIN	YIELD: 6 SERVINGS

INGREDIENTS

6 tablespoons olive oil, butter, or ghee, divided

2 medium onions, peeled and ½-inch diced

1 pound boneless, skinless chicken thighs, cut into 2-inch cubes

1 teaspoon fine sea salt

½ teaspoon freshly ground black pepper

¼ teaspoon turmeric

1 teaspoon *advieh* (Persian spice mix)

1 cup water

½ cup fresh lime juice

½ cup grape molasses

¼ teaspoon ground saffron dissolved in 2 tablespoons water

5 firm peaches, fuzz removed (by rubbing with paper towel), washed, pitted, and cut into ½-inch wedges (unpeeled)

2 tablespoons shredded fresh mint, for garnish

DIRECTIONS

1 In a medium braiser, add 3 tablespoons of the oil, butter, or ghee, and warm over medium heat. Add the onions and sauté until lightly golden, about 5 minutes. Add the chicken and sauté until browned on all sides, about 10 minutes. Add the salt, pepper, turmeric, and *advieh*, and sauté for 1 minute. Add the water, bring to a boil, reduce the heat to low, cover, and simmer for 45 minutes.

2 Add the lime juice, grape molasses, and saffron water to the chicken. Stir, cover, and simmer over low heat for 15 minutes.

3 Meanwhile, in a wide skillet, add the remaining 3 tablespoons of oil, butter, or ghee, and warm over medium heat. Add the peach wedges and sauté until golden, about 10 minutes. Transfer to the braiser, cover, and simmer 25 minutes.

4 Check to see if the chicken is tender. Adjust the seasoning taste. Cover and keep warm until ready to serve. Just before serving, garnish with mint. Serve with Plain Rice (Kateh; Chapter 12). *Nush-e joon!*

PER SERVING: *Calories 338 (From Fat 167); Fat 19g (Saturated 3g); Cholesterol 30mg; Sodium 478mg; Carbohydrate 35g (Dietary Fiber 3g); Protein 11g.*

Lamb and Quince Braise (Khoresh-e Beh)

PREP TIME: 20 MIN	COOK TIME: 2 HR	YIELD: 6 SERVINGS

INGREDIENTS

6 tablespoons olive oil, butter, or ghee, divided

2 medium onions, peeled and ½-inch diced

1 pound boneless leg of lamb, cut into 2-inch cubes

1 teaspoon fine sea salt

½ teaspoon freshly ground black pepper

½ teaspoon turmeric

¼ teaspoon ground cinnamon

3 cups water

3 medium quinces (about 2 pounds), unpeeled, washed, cored, and any hard parts or seeds removed, then cut into 1-inch cubes or wedges

½ cup grape molasses or brown sugar

¼ cup wine vinegar

¼ cup fresh lime juice

½ teaspoon ground saffron dissolved in ¼ cup rose water

⅓ cup yellow split peas

DIRECTIONS

1 In a medium braiser, add 3 tablespoons of the oil, butter, or ghee, and warm over medium heat. Add the onions and sauté until lightly golden, about 5 minutes. Add the lamb and sauté until browned on all sides, about 10 minutes. Add the salt, pepper, turmeric, and cinnamon, and sauté for 1 minute. Add the water, bring to a boil, reduce the heat to low, cover, and simmer for 1¼ hours, stirring occasionally.

2 Meanwhile, in a wide skillet, add the remaining 3 tablespoons of oil, butter, or ghee and warm over medium heat. Add the quinces and sauté, shaking the skillet often (or gently toss with a spatula — you don't want to crush the fruit), until golden brown, about 15 to 20 minutes. Transfer the quinces to the braiser.

3 To the braiser, add the grape molasses or brown sugar, vinegar, lime juice, saffron water, and peas. Cover and simmer over low heat until split peas are tender, about 30 to 45 minutes (depending on the type of yellow split peas — you want them soft but not mushy).

4 Taste and adjust the seasoning. Cover and keep warm until ready to serve. Serve with Plain Rice (Kateh; Chapter 12). *Nush-e joon!*

PER SERVING: *Calories 379 (From Fat 155); Fat 17g (Saturated 3g); Cholesterol 37mg; Sodium 366mg; Carbohydrate 43g (Dietary Fiber 5g); Protein 15g.*

VARY IT! You can use chicken thighs instead of the lamb, if you prefer. You can replace the quinces with apples. For vegetarians, eliminate the lamb, increase the yellow split peas to ½ cup, and reduce the cooking time in Step 1 to 15 minutes.

Lamb with Herbs and Dried Lime Braise (Khoresh-e Qormeh Sabzi)

PREP TIME: 25 MIN PLUS OVERNIGHT FOR SOAKING THE DRIED KIDNEY BEANS AND 30 MIN FOR SOAKING THE DRIED LIME	COOK TIME: 4 HR	YIELD: 6 SERVINGS

INGREDIENTS

1 cup kidney beans, soaked in water overnight, drained, and rinsed

6 whole dried limes, pierced and soaked in 1 cup water for 30 minutes (don't drain)

6 tablespoons olive oil, butter, or ghee, divided

2 pounds lamb shanks (bone-in)

2 medium onions, peeled and ½-inch diced

4 cloves garlic, thinly sliced

1 tablespoon fine sea salt

1 teaspoon freshly ground black pepper

1½ teaspoons turmeric

2 teaspoons ground cardamom

2 cups water

DIRECTIONS

1 In a medium braiser, add 1 tablespoon of the oil, butter, or ghee and warm over medium heat until hot. Add the lamb and sauté until browned on all sides, about 15 minutes. Remove the lamb and set aside.

2 To the braiser, add 2 tablespoons of the oil, butter, or ghee. Add the onions and garlic and sauté over medium heat until golden brown, about 10 minutes. Add the salt, pepper, turmeric, cardamom, and kidney beans, and sauté for 1 minute. Return the lamb to the braiser, add the water, bring to a boil, reduce the heat to low, cover, and simmer for 1½ hours, stirring occasionally.

3 Meanwhile, in a wide skillet, add the remaining 3 tablespoons of oil, butter, or ghee and warm over medium-low heat. Add the parsley, cilantro, chives or spring onions, and fenugreek and sauté, stirring frequently, until the herbs become fragrant, about 20 minutes. (Beware! Herbs can easily burn.)

3 cups finely chopped fresh parsley or 1 cup dried parsley

3 cups finely chopped fresh cilantro or 1 cup dried cilantro

1 cup finely chopped fresh chives or spring onions

3 tablespoons dried fenugreek leaves

¼ cup freshly squeezed lime juice

½ teaspoon ground saffron threads dissolved in ¼ cup rose water (optional)

4 To the same braiser, add the herbs, dried limes with their juice, lime juice, and saffron water. Stir, cover, and simmer over low heat for 1½ hours, stirring twice during this time. Adjust the seasoning to taste and serve with Plain Rice (Kateh; Chapter 12). *Nush-e joon!*

PER SERVING: *Calories 376 (From Fat 153); Fat 17g (Saturated 3g); Cholesterol 44mg; Sodium 1,020mg; Carbohydrate 33g (Dietary Fiber 8g); Protein 23g.*

VARY IT! For vegetarians, eliminate the meat, increase the beans to 1½ cups, and reduce the cooking time in Step 3 to 45 minutes.

TIP: If you don't have dried kidney beans, you can use 3 cups canned cooked beans, drained and rinsed, and add them during the last half-hour of cooking in Step 4.

Lamb and Potato Braise (Khoresh-e Qeymeh)

PREP TIME: 25 MIN	COOK TIME: 2 HR 5 MIN	YIELD: 6 SERVINGS

INGREDIENTS

4 whole dried limes, pierced, soaked in 1 cup of water for 30 minutes (don't drain)

3 tablespoons olive oil, butter, or ghee, plus 2 cups oil for deep frying, divided

2 medium onions, peeled and ½-inch diced

1 pound boneless leg of lamb, cut into ½-inch cubes

2 teaspoons fine sea salt

½ teaspoon freshly ground black pepper

½ teaspoon turmeric

1 teaspoon *advieh* (Persian spice mix)

4 cups water, divided

1 large tomato, peeled and pureed, or 1 cup pureed canned tomatoes

DIRECTIONS

1 In a braiser, add 3 tablespoons of the oil, butter, or ghee, and warm over medium heat. Add the onions and sauté until lightly golden, about 5 minutes. Add the lamb and sauté until browned on all sides, about 10 minutes. Add the fine sea salt, pepper, turmeric, and *advieh*, and sauté for 2 minutes. Add 1 cup of the water, bring to a boil, reduce the heat to low, cover, and simmer for 1 hour, stirring occasionally.

2 Add the limes (with the water the limes soaked in), tomato, orange peel, and saffron water. Cover and cook over low heat for another 45 minutes.

3 Meanwhile, in a saucepan, add the remaining 3 cups of water, ½ teaspoon of salt, and peas and cook for 20 minutes. Drain and add to the braiser. Stir, cover, and cook for 10 minutes. Check to see if the chicken is tender and the split peas are soft but not mushy. Adjust the seasoning to taste by adding lime juice or salt.

1 tablespoon caramelized orange peel (see Chapter 4)

½ teaspoon ground saffron dissolved in ¼ cup orange blossom water

½ teaspoon salt

¼ cup yellow split peas

1½ pounds russet potatoes (about 2), peeled and cut into matchsticks, soaked in cold water for 30 minutes, drained, rinsed, and thoroughly blot dried in a dish towel

¼ teaspoon sea salt flakes, for garnishing french fries

1 teaspoon *limu-omani* (dried Persian lime powder), for garnishing french fries

4 Meanwhile, in a deep skillet, add the remaining 2 cups of olive oil and warm over medium-high heat for about 4 minutes until hot (when you drop sliver of potato in it, it should sizzle). Add the potatoes in 3 batches and deep-fry until golden, about 5 minutes, stirring twice. Use a slotted spoon to remove the potatoes and place them on paper towels. Sprinkle with ⅓ of the sea salt flakes and the dried lime powder.

5 Just before serving, add the potatoes on top of the braise and serve with Plain Rice (Kateh; Chapter 12), Persian pickles, and a fresh herb platter on the side. *Nush-e joon!*

PER SERVING: *Calories 403 (From Fat 83); Fat 9g (Saturated 2g); Cholesterol 22mg; Sodium 857mg; Carbohydrate 61g (Dietary Fiber 12g); Protein 21g.*

VARY IT! You can use chicken thighs instead of the lamb, if you prefer. For vegetarians, eliminate the chicken and increase the split peas to ½ cup.

Spicy Chicken and Yogurt Braise (Khoresh-e Mast)

PREP TIME: 30 MIN	COOK TIME: 1 HR 40 MIN	YIELD: 6 SERVINGS

INGREDIENTS

2 tablespoons olive oil, butter, or ghee, divided

1¼ cups whole raw almonds, divided

¼ cup plus 3 tablespoons seedless raisins, divided

2 tablespoons water

1 tablespoon grape molasses

1 cup dried barberries, cleaned

¼ cup olive oil

1 small onion, peeled and ½-inch diced

2 cloves garlic, peeled and chopped

1 celery stalk, chopped

1½ pounds skinless, boneless chicken thighs, cut into 4-inch pieces

2 teaspoons fine sea salt

½ teaspoon freshly ground black pepper

½ teaspoon turmeric

¼ teaspoon red pepper flakes

2 teaspoons ground coriander

2 teaspoons ground cumin

DIRECTIONS

1 In a wide skillet, add 1 tablespoon of the oil, butter, or ghee and warm over medium heat until hot. Add 1 cup of the almonds and stir-fry for 1 minute. Add ¼ cup of the raisins, stir, and transfer to a bowl; set aside.

2 In the same skillet, place the remaining 1 tablespoon of oil, butter, or ghee; water; grape molasses; and barberries. Stir-fry over medium heat for 4 minutes. (Be careful! Barberries burn easily.) Transfer to another bowl and set aside.

3 In a medium braiser, add ¼ cup olive oil and warm over medium heat. Add the onion, garlic, and celery and sauté for 5 minutes. Add the chicken and sauté until browned on all sides, about 10 minutes. Add the salt, pepper, turmeric, red pepper flakes, coriander, cumin, cardamom, cloves, cinnamon, ginger, and bay leaves, and sauté for 1 minute. Add the tomato, reduce the heat to low, cover, and simmer for 25 minutes.

4 Meanwhile, in a food processor, grind the remaining ¼ cup of almonds and the remaining 3 tablespoons of raisins. Add the yogurt and lime juice, and mix for 5 minutes. (This is important as it helps prevent the yogurt from curdling during cooking.)

2 teaspoons ground cardamom

½ teaspoon ground cloves

½ teaspoon ground cinnamon

One 1-inch fresh gingerroot, peeled and grated

2 bay leaves

1 tomato, peeled and finely chopped

1½ cups plain yogurt

2 tablespoons fresh lime juice

1 cup fresh basil leaves, for garnish

4 Persian cucumbers, peeled and thinly sliced, for garnish

2 radishes, thinly sliced, for garnish

5 Add the yogurt sauce to the chicken and stir. Cover and simmer over low heat for 45 minutes, stirring occasionally. Discard the bay leaves.

6 Adjust the seasoning to taste. Serve over Plain Rice (Kateh; Chapter 12). Garnish with some of the prepared almonds and barberries, as well as the basil, cucumbers, and radishes. *Nush-e joon!*

PER SERVING: *Calories 481 (From Fat 281); Fat 31g (Saturated 5g); Cholesterol 15mg; Sodium 725mg; Carbohydrate 43g (Dietary Fiber 8g); Protein 14g.*

VARY IT! For vegetarians, replace the chicken with 1 pound cremini mushrooms, cleaned and thickly sliced.

Unripe Grape, Chicken, and Eggplant Braise (Khoresh-e Bademjan)

PREP TIME: 40 MIN	COOK TIME: 2 HR	YIELD: 4 SERVINGS

INGREDIENTS

6 Chinese eggplants (about 3 pounds), crowns removed, peeled, and cut in half lengthwise

5 tablespoons olive oil, butter, or ghee, plus extra to oil the sheet pan, divided

1 medium onion, peeled and ½-inch diced

2 cloves garlic, peeled and sliced

1 pound skinless, boneless chicken thighs, cut into 2-inch cubes

1 teaspoon fine sea salt

1 teaspoon freshly ground black pepper

½ teaspoon turmeric

½ teaspoon ground cinnamon

½ teaspoon ground saffron dissolved in ¼ cup hot water

3 medium fresh tomatoes, peeled and pureed, or 2 cups canned pureed tomatoes

1 cup water

½ cup *ghureh* (unripe grapes), fresh or canned, drained

2 tablespoons fresh lime juice

½ cup crispy fried onions for garnish (see Chapter 4)

DIRECTIONS

1 Preheat the oven to 450 degrees. Oil a rimmed sheet pan, and arrange the eggplants side-by-side on the pan. Brush each eggplant with a little oil (using 2 tablespoons of the oil total) and roast in the oven until golden brown, not blackened, about 30 to 40 minutes; set aside.

2 Meanwhile, in a medium braiser, add the remaining 3 table-spoons of the oil, butter, or ghee, and warm over medium heat. Add the onions and garlic and sauté until lightly golden, about 5 minutes. Add the chicken and sauté until browned on all sides, about 10 minutes. Add the salt, pepper, turmeric, and cinnamon, and sauté for 1 minute. Add the saffron water, tomatoes, water, *ghureh*, and lime juice. Bring to a boil, reduce the heat to low, cover, and simmer for 1 hour.

3 Arrange the eggplants on the chicken. Cover and cook over low heat for 45 minutes. Adjust the seasoning to taste, garnish with the fried onions, and serve with Plain Rice (Kateh; Chapter 12). *Nush-e joon!*

PER SERVING: *Calories 330 (From Fat 184); Fat 20g (Saturated 3g); Cholesterol 7mg; Sodium 526mg; Carbohydrate 35g (Dietary Fiber 14g); Protein 7g.*

VARY IT! For vegetarians, replace the chicken with 1 pound extra-firm tofu, diced into 2-inch cubes. In Step 2, reduce the simmering time to 15 minutes.

Chapter **14**

Sticking It to Kabobs and Roasts

Iranian kabobs originated as the food of the soldier, the hunter, and the herder. They're meat cooked in the most primitive way, over an open fire. That is all the Persian word, *kabab*, now familiar in various spellings the world over, means: grilled meat. It's the marination in saffron and rose water, and the tang of lime or pomegranate juice, balancing and enhancing the meat's richness and the fire's smoky tang, that gives kabobs their complexity.

When kabobs are served on top of *chelow* (rice), it's called *chelow kabab* and considered Iran's national dish.

Kabobs are served everywhere, from the grandest houses to the humblest street stalls, but the best is made in the bazaar. I remember the *chelow kababs* (plain rice and kabobs) served in the bazaar: First came the *chelow*, covered with a tin cloche to keep it warm. Then came the waiter, with as many as five skewers still smoking from the grill in his left hand and a piece of lavash bread in his right. He would hold a skewer over the rice mound, steady the meat with the bread, and pull the skewer out with a flourish, leaving the kabobs sizzling on the rice. One might have chosen *kabab-e kubideh* (ground lamb) *kabab-e barg* (fillet kabab), or the combination of both called *soltani*, meaning "kingly." Kabobs are always served with trimmings: grilled tomatoes, a fresh herb platter, raw onions, sumac, yogurt, and Persian pickles, and even a raw egg yolk and a slab of butter for mixing into the hot rice. All this was accompanied with a pitcher of *dugh* (a sparkling yogurt drink) flavored with wild mountain mint. Once in a while, my mother would allow us to have a Pepsi instead — heaven.

In my cooking classes, everyone is amazed at how easy it is to make the renowned Persian kabobs made from ground meat, *kubideh.* If you follow the steps in this book, you'll be able to make perfect ground lamb kabob — and I promise they won't fall off the skewers! Just remember, when cooking kabobs at home, make sure everything is ready because kabobs must be served hot and sizzling off the grill.

TIP

In Persian cooking, kabobs are usually cooked on a very hot charcoal grill and not covered. If you have a grill with a cover, don't cover the grill when making Persian kabobs.

TIP

Ground lamb kababs are cooked on a grill 3 inches above the coals without them touching the grill (bricks inside the barbecue on either side will make a good platform for this purpose).

For making Persian-style kabobs, I recommend using the tenderloin of lamb, veal, or beef, but you can use beef sirloin if you prefer. For chicken kabobs, I like to use organic, boneless, skinless chicken thighs, or Cornish hens cut into 8 pieces, bone-in.

REMEMBER

Make sure to wash your hands thoroughly after handling any raw poultry, meat, or fish, and clean any surfaces that the raw food touched. This will prevent salmonella poisoning. Finally, check the expiration dates and don't use poultry, meat, or fish that has expired.

Lamb Rib Chops (Shishlik)

| PREP TIME: 20 MIN PLUS 1–2 DAYS FOR MARINATING | COOK TIME: 1 HR 50 MIN | YIELD: 8 SERVINGS |

INGREDIENTS

1 large onion, peeled and thinly sliced

1 bulb garlic (10 to 12 cloves), peeled and sliced

Zest of 2 oranges

1 tablespoon honey

1 cup fresh lime juice

1 cup plain, whole yogurt

2 teaspoons fine sea salt

1 teaspoon freshly ground pepper

½ teaspoon turmeric

2 tablespoons olive oil

¼ teaspoon ground saffron threads dissolved in 2 tablespoons rose water

16 small lamb rib chops (2 racks, French cut and cut into individual chops)

2 tablespoons butter or olive oil

Juice of 2 limes

¼ teaspoon ground saffron threads

½ teaspoon sea salt flakes

1 bunch spring onions, for garnish

2 cups fresh basil leaves, for garnish

One 12-ounce package lavash bread

DIRECTIONS

1 In a glass container (preferably with a cover), place the onion, garlic, orange zest, honey, lime juice, yogurt, salt, pepper, turmeric, 2 tablespoons of olive oil, and saffron water; mix well. Add the lamb and toss well. Cover with a lid or plastic wrap and marinate for 24 to 48 hours in the refrigerator. Turn the chops once during this time.

2 Start a bed of charcoal at least 30 minutes before you want to cook. If you're using the oven broiler or an indoor grill, preheat it until very hot.

3 In a small saucepan, place the 2 tablespoons of butter or olive oil, lime juice, and saffron threads; keep warm over very low heat.

4 Thread 4 chops, flat side up, onto each of 4 flat, ½-inch-wide, swordlike skewers. (The skewer will go through the bone, which is soft.)

5 Grill the chops for 6 to 8 minutes, flipping occasionally to make sure both sides are equally grilled. The chops should be charred on the outside and juicy in the middle. Baste them just before removing from the heat. Spread a layer of lavash bread on a serving platter and place the skewers with the chops on the bread. Remove the chops from each skewer by using a piece of lavash bread to hold down several pieces of meat as you pull them off the skewer. Sprinkle with the sea salt flakes and garnish with the spring onions and basil. Serve immediately with Yogurt and Persian Shallot Salad (Mast-o Musir; Chapter 8). *Nush-e joon!*

PER SERVING: *Calories 654 (From Fat 199); Fat 22g (Saturated 8g); Cholesterol 260mg; Sodium 706mg; Carbohydrate 26g (Dietary Fiber 1g); Protein 83g.*

Ground Lamb Kabob (Kabab-e Kubideh)

PREP TIME: 20 MIN PLUS 30 MIN FOR CHILLING	COOK TIME: 5 MIN	YIELD: 6 SERVINGS

INGREDIENTS

2 medium yellow onions, peeled and minced, all juice squeezed out

4 cloves garlic, peeled and grated

2 teaspoons fine sea salt

2 teaspoons freshly ground black pepper

¼ teaspoon turmeric

¼ cup sumac powder, divided

½ teaspoon baking soda

Zest of 1 lime

2 pounds twice-ground lamb shoulder

3 roma or plum tomatoes, halved

½ cup butter or olive oil

1 tablespoon fresh lime juice

¼ teaspoon ground saffron threads dissolved in 2 tablespoons rose water

One 12-ounce package of lavash bread

2 cups fresh Persian basil leaves

DIRECTIONS

1   In a large glass bowl (preferably with a cover), add the onions, garlic, salt, pepper, turmeric, 2 tablespoons of the sumac powder, baking soda, and lime zest. Stir together until mixed. Add the ground lamb and knead with your hands for about 5 minutes. Cover the paste with plastic wrap and chill in the fridge for at least 30 minutes or up to 24 hours.

2   Prepare you barbecue so that your skewers will be 3 inches above the coals but without touching the grill (bricks on either side make a good platform). Start the barbecue at least 30 minutes before you want to cook, and let it burn until the coals are glowing evenly. For these kabobs, you want the coals as close to the meat as possible (3 inches), and at their hottest. Don't spread the charcoal too thinly. If you're using the oven broiler or an indoor grill, make sure it's preheated and very hot.

3   Using damp hands (keep a bowl of water next to you), divide the meat paste into 12 equal lumps, each about the size of a small orange. Shape each lump into a 5-inch-long sausage and mold it firmly around a skewer. Pinch both ends to firmly attach the meat to a flat metal skewer; repeat for a total of 12 skewers. Arrange side-by-side on an oiled, rimmed sheet pan. Cover with another sheet pan (inverted so it doesn't touch the kabobs), and keep in a cool place.

4   Skewer the tomatoes on 2 flat metal skewers and place them on the hot grill before the kabobs because they take longer to cook (about 5 minutes); the tomatoes should be charred and smokey.

5 For the baste, in a small saucepan, combine the butter or olive oil, lime juice, and saffron water, and keep warm on very low heat. Spread a layer of lavash bread on a serving platter.

6 Lay the skewers of kabobs on the barbecue 3 inches above the coals but without touching the grill. After 20 seconds, gently turn the skewers; then turn again 20 seconds later, to help the meat firm up on both sides and to prevent it from falling off. (These first few seconds are important for cooking ground meat kabobs.)

7 Grill the meat for 3 to 5 minutes, turning frequently. Avoid overcooking (the meat should be seared on the outside, but juicy and tender in the middle). Baste just before removing from the fire.

8 Place the kabob skewers on the lavash bread platter. Place a piece of bread over each skewer and hold the meat down while you pull out the skewer. Baste, and sprinkle sumac powder to taste. Serve immediately with the grilled tomato halves, fresh basil, and Yogurt and Persian Shallot Salad (Mast-o Musir; Chapter 8). *Nush-e joon!*

PER SERVING: *Calories 560 (From Fat 324); Fat 36g (Saturated 11g); Cholesterol 83mg; Sodium 892mg; Carbohydrate 35g (Dietary Fiber 2g); Protein 25g.*

VARY IT! Instead of the lamb, you can use a mixture of 1 pound each of ground lamb and ground beef.

TIP: Any onion juice, from the mincing, will cause ground kabob not to hold together and to fall apart during cooking.

TIP: If you're using an oven broiler, use a sheet pan so the skewers can rest on the edges of the sheet pan without the meat touching the sheet pan. Wear grilling gloves to protect your hands, and turn the kabobs gently after the first 20 seconds and then again 20 seconds later so the meat on both sides attaches itself to the skewers, preventing the meat from falling off the skewers.

Fillet Kabob (Kabab-e Barg)

PREP TIME: 20 MIN PLUS 24 HR FOR SALTING AND 20 MIN FOR MARINATING

COOK TIME: 4 MIN

YIELD: 8 SERVINGS

INGREDIENTS

2½ pounds lean lamb loin (fillet/backstrap) or beef tenderloin, rubbed all over with 1 tablespoon fine sea salt in a sheet pan, covered, and refrigerated for 24 to 48 hours, then removed and patted dry

12 Campari tomatoes or 3 large tomatoes, cut in quarters

2 large yellow onions, peeled, grated, and juice squeezed out through a fine-mesh sieve (save the juice, but discard the solids)

1 cup olive oil

1 teaspoon freshly ground black pepper

¼ teaspoon ground saffron threads dissolved in 1 tablespoon rose water

1 cup melted butter

1 tablespoon fresh lime juice

One 12-ounce package lavash bread

2 tablespoons sumac powder (optional)

DIRECTIONS

1 Place the salted loin on a moist cutting board. Press down firmly and cut it, across the grain, into 4 pieces (about 3 inches each). Then cut each piece into ½-inch strips (about 6 strips). Repeat for the rest of the meat.

2 Thread each piece of meat, against the grain, onto skewers, leaving a 2-inch gap at the top of each skewer. Use your moist hand to press down firmly to flatten the fillet on the skewers.

3 Use the edge of another metal skewer to gently pound the flattened fillet on the skewers along the length of the skewers (with the grain, about 2 minutes). Arrange the skewers side-by-side on a large, rimmed sheet pan.

4 Spear the tomatoes on 3 separate skewers.

5 In a mixing bowl, add the onions, olive oil, pepper, and saffron water. Mix together and pour over each side of the skewered kabobs. Cover with another sheet pan (inverted so it doesn't touch the kabobs), and allow to marinate for 20 minutes at room temperature. Turn the skewers in the marinade once during this period.

6 Start the barbecue at least 30 minutes before you want to cook, and let it burn until the coals are glowing evenly. If you're using the oven broiler or an indoor grill, make sure it's preheated and very hot. The secret to a good kabob is a very hot grill.

7 To prepare the baste, in a small saucepan, place the butter and lime juice over very low heat, mix, and keep warm.

8 When the grill is hot, brush the tomatoes lightly with some of the baste and place them on the grill first (they take longer to cook; you want them to be charred and smokey); cook for at least 2 minutes before adding the skewered meat. Then arrange the skewered meat on the grill. For this kabob, allow one side to sear, about 2 minutes before turning and cooking the other side, not more than a minute or two. The meat should be seared on the outside and pink and juicy on the inside.

9 Place the kabobs and grilled tomato skewers on the serving platter and pour the baste over them; keep them on the skewers and cover with lavash bread to keep warm until ready to serve. When ready to serve, remove the meat from each skewer by using a piece of lavash bread to hold down several pieces of meat as you pull them off the skewer.

10 Sprinkle the kabobs with sumac powder if you like. Serve immediately with saffron steamed rice, lavash bread, pickles, and a dish of fresh herbs that includes spring onions, basil and Yogurt and Persian Shallot Salad (Mast-o Musir; Chapter 8). *Nush-e joon!*

PER SERVING: *Calories 607 (From Fat 311); Fat 35g (Saturated 15g); Cholesterol 155mg; Sodium 1,637mg; Carbohydrate 27g (Dietary Fiber 2g); Protein 45g.*

VARY IT! Instead of the lamb, you can use beef or veal (tenderloin) if you prefer.

Sweet-and-Sour Kabab (Kabab-e Torsh)

PREP TIME: 20 MIN PLUS 24 HR FOR MARINATING	COOK TIME: 4 MIN	YIELD: 8 SERVINGS

INGREDIENTS

3 pounds boneless chicken thighs or lamb loin, cut into 2-inch pieces, rinsed, and patted dry

1 large onion, peeled and quartered

4 cloves garlic, peeled

1 cup walnuts

¼ cup fresh basil leaves

¼ cup fresh mint leaves

2 cups pomegranate juice

¼ cup lime juice

¼ cup olive oil

2 teaspoons fine sea salt, divided

1¼ teaspoons freshly ground black pepper, divided

2 teaspoons ground *golpar* (Persian hogweed seeds), divided

1 tablespoon pomegranate molasses

1 teaspoon red pepper flakes (optional)

¼ cup butter or olive oil

One 12-ounce package lavash bread

⅓ cup pomegranate arils, for garnish (optional)

DIRECTIONS

1 In a glass container or bowl (preferably with a cover), place the chicken. In a food processor, add the onion, garlic, walnuts, basil, mint, pomegranate juice, lime juice, ¼ cup of olive oil, 1 teaspoon of the salt, 1 teaspoon of the pepper, and 1 teaspoon of the *golpar*. Pulse until you have a grainy mixture. Pour over the chicken and toss well. Cover with a lid or plastic wrap and marinate in the refrigerator for 8 to 48 hours.

2 Start the barbecue 30 minutes before you want to cook. If you're using the oven broiler or an indoor grill, make sure it's preheated and very hot. For this kabob, you don't want the meat too close to the fire, because the pomegranate marinade can make the outside burn easily.

3 To make the glaze, in a small saucepan, add the pomegranate molasses, the remaining ¼ teaspoon of pepper, the remaining 1 teaspoon of salt, red pepper flakes (if using), the remaining 1 teaspoon of *golpar*, and the ¼ cup of butter or olive oil. Mix together and keep warm on very low heat until ready to use.

4 Thread 4 or 5 pieces of chicken onto a flat metal skewer, leaving at least 2 inches free at the top of the skewer; repeat for a total of 8 skewers. Place the skewers on the grill and cook for 6 to 8 minutes, flipping frequently. The best way to test for doneness is to take a piece off the skewer and check to see if the meat is firm and does not resist cutting — and of course, taste it! When done, spread a layer of lavash bread on a serving platter and place the kabobs on the bread. Baste both sides immediately with the warm glaze. Remove the meat from each skewer by using a piece of lavash bread to hold down several pieces of meat as you pull them off the skewer.

5 Sprinkle with pomegranate arils (if using) and serve immediately (kabobs should be served hot off the skewers) with Plain Rice (Kateh; Chapter 12) and Yogurt and Persian Shallot Salad (Mast-o Musir; Chapter 8). *Nush-e joon!*

VARY IT! *You can substitute the chicken with lamb or beef tenderloin.*

PER SERVING: *Calories 423 (From Fat 247); Fat 27g (Saturated 6g); Cholesterol 26mg; Sodium 627mg; Carbohydrate 37g (Dietary Fiber 2g); Protein 10g.*

Skillet Kabob (Kabab-e Tabe'i)

INGREDIENTS

Paste

1 pound ground lamb, beef, chicken, or turkey

1 medium onion, peeled and minced

4 cloves garlic, peeled and grated

1 tablespoon chopped fresh parsley

1½ teaspoons fine sea salt, divided

1½ teaspoons freshly ground black pepper, divided

½ teaspoon turmeric

¼ teaspoon ground saffron threads dissolved in 1 tablespoon rose water

2 tablespoons lime juice

¼ cup olive oil, butter, or ghee, divided

3 medium tomatoes, peeled (see Chapter 4) and cut into ¼-inch-thick round slices

1½ pounds russet potatoes, peeled and cut into ¼-inch-thick round slices

DIRECTIONS

1   In a mixing bowl, add the meat, onion, garlic, parsley, 1 teaspoon of the salt, 1 teaspoon of the pepper, turmeric, saffron water, lime juice, and 1 tablespoon of the olive oil, butter, or ghee. Knead lightly, using your hands, to create a soft paste (do not overmix).

2   Moisten your hands and shape the paste into a large meatball and place it in the center of a well-oiled wide, deep skillet. Press down with the palm of your hand so the meat covers the base of the entire skillet evenly. Raise the meat around the edges of the skillet by 1 inch to form a well.

3   Arrange the tomato slices on top and sprinkle with ¼ teaspoon of salt and ¼ teaspoon of pepper. Drizzle 1 tablespoon of oil, butter, or ghee over the tomatoes; then arrange the potato slices over the tomatoes. Sprinkle the remaining ¼ teaspoon of salt and the remaining ¼ teaspoon of pepper over the top, and drizzle the remaining 2 tablespoons of oil, butter, or ghee over the top. Cover and cook over medium-low heat for 40 minutes. Uncover and cook for another 12 to 18 minutes, until some of the juices have been absorbed.

4   Drizzle any remaining pan juices on top. Serve hot with bread or rice, green salad, and fresh herbs. *Nush-e joon!*

PER SERVING: *Calories 422 (From Fat 125); Fat 14g (Saturated 2g); Cholesterol 55mg; Sodium 793mg; Carbohydrate 42g (Dietary Fiber 4g); Protein 31g.*

Chicken Kabob (Jujeh Kabab)

PREP TIME: 20 MIN PLUS 2–3 DAYS FOR MARINATING	COOK TIME: 15 MIN	YIELD: 4 SERVINGS

INGREDIENTS

2 Cornish hens (about 4 pounds), each cut into 10 pieces, or 4 pounds of chicken drumettes, or 4 pounds boneless chicken thighs cut into 2-inch pieces

2 large onions, peeled and quartered

1 clove garlic, peeled

Zest of 2 limes

2 tablespoons fresh lime juice

2 tablespoons apple cider vinegar

½ cup olive oil

1 cup plain yogurt

2½ teaspoons fine sea salt, divided

2½ teaspoons freshly ground black pepper, divided

2 teaspoons turmeric

6 small chili peppers (optional)

6 Campari tomatoes or 3 medium tomatoes, quartered

½ cup butter

Juice of 1 lime

Two 12-ounce packages lavash bread

6 lime halves, for garnish

8 spring onions, for garnish

8 radishes, for garnish

2 cups basil leaves, for garnish

DIRECTIONS

1 In a colander, rinse the chicken under cold water and pat dry. Place in a large, glass container or bowl (preferably with a cover).

2 In a food processor, place the onions, garlic, limes, 2 tablespoons of lime juice, apple cider vinegar, olive oil, yogurt, 2 teaspoons of the salt, 2 teaspoons of the pepper, and turmeric. Pulse until you have a grainy sauce. Pour the sauce over the chicken and toss well. Cover and leave to marinate in the refrigerator for 8 to 48 hours. Turn the chicken once during this time.

3 Start a bed of charcoal at least 30 minutes before you want to cook. If you're using the oven broiler or an indoor grill, preheat it until very hot. Skewer the tomatoes on 2 flat metal skewers and place them on the hot grill before the kabobs because they take longer to cook (about 5 minutes); the tomatoes should be charred and smokey. Spear the chicken wings, breasts, and legs on different flat metal skewers (they require different cooking times), adding a chili pepper (if using) to each skewer.

4 To make the baste, in a small saucepan, place the butter, juice of 1 lime, the remaining ½ teaspoon of salt, and the remaining ½ teaspoon of pepper. Keep warm over very low heat.

(continued)

5 Place the skewers on the grill, putting the legs on first (if using), then the breasts and wings, and finally the drumettes and chicken thighs. Depending on the size of the chicken pieces, grill the kabobs for 8 to 15 minutes, turning occasionally. The chicken is done when the juice that runs out is clear rather than pink (165 degrees on a meat probe thermometer). Just before removing the kabobs from the heat, brush both sides with the basting mixture.

6 Spread a layer of lavash bread on a serving platter and place the skewers with the chops on the bread. Remove the chops from each skewer by using a piece of lavash bread to hold down several pieces of meat as you pull them off the skewer. Garnish with lime halves, spring onions, radishes, and basil leaves. Serve immediately with Cucumber and Tomato Salad (Salad-e Gojeh Khiar; Chapter 8). *Nush-e joon!*

PER SERVING: *Calories 980 (From Fat 450); Fat 50g (Saturated 23g); Cholesterol 194mg; Sodium 1,133mg; Carbohydrate 91g (Dietary Fiber 5g); Protein 42g.*

Fish Kabob with Garlic and Cilantro (Kabab-e Mahi)

PREP TIME: 20 MIN PLUS 4 HR FOR MARINATING	COOK TIME: 7 MIN	YIELD: 4 SERVINGS

INGREDIENTS

2 pounds fish fillets (swordfish, tuna, or salmon), skins and bones removed and cut into 2-inch cubes

¼ cup oil

1 medium onion, peeled and quartered

6 cloves garlic, peeled

2 tablespoons lime juice

2¼ teaspoons fine sea salt, divided

½ teaspoon freshly ground black pepper

1 teaspoon turmeric

1 teaspoon red pepper flakes

1 tablespoon coriander seeds

2 tablespoons ground hearts of dried Persian limes

1¼ cups roughly chopped fresh cilantro, divided

¼ cup olive oil, butter, or ghee

¼ cup fresh sour orange juice

DIRECTIONS

1 Place the fish in a glass container (preferably with a cover).

2 In a food processor, place the ¼ cup of oil, onion, garlic, lime juice, 2 teaspoons of the salt, pepper, turmeric, red pepper flakes, coriander, ground hearts of dried Persian limes, and 1 cup of the cilantro. Pulse until minced. Add the marinade to the fish, toss well, cover, and allow to marinate for 4 hours in the refrigerator.

3 To prepare the baste, in a small saucepan, combine the ¼ cup of oil, butter, or ghee; the remaining ¼ cup of cilantro; orange juice; and the remaining ¼ teaspoon of salt. Keep warm over very low heat.

4 Preheat the grill until very hot. Thread the fish onto 6 flat ½-inch swordlike metal skewers or place them in an oiled grill basket and lock it.

5 Grill the fish for 4 to 7 minutes (depending on type of fish), flipping gently but frequently. Avoid overcooking — the fish should be charred on the outside, and juicy and tender on the inside (overcooked fish becomes tough rather than flaky). When the fish is cooked, baste it on all sides. Serve hot with Plain Rice (Kateh; Chapter 12). *Nush-e joon!*

PER SERVING: *Calories 612 (From Fat 396); Fat 44g (Saturated 9g); Cholesterol 125mg; Sodium 608mg; Carbohydrate 5g (Dietary Fiber 1g); Protein 47g.*

TIP: If sour orange juice is not in season, use a combination of 2 tablespoons fresh orange juice and 2 tablespoons fresh lime juice instead.

Chapter **15**

Savoring Meatballs, Patties, and Casseroles

ranians love their meatballs and meat patties, and every region has its own variations. They're made not only with lamb, but also with chicken, fish, or shrimp. My favorites are made with lamb, aromatic herbs, and rice, with egg to bind them.

The casseroles in this chapter require no unusual techniques to prepare, but the interplay of sweet and tart fruits and vegetables with the chicken or lamb gives an authentic taste of Iran.

Everyone should be able to cook a simple, juicy roast chicken, and I've included two recipes in this chapter that you can use on their own or to accompany rice dishes.

Fava Bean and Dill Meatballs (Kufteh Baqali)

PREP TIME: 45 MIN	COOK TIME: 25 MIN	YIELD: 4 SERVINGS

INGREDIENTS

½ cup rice

6 cups water

8 ounces fresh or frozen fava beans, second skins removed

1 small onion, peeled and quartered

4 cloves garlic, peeled

3 cups chopped fresh dill weed or 1 cup dried dill weed

4 teaspoons fine sea salt, divided

1 teaspoon freshly ground black pepper, divided

2 teaspoons turmeric, divided

1 tablespoon plus 1 teaspoon ground cumin, divided

1 pound ground turkey thigh or lamb

3 eggs, lightly beaten

½ cup rice flour

½ cup olive oil, butter, or ghee, divided

2 onions, peeled and thinly sliced

½ teaspoon red pepper flakes

3 cups fresh tomatoes, peeled, or canned tomato puree

2 cups stock or water

DIRECTIONS

1 In a medium saucepan, place the rice and water; bring to a boil. Reduce the heat to medium and boil for 5 minutes, uncovered. Add the fava beans, and cook for another 5 minutes (the rice should be almost tender and the fava beans should be blanched). Drain (do not rinse), and allow to cool.

2 In a food processor, add the rice and fava beans, quartered onion, garlic, dill weed, 2 teaspoons of the salt, 1 teaspoon of the pepper, 1 teaspoon of the turmeric, 1 tablespoon of the cumin, and meat; pulse until grainy. Transfer to a large mixing bowl, add the egg and rice flour, and knead lightly with your hands until you have a paste. Cover and chill for 15 minutes in the refrigerator.

3 Meanwhile, In the same saucepan, add ¼ cup of the oil, butter, or ghee, and warm over medium heat. Add the sliced onions and sauté until golden, about 10 to 15 minutes. Add the remaining 2 teaspoons of salt, the remaining ½ teaspoon of pepper, the remaining 1 teaspoon of turmeric, the red pepper flakes, the remaining 1 teaspoon of cumin, the tomatoes, and the stock or water; bring to a boil. Reduce the heat to medium-low, cover, and allow to simmer for 5 minutes.

4 Preheat the oven to 450 degrees. Generously oil an 11-x-13-inch baking dish. Shape the meat paste into 16 balls, each the size of a large walnut. Gently arrange them in the baking dish and brush with the remaining ¼ cup of oil, butter, or ghee. Bake in the oven for 10 minutes.

5 Pull out the oven rack and gently pour the hot tomato sauce over the meatballs. Cover with an oiled sheet of parchment paper and bake for 7 minutes. Keep warm until ready to serve.

6 Serve with Yogurt and Persian Shallot Salad (Mast-o Musir; Chapter 8) and bread. *Nush-e joon!*

PER SERVING: *Calories 898 (From Fat 363); Fat 40g (Saturated 7g); Cholesterol 219mg; Sodium 2,217mg; Carbohydrate 94g (Dietary Fiber 19g); Protein 42g.*

VARY IT! For vegetarians, bring 2 cups of quinoa and 3 cups of water to a boil; then reduce the heat to low, cover, and cook over medium heat for 20 minutes. Allow to cool and use instead of the ground turkey.

Chickpea and Carrot Patties (Shami)

PREP TIME: 30 MIN PLUS 30 MIN TO 24 HR FOR RESTING

COOK TIME: 45 MIN

YIELD: 4 SERVINGS

INGREDIENTS

1 pound ground chicken, turkey, or lamb, or fish fillets (all small bones removed)

1 medium onion, peeled and quartered

1½ pounds carrots (about 4 large), peeled and cut into chunks

2½ teaspoons fine sea salt, divided

1 teaspoon freshly ground black pepper

1 teaspoon turmeric

2 teaspoon *advieh* (Persian spice mix)

½ cup chickpea flour

¼ cup olive oil

¼ cup grape molasses or sugar

¼ cup fresh lime juice

½ teaspoon ground saffron threads dissolved in 2 tablespoons hot water

¼ cup chopped fresh cilantro or basil, for garnish

DIRECTIONS

1 Line a sheet pan with parchment paper.

2 In a large bowl, place the chicken, turkey, lamb, or fish; set aside.

3 In a food processor, place the onion, carrots, 2 teaspoons of the salt, pepper, turmeric, and *advieh*, and pulse until you have a grainy paste. Transfer to the bowl with the meat or fish.

4 Add the chickpea flour a little at a time, and knead with your hands until all the flour has been absorbed (do not overmix). Cover and allow to rest for 30 minutes or up to 24 hours in the fridge. If the paste sticks to your hand, dust with more chickpea flour.

5 In a wide skillet, add the oil or butter and warm over medium-low heat until hot but not smoking. Shape the paste into about 3-inch-diameter patties, and make a hole in the center (like a donut). Gently place them in the skillet and cook until golden, about 5 to 7 minutes on each side. Transfer the patties to the prepared sheet pan as you make them.

6 In a small bowl, combine the grape molasses or sugar, lime juice, saffron, and the remaining ½ teaspoon of salt; stir well.

7 Return the patties to the skillet and pour the glaze over the patties. Reduce the heat to very low, cover, and allow to simmer until all the sauce has been absorbed. about 3 to 5 minutes.

8 Garnish with the cilantro and serve. *Nush-e joon!*

PER SERVING: *Calories 465 (From Fat 206); Fat 23g (Saturated 4g); Cholesterol 52mg; Sodium 1,552mg; Carbohydrate 46g (Dietary Fiber 7g); Protein 21g.*

TIP: I like to use green-leaf lettuce leaves to make wraps with the patties inside and garnish with basil.

Pistachio and Pomegranate Meatballs (Kufteh-ye Pesteh-o Anar)

PREP TIME: 20 MIN PLUS 10 MIN FOR CHILLING	COOK TIME: 20 MIN	YIELD: 8 SERVINGS

INGREDIENTS

1 large onion, peeled and quartered

1½ cups raw pistachio kernels

½ cup fresh plain breadcrumbs

3 cups chopped fresh parsley or 1 cup dried parsley

1 cup chopped fresh tarragon or ⅓ cup dried tarragon

1 cup chopped fresh cilantro or ⅓ cup dried cilantro

1 tablespoon fresh lime juice

1 teaspoon red pepper flakes

1 tablespoon ground cumin

3 teaspoons sea salt, divided

1½ teaspoons freshly ground black pepper, divided

2 pounds ground turkey thighs, lamb, or deboned fish fillets

1 egg

½ cup oil for brushing the meatballs

1 cup pomegranate molasses

⅓ cup grape molasses

½ teaspoon red pepper flakes

1 cup pomegranate arils, for garnish

DIRECTIONS

1   In a food processor, place the onion, pistachio kernels, bread-crumbs, parsley, tarragon, cilantro, lime juice, red pepper flakes, cumin, 2 teaspoons of the salt, and 1 teaspoon of the pepper; pulse until you have a grainy paste. Transfer to a large mixing bowl and add the turkey, lamb, or fish, and the egg. Knead with your hands for a few minutes (do not over-mix). Cover and chill in the refrigerator for at least 10 minutes or up to 24 hours.

2   Preheat the oven to 450 degrees. Generously oil a 12-x-14-inch baking dish (large enough to fit 24 meatballs) and set aside.

3   Remove the turkey paste from the refrigerator and, using an ice cream scoop, shape into walnut-size balls. Place the meatballs in the baking dish and brush well with the oil. Bake in the oven until lightly golden (165 degrees on a meat ther-mometer), about 10 to 15 minutes (depending on your oven).

4   Meanwhile, in another mixing bowl, add the pomegranate molasses, grape molasses, the remaining 1 teaspoon of salt, the remaining ½ teaspoon of pepper, and the red pepper flakes; stir together. Spoon the glaze over the meatballs. Bake for another 5 minutes to infuse them with the flavor of pomegran-ate. Baste and garnish with the pomegranate arils. *Nush-e joon!*

PER SERVING: *Calories 634 (From Fat 306); Fat 34g (Saturated 6g); Cholesterol 87mg; Sodium 1,136mg; Carbohydrate 62g (Dietary Fiber 5g); Protein 25g.*

VARY IT! For vegetarians, increase the pistachios to 3 cups and the eggs to 3 and leave out the turkey, lamb, or fish.

Shrimp Balls in Spicy Tomato Sauce (Chubeh)

PREP TIME: 20 MIN | COOK TIME: 50 MIN | YIELD: 4 SERVINGS

INGREDIENTS

1 shallot, peeled and quartered

4 cloves garlic, peeled

1 teaspoon red pepper flakes, divided

1½ teaspoons fine sea salt, divided

¾ teaspoon freshly ground black pepper, divided

1½ tablespoons ground dried hearts of Persian lime, divided

1 cup chopped fresh cilantro or ⅓ cup dried cilantro

1 tablespoon dried fenugreek leaves

3 tablespoons rice flour

1 pound shrimp, peeled, deveined, rinsed, and patted dry

¼ cup oil, butter or ghee for sautéing

1 teaspoon *advieh* (Persian spice mix)

½ teaspoon turmeric

2½ cups peeled fresh tomato puree or canned peeled tomato puree

1 cup chopped fresh cilantro, for garnish

DIRECTIONS

1 In a food processor, add the shallot, garlic, ½ teaspoon of the red pepper flakes, ½ teaspoon of the salt, ½ teaspoon of the pepper, ½ tablespoon of the Persian lime, the cilantro, the fenugreek, the rice flour, and the shrimp. Pulse until you have a paste.

2 Preheat the oven to 450 degrees. Line a sheet pan with parchment paper. Shape the shrimp paste into about 20 walnut-size balls and arrange them on the sheet pan. Paint the shrimp balls with 2 tablespoons of the oil, butter, or ghee. Bake in the oven for 10 minutes.

3 In a medium sauté pan, add the remaining 2 tablespoons of the oil, butter, or ghee, and warm over medium heat until hot.

4 To the pan, add the *advieh*, the remaining ½ teaspoon of red pepper flakes, the remaining 1 teaspoon of salt, the remaining ¼ teaspoon of pepper, the turmeric, and the remaining 1 tablespoon of Persian lime, and the tomato puree and give the mixture a gentle stir. Bring to a boil and add the shrimp balls. Reduce the heat to medium-low and cook, uncovered, until the sauce has thickened, about 15 to 20 minutes.

5 Adjust the seasoning to taste and garnish with the cilantro. *Nush-e joon!*

PER SERVING: *Calories 347 (From Fat 144); Fat 16g (Saturated 2g); Cholesterol 172mg; Sodium 919mg; Carbohydrate 26g (Dietary Fiber 3g); Protein 27g.*

TIP: I like to serve these shrimp balls with fresh herbs on lettuce leaves or tortillas and eat them as wraps.

Meat Patties (Kotlet-e Gusht)

PREP TIME: 45 MIN	COOK TIME: 30 MIN	YIELD: 6 SERVINGS

INGREDIENTS

1 pound ground lamb, chicken, or turkey

1 medium onion, peeled and grated

2 eggs

2 large russet potatoes (2 pounds), scored, boiled for 15 minutes, peeled, and coarsely grated

2½ teaspoons fine sea salt, divided

1½ teaspoons freshly ground black pepper, divided

1½ teaspoons turmeric, divided

2 tablespoons *advieh* (Persian spice mix)

¼ teaspoon ground saffron dissolved in 2 tablespoons hot water

¾ cup plus 2 tablespoons oil, divided

¾ cup dry breadcrumbs

4 medium ripe tomatoes (2 pounds), peeled and diced

DIRECTIONS

1 In a mixing bowl, add the meat, onion, eggs, potatoes, 2 teaspoons of the salt, 1 teaspoon of the pepper, 1 teaspoon of the turmeric, the *advieh*, and the saffron water. Knead together with your hands to form a smooth paste, about 5 minutes.

2 In a wide skillet, place ½ cup of the oil and warm over medium heat.

3 Meanwhile, dip your hands in a bowl of water to moisten them. Shape the paste into lumps the size of eggs. Flatten them into oval patties and roll in the breadcrumbs. Place the patties in the skillet and brown them on both sides (about 5 minutes on each side), adding more oil if needed. Arrange on a serving platter and keep warm.

4 Wipe the skillet. Place 2 tablespoons of the oil in the skillet and warm over medium heat. Add the tomatoes, the remaining ½ teaspoon of salt, the remaining ½ teaspoon of pepper, and the remaining ½ teaspoon of turmeric, and sauté for 5 minutes. Reduce the heat to low, cover, and simmer for 15 minutes. Pour the tomato sauce over the patties. Serve with French fries, bread, salad, fresh herbs, and *torshi* (Persian pickles). *Nush-e joon!*

PER SERVING: *Calories 585 (From Fat 355); Fat 39g (Saturated 6g); Cholesterol 111mg; Sodium 1,091mg; Carbohydrate 41g (Dietary Fiber 4g); Protein 19g.*

VARY IT! For vegetarians, in a small saucepan, place 2 cups dried lentils, 4 cups water, and ½ teaspoon fine sea salt. Bring to a boil, reduce the heat to medium, and cook for 15 minutes. Drain thoroughly, allow to cool, and use in place of the lamb in Step 1.

Chicken, Vegetable, and Fruit Casserole (Tas Kabab)

PREP TIME: 25 MIN	COOK TIME: 2 HR	YIELD: 6 SERVINGS

INGREDIENTS

1 tablespoon fine sea salt

1 teaspoon freshly ground black pepper

1 teaspoon turmeric

2 tablespoons ground dried Persian lime hearts

2 teaspoons *advieh* (Persian spice mix)

½ teaspoon red pepper flakes

¼ cup oil, butter, or ghee, divided

2 large onions, peeled and sliced into rings

3 pounds chicken thighs, skin on and bone-in

4 cloves garlic, peeled and sliced

2 quinces or apples (Fuji or Granny Smith), cored, hard parts removed, peeled, and sliced into rings

2 Chinese eggplants, peeled and sliced into rings (1 inch thick)

2 carrots, peeled and sliced into rings (1 inch thick)

DIRECTIONS

1 Preheat the oven to 400 degrees.

2 In a small bowl, add the salt, pepper, turmeric, Persian lime, *advieh*, and red pepper flakes. Mix well; set aside.

3 In a 4-quart ovenproof casserole dish, add 2 tablespoons of the oil, butter, or ghee. Layer the ingredients in the following order (sprinkling some of the spice mixture between each of the layers): onion, chicken, garlic, quince or apples, eggplant, carrot, tomato, and potato. Use the palms of your hands to press down the layers. Top with a layer of prunes, apricots, and dates, and pour the remaining 2 tablespoons of oil, butter, or ghee on top. Pour the saffron water over the chicken and vegetables.

2 tomatoes, peeled and sliced into rings (1 inch thick)

2 large russet potatoes peeled and sliced into rings (1 inch thick)

1 cup pitted prunes

1 cup dried apricots

5 Medjool dates (3 ounces), any remaining hard stalk parts removed, pitted, and halved

½ teaspoon ground saffron combined with 1 cup water and 1 teaspoon fine sea salt

4 Cover and roast in the oven for 2 hours. Remove from the oven, uncover, adjust the seasoning to taste, and baste with the sauce.

5 Serve right out of the casserole dish with bread, yogurt, salad, and fresh herbs. *Nush-e joon!*

PER SERVING: *Calories 756 (From Fat 255); Fat 28g (Saturated 7g); Cholesterol 110mg; Sodium 1,775mg; Carbohydrate 96g (Dietary Fiber 13g); Protein 37g.*

TIP: If your casserole dish doesn't have a lid, use a layer of parchment paper with a layer of aluminum foil over it and seal tightly.

VARY IT! For vegetarians, just eliminate the chicken.

Pomegranate-Infused Leg of Lamb (Barreh-ye Beriyan)

PREP TIME: 45 MIN	COOK TIME: 3 HR	YIELD: 10 SERVINGS

INGREDIENTS

1 leg of lamb, boneless (4 to 5 pounds)

10 cloves garlic, peeled

3 teaspoons fine sea salt, divided

2 teaspoons freshly ground black pepper, divided

1 teaspoon turmeric

1 tablespoon unbleached all-purpose flour

2 medium, yellow onions, peeled and quartered

1 cup walnuts

4 cups pure pomegranate juice

1 teaspoon red pepper flakes

1 tablespoon ground cardamom

1 tablespoon ground cumin

½ cup pomegranate arils, for garnish

DIRECTIONS

1 Preheat the oven to 350 degrees. Rinse the leg of lamb and thoroughly pat dry.

2 In a deep baking dish or a laminated cast-iron pot (preferably one with a lid), place the lamb. Use the point of a sharp knife to make 10 slits all over the lamb, and then insert the cloves of garlic in the slits.

3 In a small bowl, add 2 teaspoons of the salt, 1 teaspoon of the pepper, the turmeric, and the flour. Mix well, and then rub it all over the lamb.

4 In a food processor, place the onion, walnuts, pomegranate juice, the remaining 1 teaspoon of salt, red pepper flakes, the remaining 1 teaspoon of pepper, cardamom, and cumin. Pulse until you have a smooth, creamy sauce, about 1 minute. Spread the sauce over the lamb.

5 Cover and bake for 1½ hours.

6 Uncover the baking dish and turn the lamb in its sauce. Continue to bake, uncovered, until the meat is tender with a pull-apart consistency, about 30 minutes. Transfer the meat to a serving platter; remove any string or net bag and discard. Serve the lamb with the sauce on top. *Nush-e joon!*

PER SERVING: *Calories 183 (From Fat 74); Fat 8g (Saturated 1g); Cholesterol 7mg; Sodium 589mg; Carbohydrate 24g (Dietary Fiber 2g); Protein 5g.*

TIP: If you don't have a dish with a lid, use a layer of parchment paper and then a layer of aluminum foil to cover the dish.

TIP: This lamb is wonderful for accompanying any of the rice dishes, particularly Rice with Fava Beans and Dill (Baqala Polow; Chapter 12).

Sweet-and-Sour Stuffed Chicken (Morgh-e Tu Por-e Torsh-o Shirin)

PREP TIME: 30 MIN	COOK TIME: 1 HR 30 MIN	YIELD: 4 SERVINGS

INGREDIENTS

4 Cornish game hens or 2 small frying chickens

3½ teaspoons sea salt, divided

2 teaspoons freshly ground black pepper, divided

1 teaspoon turmeric

¾ cup oil, butter, or ghee, divided

1 large onion, peeled and thinly sliced

4 cloves garlic, peeled and thinly sliced

1 cup pitted prunes, finely chopped

1 apple, cored and chopped

1 cup dried apricots, finely chopped

½ cup raisins (or pitted dates, chopped)

2 teaspoons *advieh* (Persian spice mix)

1 teaspoon grape molasses

6 tablespoons fresh lime juice or vinegar, divided

¼ teaspoon ground saffron

DIRECTIONS

1   Clean and rinse the Cornish hens in cold water; pat dry.

2   In a small bowl, add 2 teaspoons of the salt, 1 teaspoon of the pepper, and the turmeric. Mix together, and then rub the hens inside and out with this mixture.

3   In a wide skillet, add ¼ cup of the oil, butter, or ghee and warm over medium heat. Add the onion and garlic and sauté until golden, about 10 minutes. Add the prunes, apple, apricots, raisins or dates, 1 teaspoon of the salt, the remaining 1 teaspoon of pepper, *advieh*, grape molasses, and 2 tablespoons of the lime juice or vinegar. Stir-fry for 1 minute; then remove from the heat and set aside.

4   Preheat the oven to 450 degrees. Stuff the hens with the filling and pin or sew the cavities shut. Place the hens in an oiled ovenproof baking dish.

5   In a saucepan, add the remaining ½ cup of oil, butter, or ghee; the remaining ¼ cup of lime juice or vinegar; the saffron; and the remaining ½ teaspoon of salt. Warm over low heat for 3 minutes, stirring well. Then baste and paint the hens all over with this mixture. Cover the hens with a layer of parchment paper and a layer of aluminum foil and seal tight. Roast in the oven for 1 hour. Uncover, baste with the pan juices, and continue to roast, uncovered, until the meat separates easily from the bone, about 20 minutes.

6   Serve with Plain Rice (Kateh; Chapter 12), salad, and fresh herbs. *Nush-e joon!*

PER SERVING: *Calories 1,021 (From Fat 548); Fat 61g (Saturated 15g); Cholesterol 337mg; Sodium 1,814mg; Carbohydrate 62g (Dietary Fiber 7g); Protein 60g.*

Lime and Turmeric Roast Chicken (Morgh-e Beriyan)

PREP TIME: 10 MIN	COOK TIME: 1 HR 45 MIN	YIELD: 4 SERVINGS

INGREDIENTS

1 organic or kosher chicken (3 to 4 pounds) or 2 Cornish hens

¼ cup olive oil mixed with ½ cup fresh lime juice (about 4 limes)

1 tablespoon fine sea salt

1 tablespoon freshly ground black pepper

1 tablespoon turmeric

1 small onion, peeled and halved

½ lime

4 cloves garlic, peeled and sliced

DIRECTIONS

1 Preheat the oven to 450 degrees. Line a rimmed sheet pan with parchment paper.

2 Place the chicken in a colander and rinse it, inside and outside, with cold water. Pat dry; then place in the lined sheet pan.

3 Spread the olive oil and lime juice mixture all over the chicken, inside and out.

4 In a small bowl, add the salt, pepper, and turmeric. Mix together, and then rub the mixture inside and over the chicken.

5 Stuff the chicken with the onion and ½ lime; insert the garlic under the skin.

6 Cover loosely with a piece of oiled parchment paper and a layer of aluminum foil and roast for 1¾ hours. Remove from the oven and baste with the pan juices or olive oil.

7 Carve and serve with your favorite rice, bread, quinoa, salad, or a fresh herb platter. *Nush-e joon!*

PER SERVING: *Calories 513 (From Fat 306); Fat 34g (Saturated 8g); Cholesterol 165mg; Sodium 1,533mg; Carbohydrate 8g (Dietary Fiber 1g); Protein 42g.*

Chapter **16**

Fixing Fish Entrees

Fish plays an important role for Iranians living near the Caspian Sea in northern Iran and those living by the Persian Gulf in southern Iran. When you enter a market in those regions, it's the fish that first impresses.

In the north, you see freshly caught Caspian *kutum* (salmon), salted and smoked fish, and pink and brown fish roe, which locals use in their omelets. They flavor their fish with salt, pepper, turmeric and lime of sour orange and serve it over plain rice.

In the south, they like their fish with a great deal of spices and flavor them with tamarind. The most interesting dishes of the Persian Gulf reflect the incredible variety of seafood in the region: tuna, mackerel, sardines, anchovies, octopus, squid, calamari, lobster, and the most delicious giant, pink shrimp, known as "tiger shrimp." Locals eat all of these, cooked in many different ways — salted, pickled, poached, fried, and grilled. One of the most beloved dishes in southern Iran is fish cooked in a tamarind, cilantro, and garlic broth.

TIP

In Persian cooking, fish is generally served with rice.

Fish with Fresh Herbs and Barberry Stuffing (Mahi-e Tu Por ba Sabzi)

PREP TIME: 30 MIN	COOK TIME: 45 MIN	YIELD: 4 SERVINGS

INGREDIENTS

3 teaspoons fine sea salt, divided

1¼ teaspoons freshly ground black pepper, divided

1 teaspoon turmeric

4 cloves garlic, peeled and grated

½ cup chopped fresh parsley

2 tablespoons chopped fresh tarragon

4 spring onions, chopped

½ cup chopped fresh cilantro

½ cup chopped fresh mint or 2 tablespoons dried mint

1 cup coarsely ground walnuts or raw pistachio kernels

½ cup dried barberries, cleaned, soaked for 10 minutes in cold water, drained, and rinsed

½ cup golden or green raisins

½ cup fresh lime juice, divided

¾ cup oil, butter, or ghee, divided

¼ teaspoon ground saffron dissolved in 2 tablespoons hot water (optional)

1 large whole striped bass, rockfish, or grouper (4–5 pounds), scaled, butterflied, and skin scored, or 2 thick fillets of fish, with the skin (about 3 pounds)

DIRECTIONS

1 Preheat the oven to 400 degrees. Line a rimmed baking sheet or dish with a layer of aluminum foil and a layer of parchment paper (overlap the baking sheet for lifting if necessary). Generously oil the parchment paper.

2 In a small bowl, add 1 teaspoon of the salt, 1 teaspoon of the pepper, and the turmeric. Mix and set aside; this is the dusting mixture.

3 In a large bowl, place the garlic; parsley; tarragon; onions; cilantro; mint; nuts; barberries; raisins; ¼ cup of lime juice; the remaining 2 teaspoons of salt; the remaining ¼ teaspoon of pepper; ¼ cup of oil, butter, or ghee; and the saffron water. Toss well and set aside; this is the filling mixture.

4 Rinse the fish in cold water and pat dry with a towel.

5 Lay the fish on the lined baking sheet. Paint it all over, inside and out, with the remaining ½ cup of the oil, butter, or ghee and the remaining ¼ cup of the lime juice. Then rub, inside and out, with the dusting mixture.

6 Reserve ¼ cup of the filling mixture for the garnish. Stuff the fish with the remaining filling mixture; then sew or pin the cavity shut.

7 Bake, uncovered, until the fish flakes easily with a fork, about 40 to 45 minutes (depending on the size of the fish). Remove from the oven and remove the skin from the fish. Baste with the pan juices. Garnish with the remaining filling mixture. Serve with Plain Rice (Kateh; Chapter 12). *Nush-e joon!*

PER SERVING: *Calories 957 (From Fat 573); Fat 64g (Saturated 9g); Cholesterol 135mg; Sodium 1,684mg; Carbohydrate 33g (Dietary Fiber 5g); Protein 68g.*

TIP: For fish fillets, place one fillet on the lined sheet pan, skin side down. Spread a layer of the filling along its length and then place the other fillet, skin side up, over it (save any extra filling to use as a garnish after the fish is cooked). Bake for only 20 to 25 minutes in Step 7.

Grilled Branzino with Tamarind and Cilantro (Mahi-e Kababi ba Tamr-e Hendi-o Gishniz)

<table>
<tr><td>PREP TIME: 20 MIN PLUS 30 MIN FOR CHILLING</td><td>COOK TIME: 35 MIN</td><td>YIELD: 4 SERVINGS</td></tr>
</table>

INGREDIENTS

5 tablespoons olive oil, butter, or ghee, divided

4 whole branzino (4–5 pounds), cleaned (gills removed, head and tail optional) and fins trimmed but scales not removed, rinsed thoroughly

5 teaspoons fine sea salt, divided

3 teaspoons turmeric, divided

1 small onion, peeled and diced

4 cloves garlic, peeled and sliced

2 spring onions, finely chopped (white and green parts)

1 cup chopped fresh cilantro or ⅓ cup dried cilantro

1 cup chopped fresh parsley or ⅓ cup dried parsley

1 cup chopped fresh dill or ⅓ cup dried dill

2 tablespoons dried fenugreek

1 tablespoon tomato paste

¼ cup tamarind paste

½ teaspoon freshly ground black pepper

4 teaspoons date molasses

¼ cup oil or melted butter

DIRECTIONS

1 Oil a rimmed sheet pan with 1 tablespoon of the oil, butter, or ghee. Rinse the fish and pat dry with a paper towel; then arrange on the sheet pan.

2 In a small bowl, add 4 teaspoons of the salt and 2 teaspoons of the turmeric and combine. Rub the inside of each fish with ¼ quarter of this mixture. Cover the fish and chill in the refrigerator.

3 In a wide skillet, add the remaining 4 tablespoons oil, butter, or ghee, and warm over medium heat. Add the onion and garlic and sauté until golden brown, about 10 to 15 minutes. Add the spring onions, cilantro, parsley, dill, fenugreek, tomato paste, tamarind paste, the remaining 1 teaspoon of salt, pepper, and the remaining 1 teaspoon of turmeric. Sauté for 2 minutes; then remove from the heat and allow to cool.

4 Preheat the grill or broiler until very hot. Spread ¼ of the filling inside each fish. Rub both sides of the outer skin of each fish with 1 teaspoon of the date molasses glaze. Spray 2 stainless-steel grill baskets with oil and place 2 stuffed fish, side-by-side, in each basket; then lock the baskets.

5 Grill the fish until the skin is blackened, about 4 to 5 minutes on each side. Remove the fish from the baskets, peel away the skins on 1 side, and drizzle with some of the oil or melted butter. Serve whole. *Nush-e joon!*

PER SERVING: *Calories 598 (From Fat 299); Fat 33g (Saturated 5g); Cholesterol 122mg; Sodium 2,545mg; Carbohydrate 17g (Dietary Fiber 2g); Protein 57g.*

TIP: If you don't want to use a grill basket for broiling, place an oven grilling rack in a half-size sheet pan, paint it with oil and arrange the fish, side-by-side, on top. Grill under the broiler per Step 5.

Spicy Sweet-and-Sour Fish with Dates (Qaliyeh-ye Khorma)

PREP TIME: 30 MIN | COOK TIME: 35 MIN | YIELD: 6 SERVINGS

INGREDIENTS

1½ teaspoons fine sea salt

½ teaspoon freshly ground black pepper

1 teaspoon turmeric

1 tablespoon unbleached all-purpose wheat flour or rice flour

6 thick fish fillets (about 2½ pounds total), such as grouper or salmon, skins and all small bones removed

4 tablespoons oil, divided

5 cloves garlic, peeled and grated

1 cup apple cider vinegar

2 tablespoons date molasses or date syrup

1 scant teaspoon cayenne or 2 red Thai chilies, thinly sliced

1 tablespoon dried fenugreek leaves

5 Medjool dates, any remaining hard stalk parts removed, pitted, and halved

1 cup chopped fresh cilantro

1 green jalapeño pepper, thinly sliced

DIRECTIONS

1 In a small bowl, add the salt, pepper, turmeric, and flour, and mix together. Set aside.

2 Line a sheet pan with parchment paper. Rinse the fish and pat dry; then place on the sheet pan. Dust both sides of the fish fillets with the flour mixture, cover, and chill until ready to cook.

3 In a medium braiser, add 2 tablespoons of the oil and warm over high heat until very hot but not smoking. Sear the fish to brown on both sides, about 1 minute each side; then remove from the pan and set aside.

4 In the same pan, add the remaining 2 tablespoons of oil and warm over medium heat. Add the garlic and stir-fry until golden brown, about 1 to 2 minutes. Add the vinegar and date molasses/syrup, cayenne or chilies, and fenugreek leaves, and stir. Return the fish to the pan, reduce the heat to low, and simmer, uncovered, until the fish is flaky, and the sauce has thickened (basting twice), about 8 to 12 minutes.

5 Adjust the seasoning to taste and keep warm until ready to serve. Garnish with the dates, cilantro, and jalapeño pepper. Serve with plain rice and Onion, Cucumber, and Coriander Quick Pickle (Torshi Hazeri-e Piaz; Chapter 17). I also love to serve this dish with fresh basil leaves on the side. *Nush-e joon!*

PER SERVING: *Calories 312 (From Fat 120); Fat 13g (Saturated 2g); Cholesterol 55mg; Sodium 532mg; Carbohydrate 23g (Dietary Fiber 2g); Protein 24g.*

Sumac Grilled Fish (Mahi-e Kababi ba Somaq)

PREP TIME: 20 MIN | COOK TIME: 10 MIN | YIELD: 4 SERVINGS

INGREDIENTS

¼ cup shelled walnuts

1 cup roughly chopped fresh parsley

1 cup roughly chopped fresh cilantro

1 cup roughly chopped fresh mint

4 cloves garlic, peeled

2 tablespoons lime juice

2½ teaspoons fine sea salt, divided

1¼ teaspoons freshly ground black pepper, divided

5 tablespoons olive oil, butter, or ghee, divided

1 teaspoon turmeric

¼ cup sumac powder

4 fillets of striped bass or catfish (each ½-inch thick, about 2 pounds total)

¼ cup olive oil combined with 2 tablespoons lime juice

DIRECTIONS

1 In a food processor, add the walnuts; parsley; cilantro; mint; garlic; lime juice; ½ teaspoon of the salt; ¼ teaspoon of the pepper; and the oil, butter, or ghee. Pulse until grainy, about 2 minutes, and then transfer to a small bowl; set aside. (This is the topping.)

2 In a small bowl, add the remaining 2 teaspoons of salt, the remaining 1 teaspoon of pepper, the turmeric, and the sumac powder. Mix and set aside. (This is the rub.)

3 Oil a rimmed sheet pan with 1 tablespoon of the oil, butter, or ghee, and arrange the fish fillets, skin sides down on it. Brush both sides with the remaining 4 tablespoons of oil, butter, or ghee, and the lime juice mixture. Sprinkle the sumac rub all over the fish. Cover and keep chilled in the refrigerator until ready to cook.

4 Shortly before you're ready to serve, turn on the broiler and allow it to get hot. Remove the cover and place the sheet pan with the fish under the broiler. Broil the fish for 4 to 5 minutes on each side.

5 Remove the fish from the oven and place ¼ of the topping on each fillet. Serve with Plain Rice (Kateh; Chapter 12). *Nush-e joon!*

PER SERVING: *Calories 493 (From Fat 370); Fat 41g (Saturated 6g); Cholesterol 60mg; Sodium 1,693mg; Carbohydrate 3g (Dietary Fiber 1g); Protein 28g.*

Fish Cooked in a Tamarind, Cilantro, and Garlic Broth (Qaliyeh-ye Mahi)

PREP TIME: 35 MIN	COOK TIME: 1 HR 30 MIN	YIELD: 6 SERVINGS

INGREDIENTS

3 tablespoons rice flour

2 cups water

3 tablespoons tamarind paste

1 teaspoon date molasses

2 tablespoons dried fenugreek leaves

½ cup olive oil, butter, or ghee

1 medium onion, peeled and finely chopped

1 bunch spring onions, coarsely chopped (1½ cups)

6 cloves garlic, peeled

6 cups roughly chopped fresh cilantro (leaves and stems)

3½ teaspoons fine sea salt, divided

1½ teaspoons freshly ground black pepper, divided

3½ teaspoons turmeric, divided

1 teaspoon ground coriander

1 teaspoon red pepper flakes, divided

1 tablespoon *advieh* (Persian spice mix)

2 pounds grouper, halibut, or salmon fillets, skins and any small bones removed, cut into 3-inch lengths

2 tablespoons oil

DIRECTIONS

1 In a small bowl, add the flour, water, tamarind paste, date molasses, and fenugreek leaves. Whisk together; set aside.

2 In a medium braiser, add the oil, butter, or ghee, and warm over medium-low heat. Add the onion and sauté until golden brown, about 10 to 15 minutes.

3 Meanwhile, in a food processor, place the spring onions, garlic, and cilantro; pulse until you have a smooth paste.

4 Add the paste to the braiser with the onion, and sauté over low heat, stirring frequently with a wooden spoon, until the aroma begins to rise, about 10 to 15 minutes. Add 2 teaspoons of the salt, ½ teaspoon of the pepper, 2 teaspoons of the turmeric, the coriander, and ½ teaspoon of the red pepper flakes; stir-fry for 1 minute. Add the flour mixture, stir well, and bring to a boil. Reduce the heat to low, cover, and simmer, stirring occasionally to prevent the sauce from sticking to the bottom of the braiser, for 30 minutes.

5 In a small bowl, add the remaining 1½ teaspoons of salt, the remaining 1 teaspoon of pepper, the remaining 1½ teaspoons of turmeric, the *advieh*, and the remaining ½ teaspoon of red pepper flakes. Mix together.

6 Rinse the fish and pat dry. Dust both sides of the fish fillets with the mixture; set aside.

7 In a wide skillet, heat the oil over medium-high heat until very hot but not smoking. Add the fish fillets to the skillet, and sear on both sides until golden brown, about 2 minutes on each side.

8 Add the fish to the braiser, cover, and cook over *low* heat for 40 minutes. Gently stir the sauce occasionally to prevent the sauce from sticking to the bottom of the braiser. Check to be sure the fish is tender and adjust the seasoning to taste by adding more date molasses or tamarind paste if needed. Cover and keep warm over *very low* heat until ready to serve. Serve with Plain Rice (Kateh; Chapter 12). Nush-e joon!

PER SERVING: *Calories 380 (From Fat 245); Fat 27g (Saturated 4g); Cholesterol 40mg; Sodium 1,453mg; Carbohydrate 15g (Dietary Fiber 2g); Protein 20g.*

Smoked Whitefish (Mahi-e Dudi)

INGREDIENTS

2 whole Canadian smoked whitefish (3 to 4 pounds)

Juice of 2 sour oranges

¼ cup olive oil, butter, or ghee, divided

½ teaspoon fine sea salt

1 teaspoon freshly ground black pepper

4 cloves garlic, peeled and thinly sliced

2 sour oranges or fresh limes, halved

DIRECTIONS

1 Preheat the oven to 350 degrees. Line a rimmed baking sheet with a layer of aluminum foil and a layer of parchment paper (large enough to overhang the baking sheet and later cover the fish).

2 Place the fish on the sheet pan, open its cavity, and pour the orange or lime juice and 2 tablespoons of the oil, butter, or ghee over the fish. Sprinkle with salt, pepper, and garlic. Wrap the fish loosely with the parchment paper and aluminum foil. Place in the oven and bake for 55 minutes.

3 Remove the fish from oven and gently transfer to a serving dish. Open the aluminum foil and parchment paper; remove the skin from the top of the fish; drizzle with the remaining 2 tablespoons of oil, butter, or ghee; and arrange the sour orange or lime halves around the fish. Serve with Rice with Fava Beans and Dill (Baqala Polow; Chapter 12). *Nush-e joon!*

PER SERVING: *Calories 340 (From Fat 101); Fat 11g (Saturated 2g); Cholesterol 75mg; Sodium 2,468mg; Carbohydrate 4g (Dietary Fiber 0g); Protein 53g.*

TIP: If you can't find sour oranges, you can use a mixture of ¼ cup fresh lime juice and ¼ cup fresh orange juice instead.

5
Side Dishes, Desserts, and Other Delights

IN THIS PART . . .

Prepare Persian pickles and preserves.

Satisfy your sweet tooth with pastries, sweets, and candies.

Make delicious Persian desserts.

Discover delicious Persian breads and street food that you can make at home.

Jazz up your Persian meal with easy-to-make, thirst-quenching, colorful drinks.

Chapter **17**

Pickles and Preserves

Whenever the *sofreh* (tablecloth) is spread for a meal, you'll find a variety of *torshis* (pickles) accompanying the main course. Most of these *torshis* consist of vegetables or fruits and spices, preserved in vinegar.

For a good *torshi*, use fresh ingredients, good vinegar, and sea salt. The fruits, vegetables, and herbs should be in season (they'll be not only tastier but also less expensive), without blemishes, and thoroughly washed and completely dried. In order for the *torshi* to keep well, not a trace of water can remain on the fruits, vegetables, and herbs. After the jars have been sealed, store them in a cool, dark place for aging. After opening the jars, keep them in the refrigerator.

Torshis are usually made by women; my mother used to say that some women have a special touch for making *torshis*. She was especially particular about the vinegar she used and who had made it — and it makes sense, because good vinegar is the foundation of a good pickle. I recommend using apple cider vinegar or malt vinegar with 5 percent acidity; the salt should be as pure as possible (use pickling salt or fine sea salt). Some pickles, such as garlic pickle, age very well. After about seven years a good garlic pickle turns black and sweet and becomes more like a preserve.

Persian preserves combine fruit, flower, rose water, cardamom, and saffron to create a heavenly taste. They're most often eaten with bread and butter, but these preserves are also good with yogurt or to sweeten tea.

Mixed Vegetable Pickle (Torshi-e Liteh)

PREP TIME: 2 HR	COOK TIME: 15 MIN	YIELD: 96 SERVINGS

INGREDIENTS

½ cup chopped fresh mint leaves or 2½ tablespoons dried mint

½ cup chopped fresh parsley or 2½ tablespoons dried parsley

½ cup chopped fresh cilantro or 2½ tablespoons dried cilantro

½ cup chopped fresh basil leaves or 2½ tablespoons dried basil

½ cup chopped fresh savory or 2½ tablespoons dried savory

½ cup chopped fresh tarragon or 2½ tablespoons dried tarragon

2 pounds Chinese eggplants (about 6), tops removed and chopped into 1-inch cubes

12 cups apple cider vinegar, divided

1 pound Persian cucumbers, washed, dried, and diced

1 pound carrots, peeled and diced

½ pound turnips, peeled and diced

3 stalks celery, stringy parts removed and diced

10 cloves garlic, peeled and diced

DIRECTIONS

1 Sterilize six 1-pint canning jars in boiling water. Drain and allow to dry thoroughly. Line a sheet pan with towels.

2 Wash the mint, parsley, cilantro, basil, savory, and tarragon. Drain, dry thoroughly, and mince. Spread the herbs on the sheet pan to dry them off (no trace of water should remain).

3 In a medium saucepan, place the eggplants and add 3 cups of the vinegar. Bring to a boil over high heat. Reduce the heat to medium and simmer for 5 minutes. Drain in a colander, discarding the vinegar, and set aside. Transfer the eggplants to a large glass container.

4 Add the cucumbers, carrots, turnips, celery, garlic, cauliflower, fenugreek, salt, peppercorns, turmeric, *golpar, advieh*, cayenne, coriander, nigella seeds, grape molasses, and 8 cups of the vinegar. Stir well with a long-handled spoon. Cover and allow to rest, at room temperature, for 8 hours (add the remaining 1 cup of vinegar if the mixture is too dry).

1 head cauliflower, separated into ¼-inch florets

2 tablespoons dried fenugreek leaves

3 tablespoons pickling salt or fine sea salt

1 tablespoon black peppercorns

1 tablespoon turmeric

4 tablespoons ground *golpar* (Persian hogweed)

3 tablespoons *advieh* (Persian spice mix)

¼ teaspoon cayenne

2 tablespoons coriander seeds

3 tablespoon nigella seeds

½ cup grape molasses

5 Adjust the seasoning to taste. Fill the jars to within 1 inch of the top with the pickle. Sprinkle with a pinch of salt and more vinegar to cover.

6 Seal (by screwing the lids on tightly), label, and date the jars. When cool, store in the refrigerator or in a cool, dark place for at least 10 days before using. *Nush-e joon!*

PER SERVING: *Calories 14 (From Fat 1); Fat 0g (Saturated 0g); Cholesterol 0mg; Sodium 186mg; Carbohydrate 3g (Dietary Fiber 1g); Protein 0g.*

TIP: You can use a food processor for chopping and dicing the vegetables and herbs. If you're dicing the vegetables by hand, aim for ¼-inch dice.

HOW TO STERILIZE CANNING JARS

To sterilize canning jars (Mason jars), follow these steps:

1. **Preheat the oven to 300 degrees.**

2. **Wash the jars and lids in a dishwasher or thoroughly with soapy water.**

3. **Place the jars (right side up) and lids (hollow side up) on a sheet pan and place in the oven for about 15 minutes.**

4. **Turn off the oven and keep the jars there until ready to fill.**

Onion Pickle (Torshi-e Piaz)

PREP TIME: 40 MIN	COOK TIME: NONE	YIELD: 24 SERVINGS

INGREDIENTS

1 pound white pearl onions

4 sprigs fresh tarragon

1 cup apple cider vinegar

1 tablespoon pickling salt or fine sea salt

DIRECTIONS

1 Sterilize a 1-pint canning jar in boiling water. Drain and allow to dry thoroughly.

2 Peel the onions, and, using a paring knife, remove the roots at the bottom; then cut a cross mark in the bottom of each onion so it will absorb the vinegar. Leave the onion tops intact.

3 Fill a pint jar almost to the top by layering the onions and sprigs of tarragon. Press down to compact them, and fill to within 1 inch of the top with the vinegar; then sprinkle the salt over the top.

4 Seal (by screwing the lids on tightly), label, and date the jar. When cool, store in the refrigerator or in a cool, dark place for at least 10 days before using. Serve as a pickle with meats. *Nush-e joon!*

PER SERVING: *Calories 10 (From Fat 0); Fat 0g (Saturated 0g); Cholesterol 0mg; Sodium 235mg; Carbohydrate 2g (Dietary Fiber 0g); Protein 0g.*

Garlic Pickle (Torshi-e Seer)

PREP TIME: 40 MIN	COOK TIME: NONE	YIELD: 20 SERVINGS

INGREDIENTS

1 pound garlic bulbs

4 sprigs thyme

1 cup apple cider vinegar

1 tablespoon pickling salt or fine sea salt

DIRECTIONS

1 Sterilize a 1-pint canning jar in boiling water. Drain and allow to dry thoroughly.

2 Separate the garlic cloves from the bulbs. Peel off all but 1 layer of skin from the cloves.

3 Fill the jars nearly to the top with alternating layers of garlic cloves and sprigs of thyme. Press down to compact them and to ensure all the cloves of garlic fit in the jar. Fill the jar to within ½ inch of the top with the vinegar. Add the salt on top.

4 Seal (by screwing the lids on tightly), label, and date the jar. Store in a cool, dark place or refrigerator for at least 7 months before using. *Nush-e joon!*

PER SERVING: *Calories 36 (From Fat 1); Fat 0g (Saturated 0g); Cholesterol 0mg; Sodium 285mg; Carbohydrate 8g (Dietary Fiber 0g); Protein 1g.*

TIP: Garlic pickle is at its best when 7 years old, when it becomes sweet like preserve.

Spicy Lime Pickle (Torshi-e Limu)

PREP TIME: 35 MIN | COOK TIME: 35 MIN | YIELD: 16 SERVINGS

INGREDIENTS

1 pound fresh limes (5–8 limes, depending on size)

¼ cup fine sea salt

5 cloves garlic, finely chopped

1½ teaspoons nigella seeds

1½ teaspoons cumin seeds

½ teaspoon mustard seeds

1½ teaspoons coriander seeds

½ teaspoon fenugreek seeds

¼ cup oil

½ teaspoon turmeric

1½ teaspoons red pepper flakes

1¼ cup fresh lime juice

DIRECTIONS

1 Sterilize a 1-pint canning jar in boiling water. Drain and allow to dry completely.

2 Wash and scrub the limes. Cut each lime vertically into quarters. Remove the seeds, cut into 1 inch cubes, and rub all over with the salt. Arrange the lime cubes and the garlic in the jar in alternate layers.

3 Heat a wide skillet over low heat. Add the nigella, cumin, mustard, coriander, and fenugreek. Cover and toast, moving the skillet back and forth, until fragrant, about 30 to 35 minutes.

4 Add the oil, turmeric, and red pepper flakes to the skillet and stir-fry for 1 minute. Transfer the spice mixture to the jar and fill it to within ½ inch of the top with the lime juice.

5 Seal (by screwing the lids on tightly), label, and date the jar. Store in a cool, dark place or refrigerator for at least 10 days before using. *Nush-e joon!*

PER SERVING: *Calories 46 (From Fat 32); Fat 4g (Saturated 0g); Cholesterol 0mg; Sodium 1,406mg; Carbohydrate 5g (Dietary Fiber 1g); Protein 0g.*

Black Carrot Quick Pickle (Torshi-e Gazar)

PREP TIME: 15 MIN PLUS 30 MIN FOR PICKLING	COOK TIME: NONE	YIELD: 20 SERVINGS

INGREDIENTS

2 pounds black or regular carrots, peeled and roughly chopped

10 cloves garlic, peeled

4 teaspoons fine sea salt

1 tablespoon date molasses or sugar

1 teaspoon freshly ground black pepper

2 tablespoons cilantro leaves

¾ cup freshly squeezed lime juice or apple cider vinegar

DIRECTIONS

1 In a food processor, place the carrots, garlic, salt, date molasses or sugar, pepper, and cilantro. Pulse until finely chopped; then transfer to a large glass bowl, add the lime juice, and stir well.

2 Cover and allow to sit for at least 30 minutes before serving. Serve right away as a condiment. *Nush-e joon!*

PER SERVING: *Calories 26 (From Fat 1); Fat 0g (Saturated 0g); Cholesterol 0mg; Sodium 1,155mg; Carbohydrate 6g (Dietary Fiber 1g); Protein 1g.*

VARY IT! You can replace the carrots with parsnip, beets, or cabbage.

TIP: Store any leftover pickle in a covered glass container in the refrigerator for up to 1 week and use as needed.

Onion, Cucumber, and Coriander Quick Pickle (Torshi Hazeri-e Piaz)

PREP TIME: 20 MIN	COOK TIME: 3 MIN	YIELD: 12 SERVINGS

INGREDIENTS

¼ cup coriander seeds

1 pound red onion (1 large), peeled and thinly sliced lengthwise (with the grain)

12 Persian cucumbers, sliced

2 teaspoons fine sea salt

¼ teaspoon red pepper flakes (optional)

¼ cup apple cider vinegar

DIRECTIONS

1 In a small skillet, place the coriander seeds and toast over medium-high heat, shaking the skillet constantly, until the color darkens and the aroma rises, about 2 to 3 minutes. Remove from the heat and set aside.

2 In a large glass mixing bowl, add the onion, cucumber, salt, red pepper flakes (if using), and toasted coriander seeds; mix well. Add the vinegar, and toss well.

3 Serve immediately as a condiment. *Nush-e joon!*

PER SERVING: *Calories 40 (From Fat 5); Fat 1g (Saturated 0g); Cholesterol 0mg; Sodium 318mg; Carbohydrate 8g (Dietary Fiber 2g); Protein 2g.*

TIP: You can store any leftover pickle in the refrigerator in a covered glass container for up to 3 days.

Sour Cherry Preserve (Moraba-ye Albalu)

PREP TIME: 1 HR PLUS OVERNIGHT FOR MACERATING	COOK TIME: 1 HR	YIELD: 32 SERVINGS

INGREDIENTS

3 pounds fresh sour cherries or 2 pounds pitted fresh or frozen sour cherries

4 cups sugar

1 tablespoon lime juice

¼ teaspoon vanilla

DIRECTIONS

1 Sterilize two 1-pint canning jars in boiling water. Drain and allow to dry completely.

2 Wash the cherries and remove the stems and pits. In a medium laminated pot, place the cherries and sugar. Cover and allow to macerate overnight.

3 Place the pot of cherries over high heat and bring to a boil. Reduce the heat to medium and simmer, uncovered, for about 45 minutes. Gently stir occasionally to prevent burning.

4 Add the lime juice and vanilla, and simmer over medium heat until the syrup is thick enough to coat the back of a spoon, about 10 to 15 minutes. Remove from the heat.

5 Fill the jars with hot preserve within ½ inch of the top.

6 Seal (by screwing the lids on tightly), label, and date the jars. Use as soon as cool, or cover again and store in the refrigerator. *Nush-e joon!*

PER SERVING: *Calories 116 (From Fat 1); Fat 0g (Saturated 0g); Cholesterol 0mg; Sodium 1mg; Carbohydrate 30g (Dietary Fiber 1g); Protein 0g.*

Quince Preserve (Moraba-ye Beh)

PREP TIME: 25 MIN	COOK TIME: 2 HR 45 MIN	YIELD: 16 SERVINGS

INGREDIENTS

2 pounds quinces (3 medium)

2 tablespoons vinegar

1½ cups water

4 cups sugar

¼ teaspoon pure vanilla extract

1 cinnamon stick

¼ cup fresh lime juice

DIRECTIONS

1 Sterilize a 1-pint canning jar in boiling water. Drain and allow to dry completely.

2 Quarter the quinces and remove the cores (do not peel). Slice the quarters into wedges. Place in a container full of cold water with the vinegar to prevent the quince wedges from turning black. Drain and rinse.

3 In a medium pot (ideally, a copper pot), place the quince wedges and water. Bring to a boil over high heat, reduce the heat to low, cover, and simmer for 15 minutes.

4 Add the sugar, vanilla, and cinnamon. To steep the quince, wrap the lid of the pot with a clean dish towel and cover firmly. Simmer over low heat for 1 hour.

5 Add the lime juice. Cover and simmer over low heat, stirring gently from time to time, until the syrup has thickened and the quince has turned red, about 1¼ to 1½ hours. Remove from the heat and allow to cool. Then fill the jar with hot preserve to within 1 inch of the top.

6 Seal (by screwing the lids on tightly), label, and date the jar. Use as soon as cool, or cover again and store in the refrigerator. *Nush-e joon!*

PER SERVING: *Calories 227 (From Fat 1); Fat 0g (Saturated 0g); Cholesterol 0mg; Sodium 3mg; Carbohydrate 59g (Dietary Fiber 1g); Protein 0g.*

Barberry Preserve (Moraba-ye Zereshk)

PREP TIME: 35 MIN	COOK TIME: 55 MIN	YIELD: 16 SERVINGS

INGREDIENTS

2 cups dried barberries, washed and cleaned

2½ cups pure apple cider

2 cups sugar

½ teaspoon cinnamon

½ teaspoon cardamom powder

¼ teaspoon ground saffron dissolved in 2 tablespoons rose water

2 tablespoons fresh lime juice

DIRECTIONS

1 Sterilize a 1-pint canning jar in boiling water. Drain and allow to dry completely.

2 In a medium laminated pot, place the barberries and apple cider and bring to a boil over high heat.

3 Add the sugar, cinnamon, cardamom, saffron water, and lime juice. Return to a boil, stirring frequently. Simmer over medium heat until the syrup is thick enough to coat the back of a spoon, about 35 to 40 minutes. Fill the jar with preserve to within 1 inch of the top.

4 Seal (by screwing the lids on tightly), label, and date the jar. Use as soon as cool, or cover again and store in the refrigerator. *Nush-e joon!*

PER SERVING: *Calories 154 (From Fat 0); Fat 0g (Saturated 0g); Cholesterol 0mg; Sodium 34mg; Carbohydrate 39g (Dietary Fiber 2g); Protein 2g.*

Carrot Preserve (Moraba-ye Havij)

| PREP TIME: 35 MIN | COOK TIME: 1 HR 10 MIN | YIELD: 24 SERVINGS |

INGREDIENTS

1 pound carrots (or use ready-made julienned carrots)

2½ cups sugar

1½ cups water

¼ cup slivered orange peel, bitterness removed (see Chapter 4)

3 tablespoons fresh lime juice

½ teaspoon ground cardamom

⅛ teaspoon ground saffron threads

1 tablespoon orange blossom water

2 tablespoons slivered pistachios

2 tablespoons blanched slivered almonds

DIRECTIONS

1 Sterilize a 1-pint canning jar in boiling water. Drain and allow to dry completely.

2 Scrape, wash, drain, and julienne the carrots.

3 In a medium laminated pot, add the sugar, water, orange peel, and carrots. Bring to a boil over high heat. Then reduce the heat to medium, stir, cover, and cook for 45 minutes.

4 Add the lime juice, cardamom, saffron, orange blossom water, pistachios, and almonds, and simmer over medium heat until the syrup has thickened enough to coat the back of a spoon, about 5 to 10 minutes. Remove from the heat and fill the jar with the hot preserve to within 1 inch of the top.

5 Seal (by screwing the lids on tightly), label, and date the jar. Use as soon as cool, or cover again and store in the refrigerator. *Nush-e joon!*

PER SERVING: *Calories 98 (From Fat 6); Fat 1g (Saturated 0g); Cholesterol 0mg; Sodium 16mg; Carbohydrate 23g (Dietary Fiber 1g); Protein 0g.*

Fig Preserve (Moraba-ye Anjir)

PREP TIME: 20 MIN PLUS OVERNIGHT FOR MACERATING	COOK TIME: 1 HR 10 MIN	YIELD: 20 SERVINGS

INGREDIENTS

2 pounds firm, seedless, fresh green figs or 1 pound dried yellow Persian figs with stems (available at Persian markets)

3 cups sugar

2 cups water

½ teaspoon ground cardamom

½ teaspoon vanilla extract

2 tablespoons rose water

2 tablespoons lime juice

DIRECTIONS

1 Sterilize two 1-pint canning jars in boiling water. Drain and allow to dry completely.

2 Wash the figs, but do *not* remove the stems. In a laminated pot, place the figs and sugar in alternating layers. Cover and macerate overnight.

3 Add the water to the pot, bring to a boil, cover, and let simmer over medium-low heat for 45 minutes. Add cardamom, vanilla, rose water, and lime juice. Continue simmering over medium heat until the syrup has thickened enough to coat the back of a spoon, about 5 to 10 minutes. Fill the jars with hot preserve to within 1 inch of the top.

4 Seal (by screwing the lids on tightly), label, and date the jar. Use as soon as cool, or cover again and store in the refrigerator. *Nush-e joon!*

PER SERVING: *Calories 150 (From Fat 1); Fat 0g (Saturated 0g); Cholesterol 0mg; Sodium 1mg; Carbohydrate 39g (Dietary Fiber 1g); Protein 0g.*

TIP: If you use dried figs, in Step 2 add 7 cups of water with only 1½ cups sugar to hydrate the dried figs; then allow to macerate overnight per Step 2. Continue with Step 3 without adding any more water.

Rose Petal Preserve (Moraba-ye Gol)

PREP TIME: 25 MIN PLUS 2 HR FOR STEEPING	COOK TIME: 1 HR	YIELD: 16 SERVINGS

INGREDIENTS

6 cups fresh organic damask rose petals or 2 cups dried organic damask rose petals

1 cup boiling water

2 cups sugar

1½ cups water

1 tablespoon rose water

2 tablespoons fresh lime juice or ½ teaspoon citric acid

1 cup walnuts or raw pistachio kernels, coarsely chopped

DIRECTIONS

1   Sterilize a 1-pint canning jar in boiling water. Drain and allow to dry completely.

2   If using fresh rose petals, soak them in water, pick out any impurities, drain, and rinse thoroughly.

3   In a wide skillet, place the rose petals and toast over low heat, stirring constantly, until crispy and toasted, about 4 to 5 minutes. Transfer to a spice grinder and coarsely grind. Transfer to a small bowl, add the boiling water, and stir. Cover with plastic wrap and allow to macerate for 10 minutes.

4   In a medium pot, place the sugar and water and bring to a boil over high heat. Reduce the heat to medium and simmer until the syrup has thickened, about 15 to 20 minutes.

5   Add the macerated rose petal and its liquid, the rose water, and the lime juice or citric acid to the pot, cover, and cook over low heat for 20 minutes. Add the walnuts or pistachios, stir gently, and cook until the syrup is thick enough to coat the back of a spoon, about 5 to 10 minutes. Remove from the heat and immediately cover; allow to steep for about 1 hour. Then fill the jar with the warm preserve to within 1 inch of the top.

6   Seal (by screwing the lids on tightly), label, and date the jar. Use as soon as cool, or cover again and store in the refrigerator. *Nush-e joon!*

PER SERVING: *Calories 228 (From Fat 37); Fat 4g (Saturated 0g); Cholesterol 0mg; Sodium 0mg; Carbohydrate 26g (Dietary Fiber 0g); Protein 1g.*

Chapter **18**

Pastries, Sweets, and Candies

In this chapter, you find easy recipes for delicious cookies: cardamom rice cookies, chickpea cookies, almond cookies, honey–almond brittle, and perhaps best of all, the unique Persian baklava. But that's not all! I include recipes for cakes and candies here, too.

Did you know that the English word *candy* comes from the Persian word for cane sugar, *qand.* Persian candies are easy to make, not overly sweet, and rewarding to try.

Rice Cookies (Nan-e Berenji)

PREP TIME: 30 MIN PLUS 30 MIN FOR RESTING	COOK TIME: 20 MIN	YIELD: 36 SERVINGS

INGREDIENTS

1½ cups sugar

½ cup water

¼ cup rose water

½ teaspoon lime juice

4 egg yolks, at room temperature

1 cup olive oil or clarified butter

2 teaspoons cardamom powder

¼ teaspoon fine sea salt

3 cups rice flour

2 tablespoons poppy seeds

2 tablespoons dried rose petals, crushed

2 tablespoons ground raw pistachios

DIRECTIONS

1 In a saucepan, add the sugar and water. Stir well until the sugar dissolves completely. Bring to a boil, reduce the heat to medium, and simmer for 2 minutes. Be careful not to overboil (it shouldn't be too thick). Remove from the heat, add the rose water and lime juice, and allow to cool. The syrup should be at room temperature and not too thick.

2 In a mixing bowl, add the egg yolks and whisk until creamy. Add the cooled, prepared syrup and whisk for 1 minute. Set aside.

3 In another mixing bowl, add the oil or butter, cardamom, salt, and rice flour *gradually*; use a handheld mixer or a mixer with a paddle to mix until you have a creamy dough.

4 Add the egg yolk mixture to the rice flour mixture. Use a rubber spatula to fold it in until you have a soft dough. Cover and chill in the refrigerator for at least 30 minutes (or up to 24 hours).

5 When you're ready to bake the cookies, place the rack in the center of the oven and preheat the oven to 350 degrees. Line several sheet pans with parchment paper. Use an ice cream scoop to small scoop a walnut-size amount of dough and place it on the parchment paper. Flatten the dough slightly using an offset spatula. Repeat, making 36 cookies total, with 2½ inches between each cookie. Draw geometric patterns on the cookies and decorate with the poppy seeds, rose petals, and pistachios. Bake until the bottom edges are lightly golden, about 10 minutes. The cookies should be white when they're done.

6 Remove from the oven and allow to cool. These cookies crumble very easily, so remove them carefully from the sheet pan using an offset spatula. Serve right away or store in an airtight glass container in the refrigerator up to 10 days or in the freezer up to 3 months. *Nush-e joon!*

PER SERVING: *Calories 143 (From Fat 63); Fat 7g (Saturated 1g); Cholesterol 23mg; Sodium 15mg; Carbohydrate 19g (Dietary Fiber 0g); Protein 1g.*

TIP: When storing, use parchment paper between the layers.

Chickpea Cookies (Nan-e Nokhodchi)

PREP TIME: 15 MIN PLUS 30 MIN FOR RESTING	COOK TIME: 30 MIN	YIELD: 40 SERVINGS

INGREDIENTS

1 cup olive oil, butter, or ghee

1 cup powdered sugar

4 teaspoons ground cardamom

1 tablespoon rose water

3¾ cups fine roasted chickpea flour, twice sifted (at least) with ¼ cup unbleached all-purpose wheat flour

3 tablespoons slivered raw pistachios

DIRECTIONS

1 In the bowl of an electric mixer, add the oil, butter, or ghee; sugar; cardamom; and rose water. Mix until creamy, about 2 to 3 minutes. Add the chickpea flour mixture, and mix until you have a soft dough that doesn't stick to your hands, about 5 minutes. (Do not overmix.)

2 Line a sheet pan with parchment paper and dust it with chickpea flour. Place the dough on top and use your hands to flatten and shape it into a ½-inch-thick square.

3 Cover the entire sheet pan with plastic wrap and, using a rolling pin, gently roll over it to even out the dough. Allow to rest at room temperature for 30 minutes (or up to 24 hours in the refrigerator).

4 When you're ready to bake the cookies, line 2 sheet pans with parchment paper. Place the rack in the center of the oven and preheat the oven to 300 degrees.

5 Use a 1½-inch diameter cloverleaf cookie cutter (available in a mixed box of them in the United States — the traditional Iranian ones are smaller, about ¾ inch in diameter) dipped in chickpea flour to cut out a total of 40 cookies. Place them on the lined sheet pans, leaving 1 inch between the cookies. Decorate each cookie with the pistachios.

(continued)

6 Bake for 30 minutes, remove from the oven, and place the sheet pans on a cooling rack. When the cookies have thoroughly cooled, carefully lift them from the pans using an offset spatula. (Be careful — these cookies crumble very easily.) Serve right away on a platter or store in an airtight glass container in the fridge up to 10 days or in the freezer up to 3 months. *Nush-e joon!*

PER SERVING: *Calories 99 (From Fat 57); Fat 6g (Saturated 1g); Cholesterol 0mg; Sodium 8mg; Carbohydrate 9g (Dietary Fiber 1g); Protein 2g.*

VARY IT! For gluten-free cookies, replace the all-purpose flour with rice flour.

TIP: You can freeze the flattened chickpea dough for up to 3 weeks.

Almond Cookies (Nan-e Badami)

PREP TIME: 40 MIN | COOK TIME: 20 MIN | YIELD: 20 SERVINGS

INGREDIENTS

2 egg whites

1½ cups confectioners' sugar

¼ teaspoon fine sea salt

2 tablespoons rose water

4 cups almond flour

1 teaspoon ground cardamom

¼ cup almond slices

2 tablespoons dried rose petals, crushed

DIRECTIONS

1 Place the rack in the center of the oven and preheat the oven to 350 degrees. Line 2 sheet pans with parchment paper.

2 In a bowl, add the egg whites, sugar, salt, and rose water and lightly beat until frothy, about 2 minutes.

3 Add the almond flour and cardamom, and fold in using a rubber spatula until a firm dough is formed, about 5 minutes.

4 Use an ice cream scoop to scoop up some of the dough (the size of a walnut). Drop it on 1 of the prepared sheet pans. Continue to make a total of 10 cookies for each sheet pan, leaving 1 inch between each piece. Decorate with the almond slices and crushed rose petals. Bake in 2 batches until lightly golden, about 12 to 15 minutes for each sheet pan.

5 Remove the sheet pan from the oven and allow to cool on a cooling rack. Transfer the cookies from the sheet pan using an offset spatula. Serve right away on a platter or store in an airtight glass container in the refrigerator up to 10 days or in the freezer up to 3 months. *Nush-e joon!*

PER SERVING: *Calories 176 (From Fat 109); Fat 12g (Saturated 1g); Cholesterol 0mg; Sodium 29mg; Carbohydrate 14g (Dietary Fiber 3g); Protein 6g.*

Raisin Cookies (Nan-e Keshmeshy)

PREP TIME: 15 MIN   COOK TIME: 15 MIN   YIELD: 32 SERVINGS

INGREDIENTS

1¼ cups olive oil, butter, or ghee

1 teaspoon vanilla extract

2 tablespoons rose water

¼ teaspoon fine sea salt

1¼ cups sugar

4 large eggs

1¼ cups raisins

2 cups unbleached all-purpose flour

DIRECTIONS

1 Place the rack in the center of the oven and preheat the oven to 350 degrees. Line several sheet pans with parchment paper.

2 In a large bowl, add the oil, butter, or ghee; vanilla; rose water; salt; and sugar. Whisk together until smooth. Whisk in the eggs, one at a time, until the mixture is creamy.

3 Stir in the raisins. Fold in the flour using a rubber spatula until a thick batter forms (add more flour if necessary).

4 Use a small ice cream scoop to pick up a spoonful of the batter and place it on the lined sheet pans. Make a total of 32 cookies, leaving about 2 inches between each scoop.

5 Bake until the edges of the cookies are golden brown, about 10 to 15 minutes.

6 Remove the sheet pans from the oven and place on a cooling rack. When cool, loosen the cookies from the parchment paper with an offset spatula.

7 Serve right away on a platter or store in an airtight glass container in the refrigerator up to 10 days or in the freezer up to 3 months. *Nush-e joon!*

PER SERVING: *Calories 159 (From Fat 82); Fat 9g (Saturated 1g); Cholesterol 26mg; Sodium 24mg; Carbohydrate 18g (Dietary Fiber 0g); Protein 2g.*

Yazdi Cupcakes (Cayk-e Yazdi)

PREP TIME: 15 MIN   COOK TIME: 25 MIN   YIELD: 24 SERVINGS

INGREDIENTS

1 cup olive oil, butter, or ghee

1½ cups light brown sugar

Zest of 1 lime

3 tablespoons rose water

4 eggs, separated, at room temperature, divided

1 cup whole plain yogurt

1 teaspoon baking soda

2 teaspoons baking powder

¼ teaspoon fine sea salt

1 tablespoon ground cardamom

¼ cup rice flour

1¾ cups unbleached all-purpose flour

¼ cup ground pistachios

2 tablespoons dried, crushed rose petals mixed with ¼ teaspoon plain sanding sugar (optional)

DIRECTIONS

1 Place the rack in the center of the oven and preheat the oven to 350 degrees. Line 2 muffin pans (capable of holding 12 muffins each) with paper cups.

2 In the bowl of an electric mixer, blend the oil, butter, or ghee; sugar; lime zest; and rose water. While the mixer is running, add the 4 egg yolks, one by one. Add the yogurt and continue to blend until creamy, about 5 minutes.

3 In a mixing bowl, add the baking soda, baking powder, salt, cardamom, rice flour, and all-purpose flour; whisk together. Gradually add this mixture to the egg yolk mixture and mix for 3 minutes (do not overmix).

4 In another bowl, add the 4 egg whites and beat until stiff; add them to the flour mixture and fold in using a rubber spatula until you have a light batter. Pour the batter into the lined molds, leaving ¼ inch on top. Decorate with the pistachios and rose petals.

5 Bake until a tester comes out clean and the cupcakes are golden, about 25 to 30 minutes. Remove the pans from the oven and allow to cool on a cooling rack. Remove the cupcakes from the pans, transfer to a serving platter and allow to cool completely. Serve right away on a platter or store in an air-tight glass container in the refrigerator up to 10 days or in the freezer up to 3 months. *Nush-e joon!*

PER SERVING: *Calories 156 (From Fat 95); Fat 11g (Saturated 2g); Cholesterol 37mg; Sodium 41mg; Carbohydrate 14g (Dietary Fiber 0g); Protein 2g.*

Pistachio Cake (Kayk-e Pesteh)

PREP TIME: 40 MIN	COOK TIME: 40 MIN	YIELD: 8 SERVINGS

INGREDIENTS

1 cup sugar

1¼ cups raw pistachio kernels, divided

4 eggs, separated, at room temperature, divided

Zest of 1 orange

½ teaspoon vanilla extract

2 tablespoons rose water

1 cup plain yogurt

½ cup olive oil, butter, or ghee

½ teaspoon fine sea salt

2 teaspoons baking powder

1 teaspoon baking soda

2 cups unbleached all-purpose wheat flour

½ teaspoon cardamom powder

1 teaspoon dried rose petals

2 tablespoons confectioners' sugar (optional)

DIRECTIONS

1 Place the rack in the center of the oven and preheat the oven to 350 degrees. Butter an 8-inch springform cake pan and line the base with parchment paper. Then butter and dust the top of the parchment paper with flour.

2 In a food processor, place the sugar and 1 cup of the pistachios and blend until finely ground.

3 In a bowl, place the egg yolks; orange zest; vanilla; rose water; yogurt; and oil, butter, or ghee. Mix until creamy, about 5 minutes. Using a rubber spatula, fold in the sugar and pistachio mixture.

4 In a separate bowl, sift together the salt, baking powder, baking soda, and flour; then use a rubber spatula to fold this mixture into the egg yolk mixture.

5 In a separate bowl, beat the egg whites until soft peaks form, about 4 minutes. Add the flour mixture and fold in until you have smooth batter, about 5 minutes.

6 Gently pour the batter into the cake pan and bake until a tester comes out clean, about 45 to 50 minutes. Remove from the oven and allow to cool on a rack for 10 minutes.

7 Tap the pan to release the cake. Turn the cake out onto the rack and remove the mold, peel off the parchment paper, and turn the cake over. Decorate with the remaining ¼ cup of pistachios, the cardamom powder, and the rose petals. Dust with confectioners' sugar (if using). Allow to cool completely before serving. *Nush-e joon!*

PER SERVING: *Calories 486 (From Fat 241); Fat 27g (Saturated 4g); Cholesterol 110mg; Sodium 229mg; Carbohydrate 54g (Dietary Fiber 6g); Protein 13g.*

Baklava (Baqlava)

PREP TIME: 35 MIN PLUS 4 HR FOR RESTING	COOK TIME: 35 MIN	YIELD: 50 SERVINGS

INGREDIENTS

4 cups sugar, divided

1½ cups water

¾ cup plus 1 tablespoon rose water, divided

2 tablespoons fresh lime juice

¼ cup plain whole milk

½ cup olive oil, butter, or ghee, plus 6 tablespoons oil for baking, divided

1 egg

2½ cups unbleached all-purpose flour, sifted

8 cups almond flour

3 tablespoons ground cardamom

2 tablespoons slivered raw pistachios

2 tablespoons dried rose petals

DIRECTIONS

1 To make the syrup, in a small saucepan, combine 2½ cups of the sugar and the water, stir well until the sugar has dissolved, and bring to a boil (do not overboil — syrup should not be too thick). Add ½ cup of the rose water and the lime juice; set aside.

2 To make the dough, in a food processor, combine the milk; oil, butter, or ghee; 1 tablespoon of the syrup (at room temperature); ¼ cup of the rose water; and the egg. Gradually add the flour, and mix well to form a dough that doesn't stick to your hands and is elastic, about 5 to 10 minutes. Divide the dough into 2 balls of equal size and immediately wrap in plastic. Set aside.

3 To make the filling, in a food processor, add the ground almonds or almond flour, the remaining 1½ cups of sugar, the cardamom, and the remaining 1 tablespoon of rose water. Mix until you have a thick paste. Remove from the food processor and then set aside.

4 Brush an 11-x-17-x-1 inch rimmed sheet pan with 2 tablespoons of the oil. Place the rack in the center of the oven and preheat the oven to 350 degrees.

5 To make the crust, dust a large, wide surface with flour for rolling out the dough. Unwrap 1 ball of dough and roll out into a very thin rectangular layer with a thin wooden rolling pin (the rolled dough should be thinner than a pie crust). Roll the dough from the center to the outside edge in all directions, giving it a quarter turn occasionally for an even thickness; dust the dough with flour as necessary. The finished dough should be larger than the sheet pan.

(continued)

6   Roll the thin layer of dough around the wooden rolling pin and transfer it to the oiled sheet pan. Unroll the dough until it covers the whole sheet pan. Don't cut off the excess dough; let the dough hang over the edge of the sheet pan, 1 inch on all sides.

7   Spread all the filling mixture on top of the dough. Spread, press down, and smooth it out using your hands. Place parchment paper on top and use a small rolling pin (or another sheet pan on top) to even it out and pack it down firmly (this is important to achieve a tight, firm baklava when baked).

8   Roll out the second ball of dough into a very thin rectangular layer as you did in Step 6 for the first one. Transfer the dough sheet on top of the filling, allowing it to hang over all sides like the bottom layer. Press down on the dough evenly with your hands and smooth out the surface of the dough.

9   Fold and roll the overhanging dough from the top layer under the dough from the bottom layer. Press together and pinch the top and bottom edges together to seal like a pie, forming a rim around the edge of the baking pan.

10   Hold down the dough with one hand, pressing down with your palm while cutting the dough with a sharp knife (all the way through) into diamond shapes. Use a brush to evenly paint the dough with 1/4 cup of the oil.

11   Bake until the baklava is golden or pinkish in color, about 30 to 35 minutes.

12   Spread a damp towel on the counter. When the baklava is pink, remove it from the oven and place it on the towel. Evenly pour only 2 cups of the syrup all over the top (add more warm syrup later, when the baklava has cooled, if you prefer your baklava moister).

13 Decorate the baklava with the pistachios and rose petals. Cover immediately with a layer of plastic wrap and a layer of aluminum foil, and seal tightly. Let stand at room temperature at least 4 hours before serving. Make sure that the baklava remains covered — it will dry out very easily.

14 When ready to serve, use a sharp knife to lift 2 of the diamond pieces out of the sheet pan (to create an opening); then carefully lift 1 diamond at a time and arrange on a serving dish. Or transfer to a covered glass container and store in the refrigerator up to 10 days or in the freezer up to 3 months. *Nush-e joon!*

PER SERVING: *Calories 212 (From Fat 103); Fat 11g (Saturated 1g); Cholesterol 4mg; Sodium 3mg; Carbohydrate 25g (Dietary Fiber 2g); Protein 5g.*

TIP: It's important to use a food processor as opposed to a dough maker because the heat generated by the food processor helps develop the dough.

Saffroned Marzipan (Loz-e Badam)

PREP TIME: 20 MIN PLUS 48 HR FOR CHILLING	COOK TIME: 10 MIN	YIELD: 48 SERVINGS

INGREDIENTS

2 cups sugar

1 cup water

½ teaspoon ground saffron threads dissolved in ¼ cup rose water

9 cups almond flour

2 tablespoons ground pistachios mixed with 1 teaspoon ground cardamom

DIRECTIONS

1 Spray a quarter-size rimmed sheet pan (9½ x 13 inches) with oil. Line with parchment paper and paint or spray evenly with oil on top of the parchment paper.

2 In a saucepan, place the sugar and water; stir well, and bring to a boil. Reduce the heat to medium and simmer for 1 minute. Remove from the heat, add the saffron water, stir well, and allow to cool completely.

3 Transfer the cooled syrup to the bowl of an electric mixer and beat for 3 minutes. Gradually add the almond flour to the syrup and mix until you have a thick dough, about 10 minutes.

4 Transfer the almond paste to the prepared sheet pan. Place a sheet of oiled parchment paper on top of the almond paste (oiled side down) and flatten the paste by pressing with your hands on the parchment paper. Use a rolling pin over the parchment paper to further flatten and even out the surface.

5 Refrigerate (still covered with parchment paper) for at least 48 hours and up to 3 days to firm up the paste.

6 Oil a knife and cut into squares or diamond shapes. Decorate with the pistachio and cardamom mixture. Cover tightly with plastic wrap to prevent the marzipan from drying and store in the fridge. When you want to serve the marzipan, dust a little almond flour over it to help you separate the pieces for placing on a plate. *Nush-e joon!*

PER SERVING: *Calories 156 (From Fat 96); Fat 11g (Saturated 1g); Cholesterol 0mg; Sodium 1mg; Carbohydrate 13g (Dietary Fiber 3g); Protein 5g.*

Sprouted Wheat Flour, Date, and Walnut Pie (Komaj-e Sen)

PREP TIME: 30 MIN PLUS 2 HR FOR RESTING	COOK TIME: 25 MIN	YIELD: 16 SERVINGS

INGREDIENTS

3 cups sprouted wheat flour whisked with 1 cup unbleached all-purpose flour

1 teaspoon ground cumin

1 teaspoon turmeric

½ teaspoon ground cinnamon

2 teaspoons ground fennel seeds

1 teaspoon safflower petals

1 teaspoon nigella seeds

1½ cups olive oil, butter, or ghee

3 tablespoons date molasses

2¼ teaspoons instant yeast dissolved in 1 cup warm water (100 degrees)

2 cups Medjool dates (about 20), pitted and any hard stalk parts removed

1 cup walnuts, coarsely chopped

2 tablespoons sesame oil

½ cup ground pistachio kernels

½ teaspoon safflower petals

½ teaspoon toasted sesame seeds

½ teaspoon toasted nigella seeds

DIRECTIONS

1 In the bowl of an electric mixer, add the flour mixture, cumin, turmeric, cinnamon, fennel, safflower petals, and nigella seeds; mix together.

2 Add the oil, butter, or ghee; date molasses; and yeast mixture. Knead well until you have a dough that doesn't stick to your hands, about 10 to 15 minutes. Add more warm water if it's too dry (you need to have a pliable dough). Remove the bowl from the electric mixer, cover with plastic wrap, and allow to rest in the refrigerator for 2 to 24 hours.

3 Meanwhile, to make the filling, place the dates, walnuts, and sesame oil in a food processor and pulse until you have a grainy paste. Set aside.

4 Preheat the oven to 350 degrees. Oil an 11-x-17-inch rimmed sheet pan, and line it with parchment paper. Use your hands to roll out the dough on the prepared sheet pan to a ½-inch-thick disk. Spread the filling in the center.

5 Gently gather together the edges of the pastry to enclose the filling and pinch the edges together to seal the filling inside. Then pat down the filled pastry and lightly press down the rolling pin until you have an evenly round, 9-inch-diameter cake. With a sharp knife cut the pie all the way through to create about 16 diamond shapes.

6 Bake until a tester comes out clean, about 20 to 25 minutes. While still hot, decorate with the pistachios, safflower petals, sesame seeds, and nigella seeds. *Nush-e joon!*

PER SERVING: *Calories 468 (From Fat 265); Fat 29g (Saturated 4g); Cholesterol 0mg; Sodium 16mg; Carbohydrate 50g (Dietary Fiber 6g); Protein 7g.*

TIP: Serve as a nutritious vegan snack with tea or coffee.

Honey Almond Brittle (Sohan Asal)

INGREDIENTS

1 cup sugar

3 tablespoons pure honey

¼ cup olive oil, butter, or ghee

1½ cups blanched slivered almonds

¼ teaspoon ground saffron dissolved in 2 tablespoons rose water

¼ cup chopped raw pistachios

DIRECTIONS

1 Line 2 sheet pans with parchment paper. Place a bowl of ice water next to the stove.

2 In a small, heavy-bottomed saucepan, add the sugar; honey; and oil, butter, or ghee. Cook over medium-high heat, stirring occasionally with a wooden spoon, for about 3 minutes. At this stage, the sugar should be slightly discolored and foaming lightly around the edges.

3 Reduce the heat to medium-low. Add the almonds to the mixture, giving them a quick stir with the wooden spoon. Continue to cook until the mixture thickens, is golden, and is covered with small bubbles, about 3 to 4 minutes.

4 Add the saffron water mixture, gently stirring with a wooden spoon (be careful not to burn yourself). Cook for another 1 to 2 minutes, stirring occasionally, until the mixture is golden brown with large bubbles on the surface. Be careful — it should not be dark brown. (This step is tricky because if you over cook, it will burn, and if you under cook, it will be stretchy and not brittle.)

5 To be sure the mixture is ready, drop a spoonful of the hot almond mixture in the ice water. If it hardens immediately and doesn't stick to your teeth, the brittle is ready. Using a potholder, remove from the heat. Using a wooden spoon, stir.

6 Place about 1 teaspoon of the mixture on the parchment paper. Repeat to make a total of 25 pieces, leaving 1 inch between each. (Use 2 teaspoons, one for scooping and another for scraping off. Change spoons if they get too hot to handle.) Immediately decorate with pinches of chopped pistachios. Allow the brittle to cool completely, at least 1 hour. Remove from the paper using an offset spatula. Serve or store in an airtight glass container in the refrigerator up to 3 weeks or the freezer up to 3 months. *Nush-e joon!*

PER SERVING: *Calories 113 (From Fat 62); Fat 7g (Saturated 1g); Cholesterol 0mg; Sodium 4mg; Carbohydrate 12g (Dietary Fiber 1g); Protein 2g.*

Chapter **19**

Delicious Desserts

The word *dessert* comes from the French verb *desservir*, meaning "to clear the table of what has been served." The word was first introduced in France in the 16th century. Dessert was usually spiced wine and fresh or dried fruit, crisp thin wafers, or candied spices or nuts. However, the concept and the tradition of serving wine accompanied by a sweet course after the main meal goes back more than 2,500 years to the ancient Persian royal courts. Persians believed that finishing the meal with sweets helped the digestion. Herodotus wrote, "The Persians believe that the Greeks finish their dinner still hungry because they don't have any worthwhile desserts."

Several Persian desserts are associated with special events. Saffroned Wheat Halva (Halva) is associated with remembrance ceremonies. Saffron Rice Pudding (Sholeh Zard) is often served as thanksgiving for a wish come true.

Celebrations aside, Iranians are quite fond of sweets. Cookies, pastries, and puddings are served not just as dessert but at any time of day.

As for everyday meals, a favorite Persian dessert is seasonal fruit. Fruits make a happy ending to any dinner, as do the special desserts on the following pages. Whatever you choose should be pretty and fragrant, as well as light. Dessert is meant to refresh both the eyes and the palate.

Saffron Rice Pudding (Sholeh Zard)

PREP TIME: 5 MIN | COOK TIME: 1 HR 25 MIN | YIELD: 8 SERVINGS

INGREDIENTS

1 cup jasmine rice, soaked for 30 minutes, drained, and rinsed

½ teaspoon fine sea salt

7 cups warm water, divided

1 cup orange peel, diced and bitterness removed (see Chapter 4)

1½ cups fresh orange juice mixed with 1 tablespoon orange blossom water

2 cups sugar, divided

¼ cup olive oil, butter, or ghee

½ cup raw blanched almonds

½ teaspoon ground saffron dissolved in ½ cup rose water

1 tablespoon ground cardamom

1 teaspoon ground cinnamon

2 teaspoons slivered almonds

2 teaspoons slivered pistachios

DIRECTIONS

1 In a large nonstick pot, place the rice, salt, and 5 cups of water, and bring to a boil, skimming the foam as it rises. Reduce the heat to low, cover, and simmer, stirring occasionally with a long-handled wooden spoon, until the rice is quite soft, about 40 minutes.

2 Meanwhile, in a small saucepan, place the orange peel, orange juice mixture, and 1 cup of the sugar, and bring to a boil. Reduce the heat to medium and simmer, uncovered, for 25 minutes. Remove from the heat and set aside.

3 Add the remaining 2 cups of water and the remaining 1 cup of sugar to the rice and bring back to a boil, over medium heat, stirring frequently, for 15 minutes. Add the oil, butter, or ghee; almonds; saffron water; cardamom; and caramelized orange peel with its syrup (reserving 2 tablespoons of the caramelized orange peel for decoration). Stir well with a wooden spoon for 2 minutes. Reduce the heat to very low, wrap the lid with a clean towel, and cover tightly; allow to simmer for 40 minutes.

4 Remove from the heat, stir, and immediately spoon the pudding into individual serving bowls. Decorate, while still hot, with the cinnamon, almonds, and pistachios. Allow to cool at room temperature, cover, and chill in the refrigerator. *Nush-e joon!*

PER SERVING: *Calories 415 (From Fat 106); Fat 12g (Saturated 1g); Cholesterol 0mg; Sodium 123mg; Carbohydrate 76g (Dietary Fiber 2g); Protein 4g.*

Paradise Custard (Yakh dar Behesht)

PREP TIME: 20 MIN PLUS 4 HR FOR CHILLING	COOK TIME: 25 MIN	YIELD: 6 SERVINGS

INGREDIENTS

½ cup rice flour

¼ cup cornstarch

4 cups milk or your favorite plant-based milk

¾ cup sugar

Seeds of 5 cardamom pods

¼ cup rose water

2 tablespoons sliced almonds, toasted

2 tablespoons sliced, raw pistachio kernels

2 teaspoons rose petals, crushed

DIRECTIONS

1 In a medium, heavy-bottomed saucepan, add the rice flour, cornstarch, and milk and whisk until smooth. Cook over medium-low heat, stirring frequently, for 10 minutes.

2 Add the sugar, cardamom seeds, and rose water. Cook, stirring constantly to prevent sticking and lumping, until the mixture reaches the consistency of a smooth, glossy custard, about 5 to 10 minutes.

3 Remove from the heat and immediately spoon the pudding into individual serving bowls. Decorate, while still hot, with the almonds, pistachios, and rose petals. Allow to cool at room temperature; then cover and chill in the refrigerator for at least 4 hours. Serve chilled. *Nush-e joon!*

PER SERVING: *Calories 280 (From Fat 57); Fat 6g (Saturated 2g); Cholesterol 13mg; Sodium 77mg; Carbohydrate 49g (Dietary Fiber 1g); Protein 7g.*

Saffroned Wheat Halva (Halva)

PREP TIME: 10 MIN | COOK TIME: 30 MIN | YIELD: 4 SERVINGS

INGREDIENTS

1½ cups water

1½ cups sugar

1 teaspoon ground saffron dissolved in 1 cup rose water

1 teaspoon ground cardamom

1 cup olive oil, butter, or ghee

1 cup all-purpose flour

1 cup whole-wheat flour

2 tablespoons slivered pistachio kernels

DIRECTIONS

1 In a medium saucepan, add the water and sugar and bring to a boil over high heat. Remove from the heat and add the saffron water and cardamom. Mix well and set aside.

2 In a wide, shallow, nonstick pot, add the oil, butter, or ghee and warm over medium heat until hot. Add the all-purpose flour and whole-wheat flour. Stir constantly with a long, wooden spoon until golden brown, about 20 to 25 minutes. (This stage is very important: Be careful that the flour isn't overcooked [too dark] or undercooked [too light and the aroma hasn't risen].) Remove the pot from the heat.

3 Put on mittens. Carefully and gradually stir the syrup into the hot flour mixture, stirring quickly and constantly with the wooden spoon until all the syrup has been absorbed, about 5 minutes. Continue stirring until you get a thick, smooth paste.

4 Hold the pot by both handles and rock it from side to side until it becomes a roll and separated from the pot, about 3 minutes (see Figure 19-1). This helps develop the texture and taste of the *halva*.

5 Transfer the soft paste to a flat dish and pack firmly and quickly with a spoon. Decorate with the pistachios.

6 Allow to cool; then cover and chill in the refrigerator, to allow it to firm up more. Cut into small pieces and serve chilled on its own or as a wrap in lavash bread. *Nush-e joon!*

PER SERVING: *Calories 994 (From Fat 502); Fat 56g (Saturated 8g); Cholesterol 0mg; Sodium 10mg; Carbohydrate 121g (Dietary Fiber 5g); Protein 8g.*

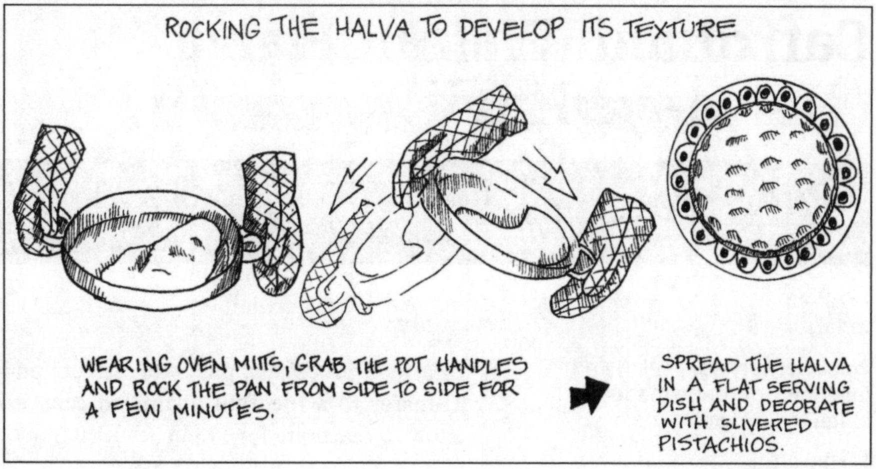

ROCKING THE HALVA TO DEVELOP ITS TEXTURE

WEARING OVEN MITTS, GRAB THE POT HANDLES AND ROCK THE PAN FROM SIDE TO SIDE FOR A FEW MINUTES.

SPREAD THE HALVA IN A FLAT SERVING DISH AND DECORATE WITH SLIVERED PISTACHIOS.

FIGURE 19-1:
Making *halva*.

Illustration by Elizabeth Kurtzman

Carrot and Walnut Halva (Halva-ye Havij)

PREP TIME: 30 MIN PLUS 1 HR FOR MACERATING	COOK TIME: 30 MIN	YIELD: 12 SERVINGS

INGREDIENTS

2 pounds carrots, peeled and julienned, or ready-made julienned carrots

½ cup sugar

1 cup grape molasses

2 cups walnuts, toasted and coarsely ground

½ teaspoon ground saffron threads dissolved in ¼ cup rose water

1 tablespoon ground cardamom

½ teaspoon ground cinnamon

2 tablespoons slivered pistachio kernels

1 tablespoon sliced almonds

¼ cup coarsely chopped walnuts

DIRECTIONS

1 In a food processor, place the carrots and sugar and puree. Transfer to a medium enameled cast-iron pot. Cover and allow to macerate for 1 hour.

2 Place the pot over low heat, cover, and cook until the pureed carrots have caramelized and become smooth, about 20 to 25 minutes. Set aside 2 tablespoons for the garnish.

3 Add the grape molasses, stirring constantly with a wooden spoon for 2 minutes.

4 Add the toasted walnuts, saffron water, cardamom, and cinnamon, stirring constantly until you have a thick, grainy *halva*, about 2 to 4 minutes.

5 Transfer to a serving platter, smooth the top, and decorate with the reserved carrots, pistachios, almonds, and chopped walnuts. Allow to cool and serve chilled either on its own with lavash bread or with tea or coffee. *Nush-e joon!*

PER SERVING: *Calories 279 (From Fat 121); Fat 13g (Saturated 1g); Cholesterol 0mg; Sodium 63mg; Carbohydrate 39g (Dietary Fiber 4g); Protein 4g.*

TIP: Using ready-made julienned carrots makes this recipe even quicker and easier.

Saffron Ice Cream (Bastani-e Gol-o Bolbol)

PREP TIME: 35 MIN PLUS 1 HR 40 MIN FOR ICE CREAM MACHINE

COOK TIME: NONE

YIELD: 4 SERVINGS

INGREDIENTS

1 cup heavy cream

¼ cup *sahlab* mixture (Cortas brand)

4 cups whole milk or plant-based milk, divided

¾ cup sugar or date molasses

½ teaspoon salt

¼ teaspoon ground saffron threads dissolved in 2 tablespoons rose water

¼ teaspoon ground cardamom (optional)

½ teaspoon mastic ground with 1 teaspoon sugar

¼ cup shelled, raw pistachios

8 ice cream wafers

DIRECTIONS

1 In a 9-inch freezer-proof pie dish, add the cream and place in the freezer.

2 Meanwhile, to make the ice cream base, in a small bowl, add the *sahlab* and 1 cup of the milk; stir well until the *sahlab* mixture has dissolved and become quite smooth. Set aside.

3 In a medium saucepan, add the remaining 3 cups of milk and the sugar or date molasses and bring it almost to a boil. Reduce the heat to very low and add the *sahlab* mixture, gradually while stirring. Add the salt, saffron water, cardamom (if using), and mastic-sugar mixture. Bring back to a boil; then reduce the heat to medium-high, whisking constantly until thick enough for the mixture to coat the back of a spoon, about 10 to 20 minutes. Remove from the heat and allow to cool; then chill in the refrigerator.

4 Pour into a chilled ice cream maker and follow the manufacturer's instructions for making ice cream. At the end of the process (30 minutes to 1 hour), the resulting ice cream should be thick and stretchy.

(continued)

5 Remove the cream from the freezer and allow to sit for a few minutes before unmolding it from the pan and breaking it into ¼-inch pieces. Add it to the ice cream in the machine. Add the pistachios, and continue to turn in the machine for another 1 to 2 minutes.

6 Transfer the ice cream to an ice-cream tub or a freezer-proof glass container with a press-in-place lid. Cover tightly and serve. Or freeze the ice cream; then, 20 minutes before serving, remove the ice cream from the freezer and refrigerate. Serve individual portions with wafers. *Nush-e joon!*

PER SERVING: *Calories 613 (From Fat 318); Fat 35g (Saturated 19g); Cholesterol 106mg; Sodium 397mg; Carbohydrate 66g (Dietary Fiber 1g); Protein 11g.*

Rice Stick Sorbet with Sour Cherries (Paludeh-ye Shirazi)

PREP TIME: 40 MIN PLUS 1 HR 5 MIN FOR FREEZING	COOK TIME: NONE	YIELD: 6 SERVINGS

INGREDIENTS

4 ounces thin rice stick noodles or rice vermicelli

10½ cups water, divided

2 cups sugar

2 tablespoons light corn syrup (optional)

¼ teaspoon sea salt

½ cup fresh lime juice, divided

1 tablespoon cooking rose water

2 tablespoons slivered pistachio kernels

¼ cup sour cherry preserve

3 fresh limes, halved

DIRECTIONS

1 Using scissors, snip the noodles into 1½-inch lengths. In a medium saucepan, add 8 cups of the water and bring to a boil; then add the noodles. Boil until tender, about 12 to 15 minutes. Drain immediately in a fine-mesh colander and rinse thoroughly with cold water to give the noodles a shock and to stop the cooking. Place the noodles in a bowl, cover, and chill in the refrigerator until ready to use in Step 3.

2 In the same saucepan, combine the remaining 2½ cups of water and the sugar; stir well and bring to a boil to dissolve the sugar. Remove from the heat and add the corn syrup (if using), salt, ¼ cup of the lime juice, and rose water. Stir well and set aside to cool.

3 Pour the syrup into an ice cream maker or sorbet machine and start the machine. When the syrup has a white, snowy consistency (about 45 minutes), start adding the noodles, a little at a time. Run the machine until the noodles have frozen properly (about 20 minutes); they won't have a rubbery texture.

4 Transfer to an ice-cream tub. Scoop some sorbet into individual dishes and decorate with a sprinkle of pistachios, a drizzled of sour cherry preserve, and the remaining ¼ cup of fresh lime juice. Place 1 lime half on the side of each dish for a last-minute fresh squeeze. *Nush-e joon!*

PER SERVING: *Calories 377 (From Fat 6); Fat 1g (Saturated 0g); Cholesterol 0mg; Sodium 122mg; Carbohydrate 94g (Dietary Fiber 1g); Protein 1g.*

Chapter **20**

Breads and Street Food

Bread, called *nan* in Persian, is the staple food of Iran in all regions except around the Caspian Sea, where rice supplants it. *Nan* is a Persian word that other languages borrowed. There are many types of Persian breads, but in this chapter, I have recipes for the most popular ones.

As children, my sisters and I loved the street foods of Iran, but our mother forbade us from indulging — she thought these snacks were unhygienic and could make us sick. But because they were forbidden, they were naturally even more desirable and tasty! Street foods could be found everywhere — in front of schools, near movie theaters, at busy street corners, and in and around the bazaar (like hot dogs and pretzels are in New York City today).

Vendors sold fruit and nut snacks seasonally, starting in the early spring with unripe almonds and plums sold with sprinkles of salt, wrapped in newspapers. Summer was a time for corn on the cob, roasted on an open fire, then dropped into salted water and served hot. Popular winter street foods were beets, roasted in *tanur* (bread ovens), kept on a steamer in the street vendors' carts, sold, peeled, and sliced. Another winter snack was steamed fava beans garnished with a splash of vinegar, *golpar* (Persian hogweed), and paprika. I've included the recipes for these in this chapter.

Barbari Bread (Nan-e Barbari)

PREP TIME: 40 MIN PLUS 6 HR FOR RISING	COOK TIME: 1 HR	YIELD: 6 SERVINGS

INGREDIENTS

1 envelope or 2¼ teaspoons dry active yeast

3 cups warm water (100 degrees)

1 tablespoon sugar

2 teaspoons sea salt

6½–8½ cups unbleached all-purpose flour or bread flour, sifted, divided

¼ cup oil or butter, divided

½ cup yellow cornmeal, for dusting, divided

1 tablespoon sesame seeds, divided

1 tablespoon nigella seeds, divided

1 egg mixed with 1 tablespoon plain whole yogurt

DIRECTIONS

1 In the bowl of an electric mixer, add the yeast and water and allow to dissolve. Add the sugar and set aside for 10 minutes.

2 Add the salt and mix well. Gradually add the flour and mix, until 6½ cups of flour has been added and you have a sticky dough, about 5 minutes. Add 1 tablespoon of the oil or butter and mix for 2 minutes. Gradually add more flour until the dough is no longer sticky.

3 Remove the mixing bowl from the machine; lift the dough in the mixing bowl and pour the remaining 3 tablespoons of oil or butter into it. Turn the dough so it's coated all over with the oil or butter. Cover the entire bowl with a clean damp dish towel and place it in a warm place (I use the oven with just the light on); allow the dough to rise for 4 hours, without moving it.

4 Punch the air out of the dough while it's still in the bowl and flip it over. Cover again with the damp dish towel and allow to rise for 2 more hours.

5 Preheat the oven to 500 degrees. With oily hands, divide the dough into 4 balls. Use an oiled rolling pin to roll each ball out to an approximately 11-x-6-inch oval shape.

6 Dust 4 sheet pans with 2 tablespoons each of the cornmeal and transfer a loaf to it. Cover with dishtowels, and leave at room temperature for 20 minutes.

7 Brush with ¼ of the egg wash and make dents along the length of the top of the loaf; sprinkle ¾ teaspoon of the sesame seeds and ¾ teaspoon of the nigella seeds on top. Bake until golden, about 12 to 15 minutes. Remove the bread from the oven and place it on a cooling rack.

8 Repeat Step 6 with the remaining loaves. If you aren't serving the bread right away, wrap in aluminum foil and keep in the refrigerator. When ready to serve, unwrap and either cut into rectangles and toast, or place in a 200-degree oven for 5 to 10 minutes. *Nush-e joon!*

PER SERVING: *Calories 652 (From Fat 120); Fat 13g (Saturated 2g); Cholesterol 35mg; Sodium 640mg; Carbohydrate 114g (Dietary Fiber 5g); Protein 17g.*

TIP: *Barbari* bread is a flat oval or round flatbread, 1 to 1½ inches thick. It's at its best when eaten fresh, as you would a French baguette.

Lavash Bread (Nan-e Lavash)

PREP TIME: 5 MIN PLUS 1 HR FOR RESTING	COOK TIME: 8 MIN	YIELD: 4 SERVINGS

INGREDIENTS

1½ tablespoons active dry yeast

1 cup warm water (100 degrees)

½ cup olive oil

3½ cups pizza flour (00) mixed with 1 teaspoon fine sea salt

½ cup flour, for dusting

DIRECTIONS

1 In the bowl of an electric mixer, add the yeast and warm water and dissolve; mix, cover, and allow to rest for 10 minutes. Add the oil, and mix for 1 minute.

2 Gradually add the flour mixture, and mix, at low speed, until all the flour has been absorbed. Continue to mix, at high speed, until the dough doesn't stick to your hands, about 5 minutes. Cover with a clean dish towel and allow to rest, at room temperature, for 1 hour.

3 Transfer the dough to your work area and knead with your hands for a few minutes, until smooth. Shape the dough into a log and divide it into 8 pieces; then shape those pieces into balls.

4 Dust a sheet pan with the flour and transfer the 8 balls onto it, leaving space between them. Cover and allow to rest at room temperature for 20 minutes.

5 Line a sheet pan with parchment paper. Heat a griddle pan over medium-high heat until very hot.

6 Place a ball of dough on a generously floured surface and use your hand to flatten it to a 4-inch-diameter disk. Flip over and use a rolling pin to roll out until it's about 10 inches in diameter.

7 Flip the dough across the back of your hands to stretch it a little and to shake off any extra flour.

8 Slide the loaf onto the hot griddle. Cook until bubbles appear over the entire surface, about 20 seconds. Use an offset spatula to flip the bread to cook the other side until lightly golden and brown spots appear on the surface, about 20 seconds.

9 Use the spatula to remove the bread from the griddle and immediately place on the prepared sheet pan. Cover with a clean dish towel to keep it soft. Repeat for the rest of the dough. To store, while still warm, transfer to a resealable bag and store in the fridge until ready to use. To serve, remove from the bag and warm up either on a griddle or on a sheet pan in a 200-degree oven for 5 minutes. *Nush-e joon!*

PER SERVING: *Calories 588 (From Fat 134); Fat 15g (Saturated 2g); Cholesterol 0mg; Sodium 941mg; Carbohydrate 97g (Dietary Fiber 4g); Protein 15g.*

Stone-Baked Bread (Nan-e Sangak)

PREP TIME: 30 MIN PLUS 24 HR FOR STARTER PLUS 2 HR FOR RESTING	COOK TIME: 45 MIN	YIELD: 6 SERVINGS

INGREDIENTS

1½ teaspoons instant dry yeast (or 1 tablespoon fresh yeast, grated)

2 teaspoons sea salt, divided

1 tablespoon sugar, divided

3 cups warm water (100 degrees), divided

1 cup whole-wheat flour

1 cup whole-wheat flour mixed with 2 cups bread flour

2 tablespoons sesame seeds, divided

2 tablespoons poppy seeds, divided

2 tablespoons cumin seeds, divided

2 tablespoons nigella seeds, divided

DIRECTIONS

1 In a large bowl, add the yeast, 1 teaspoon of the salt, 1 teaspoon of the sugar, 1 cup of the water, and the whole-wheat flour. Whisk until soft and stretchy, about 10 minutes. Cover with plastic wrap and allow to rest in the refrigerator for 24 hours.

2 In the bowl of an electric mixer, add the whole-wheat flour mixed with bread flour, the remaining 1 teaspoon of salt, and the remaining 2 teaspoons of sugar; mix, on low speed for 1 minute. Then gradually add the remaining 2 cups of water and continue to mix, still on low speed, for another 2 minutes. Increase the speed to high and continue to mix until you have a soft, stretchy, and smooth dough, about 5 minutes.

3 Add the yeast mixture to the dough and mix, at high speed, until you have a soft stretchy dough, about 5 to 7 minutes. Cover with plastic wrap and place a dish towel over it; allow to rise for 2 hours in a warm place (I put mine in the oven with just the light on) or up to 24 hours in the refrigerator.

4 Preheat the oven to 450 degrees. Line 3 sheet pans with parchment paper. Place a bowl of warm water beside you.

5 Transfer a ladle of dough (about 1½ cups) to the lined sheet pan and use moist hands to spread it to a ¼-inch-thick oval loaf; then perforate it all over with your moist fingers. Sprinkle 2 teaspoons of the sesame seeds, 2 teaspoons of the poppy seeds, 2 teaspoons of the cumin seeds, and 2 teaspoons of the nigella seeds on top. Bake until slightly golden, about 12 to 15 minutes. Remove the sheet pan from the oven and allow to cool on a cooling rack.

6 Repeat Step 5 for the remaining dough to make 2 more loaves.

7 If you are not using the bread right away, cut into 4-x-6-inch strips and place in a resealable bag in the refrigerator; toast just before serving. *Nush-e joon!*

PER SERVING: *Calories 368 (From Fat 58); Fat 6g (Saturated 1g); Cholesterol 0mg; Sodium 634mg; Carbohydrate 67g (Dietary Fiber 8g); Protein 13g.*

Sweet Sesame Buns (Nan-e Komaj)

PREP TIME: 15 MIN PLUS 6 HR FOR RESTING	COOK TIME: 25 MIN	YIELD: 10 SERVINGS

INGREDIENTS

1 envelope or 2¼ teaspoons active dry yeast

1¼ cups warm milk (100 degrees)

¾ cup sugar

1 egg

¼ cup tahini paste or oil

2 tablespoons rose water

6 cups unbleached all-purpose flour plus ¼ cup for dusting

1 teaspoon baking powder

¼ teaspoon fine sea salt

1 teaspoon turmeric or ¼ teaspoon ground saffron threads

1 tablespoon oil

1 egg yolk mixed with 1 teaspoon milk until smooth

2 tablespoons sesame seeds

DIRECTIONS

1 In the bowl of an electric mixer, add the yeast and the milk and allow the yeast to dissolve. Add the sugar, cover, and allow to rest for 10 minutes undisturbed.

2 Add the egg, tahini paste or oil, and rose water; mix until creamy.

3 In a bowl, sift together the 6 cups of flour, baking powder, salt, and turmeric or saffron. Gradually add the flour mixture to the yeast, and mix until you have a soft dough, about 10 minutes.

4 Remove the mixing bowl from the machine, lift up the dough, and add the 1 tablespoon of oil. Turn the dough in the oil to ensure it's evenly coated all over. Cover with plastic wrap, place a clean dish towel over it, and allow it to rise at room temperature for 4 hours (or up to 24 hours in the refrigerator).

5 Turn the dough out onto a floured work surface, punch it down, and knead it, adding more flour if necessary until you have a dough that doesn't stick to your hands. Divide it into 10 portions and roll each portion into a tangerine-size ball.

6 Use your hands to flatten each ball to a 4-inch diameter disk. Place 5 buns on each sheet pan, spaced apart; cover with a moist dish towel, and allow to rest for 2 hours.

7 Preheat the oven to 325 degrees. Line 2 sheet pans with parchment paper. Use the edge of a cookie cutter to stamp the tops according to your fancy. Generously brush the buns with the egg wash and decorate with sesame seeds. Bake in the oven until golden brown, about 20 to 25 minutes. Remove from the oven and allow to cool briefly on a cooling rack. *Nush-e joon!*

PER SERVING: *Calories 435 (From Fat 74); Fat 8g (Saturated 2g); Cholesterol 45mg; Sodium 73mg; Carbohydrate 78g (Dietary Fiber 3g); Protein 12g.*

Roasted Beets (Labu)

INGREDIENTS

2 pounds large beets

2 tablespoons sugar

5 cups water

DIRECTIONS

1 Preheat the oven to 350 degrees.

2 Place the beets, unpeeled, in a medium baking dish. Add the sugar and water, and bake, uncovered, in the oven until the beets are tender and most of the water has been absorbed, about 2½ to 3 hours (depending on the size of the beets).

3 Peel, slice, and serve the beets on their own or use in a yogurt salad. *Nush-e joon!*

PER SERVING: *Calories 122 (From Fat 3); Fat 0g (Saturated 0g); Cholesterol 0mg; Sodium 177mg; Carbohydrate 28g (Dietary Fiber 6g); Protein 4g.*

Hot Fava Beans in the Pod (Baqala Pokhteh)

INGREDIENTS

8 cups water

3 tablespoons fine sea salt

2 pounds fresh fava beans in the pod or 1 pound shelled fava beans, fresh or frozen

2 tablespoons apple cider vinegar

1 teaspoon ground *golpar* (Persian hogweed)

½ teaspoon red pepper flakes or paprika

DIRECTIONS

1 In a large pot, combine the water and salt, and bring to a boil.

2 Add the fava beans and boil briskly for 10 to 15 minutes. (If using shelled fava beans, cook until tender, about 5 minutes.)

3 Drain and transfer to a platter. Sprinkle with the vinegar, *golpar*, and red pepper flakes or paprika. Serve hot as a snack or appetizer. *Nush-e joon!*

PER SERVING: *Calories 100 (From Fat 7); Fat 1g (Saturated 0g); Cholesterol 0mg; Sodium 731mg; Carbohydrate 20g (Dietary Fiber 0g); Protein 9g.*

Charcoal-Roasted Corn on the Cob (Balal)

PREP TIME: 20 MIN | COOK TIME: 15 MIN | YIELD: 4 SERVINGS

INGREDIENTS

8 cups warm water

3 tablespoons fine sea salt

4 ears of corn

DIRECTIONS

1 Prepare a charcoal grill outside or preheat an indoor grill until very hot.

2 In a large container, add the water and salt, and allow the salt to dissolve.

3 When the grill is ready, shuck the corn (keeping the husks for serving).

4 Grill the corn, turning them frequently, until all sides have solid grill marks and some of the corn has blackened.

5 When all sides are well roasted, remove from the grill using tongs and immediately plunge them into the brine for 1 minute.

6 Serve hot on a piece of the husk. *Nush-e joon!*

PER SERVING: *Calories 123 (From Fat 15); Fat 2g (Saturated 0g); Cholesterol 0mg; Sodium 255mg; Carbohydrate 27g (Dietary Fiber 4g); Protein 5g.*

Chapter **21**

Thirst-Quenching Beverages

Iranians used to be coffee drinkers, but for the past 150 years, black tea has become the national drink. A glass of tea must please all the senses. Its color — light red rather than dark brown — should be appreciated, so it's served in a small glass. Tea should be steeped, but not for more than 10 minutes. The temperature and perfume are also important — it must be hot, with a heavenly aroma. Tea is offered almost everywhere; it's a sign of hospitality. If you go to someone's home and they don't offer you a hot glass of tea, you get the message.

The basis for *sharbat* (sherbet) or the shrubs that are seeing a comeback in the West was the ice and snow that ancient Iranians learned to preserve during the hot summer months in spectacular domed ice wells on the edges of towns and along caravan routes. The flavorings were syrups, made by combining fruit or vegetable juice with honey, sugar, or date or grape molasses and boiling the mixture down to intensify the flavor. Sipped through a mound of crushed ice or snow, the syrup became a delightful drink. The Vinegar and Mint Sherbet (Sharbat-e Sekanjebin) recipe in this chapter, flavored with aromatic herbs, and garnished with lime and cucumbers, is one of my favorites.

TEA AND MORE TEA

Black tea is the most popular drink, by far, throughout Iran, but no one really knows how it managed to replace coffee as the stimulant drink of choice in Iran in the 19th century.

Tu was the southern Chinese pronunciation for the drink, which was pronounced *tea* when it reached Europe. *Cha,* on the other hand, was the pronunciation in northern China, which became *cha* and *chai* in Iran, Russia, and other countries in the East.

Herbal teas, such as those made from borage and valerian, as well as tea made from the fruit of the *jujube* (Chinese date), have a much longer history and remain popular in Iran.

CULTURAL WISDOM

The word *shrub* comes from the Persian *sharbat*. In England, it was first used for medicinal sweet drinks in the 15th century. It became a popular drink in 17th-century England. By the 19th century, typical American recipes for shrubs used vinegar poured over fruit. The sweet-and-sour syrup could be mixed with either water or soda water and served as a soft drink, or it could be used as a mixer in alcoholic cocktails. Shrubs fell out of popularity but became popular again around 2011 in American, Canadian, and London restaurants and bars.

Tea (Chai)

INGREDIENTS

6 cups water, divided

2 tablespoons black aromatic tea leaves (Earl Grey)

1 teaspoon orange blossom water

DIRECTIONS

1   Bring 6 cups of water to a boil in a samovar or tea kettle. Transfer ½ cup of boiling water to a teapot, swirl it around to warm the pot, and then pour it out. Place the tea leaves and orange blossom water in the pot.

2   Fill the teapot with the remaining 5½ cups of boiling water. Replace the lid, cover the pot with a cozy, and let the tea steep for 10 minutes — don't steep for any longer than this because the quality will deteriorate. If you're using a samovar, steep the tea on top.

3   Pour out a glassful of tea and return it to the pot to make sure the tea is evenly mixed.

4   Fill each glass or cup up to halfway with tea, using a tea strainer if you like. Add boiling water from the kettle to dilute the tea to the desired color and taste (some people prefer their tea weak; others, strong). Keep the pot covered with the cozy while you drink the first glasses. Persian-style tea should always be served hot. Refill the glasses frequently (until you've had enough of company and it's time for your guests to leave — I love this kind of subtle sign language). *Nush-e joon!*

PER SERVING: *Calories 2 (From Fat 0); Fat 0g (Saturated 0g); Cholesterol 0mg; Sodium 4mg; Carbohydrate 0g (Dietary Fiber 0g); Protein 0g.*

Coffee (Qahveh)

PREP TIME: ABOUT 5 MIN | COOK TIME: 10 MIN | YIELD: 4 SERVINGS

INGREDIENTS

1¼ cups water

4 teaspoons very finely ground coffee (Turkish coffee)

2 teaspoons sugar

1 teaspoon rose water

⅛ teaspoon ground saffron threads (optional)

½ teaspoon ground cardamom (optional)

DIRECTIONS

1 In a small saucepan or *ibriq* (coffee pot), place the water, coffee, sugar, rose water, saffron (if using), and cardamom (if using).

2 Stir well for 1 minute until the coffee dissolves.

3 Cook, over low heat, undisturbed (don't walk away — this coffee needs supervision because it can froth up at any moment).

4 As soon as you see it begin to boil, the froth begin to rise to the top, and the surface covered with bubbles (about 10 minutes), remove from the heat.

5 To make sure that every cup of coffee has the same consistency, gently fill each demitasse cup a little at a time, until each is full. Sip the coffee carefully so as not to disturb any grounds. *Nush-e joon!*

PER SERVING: *Calories 11 (From Fat 0); Fat 0g (Saturated 0g); Cholesterol 0mg; Sodium 0mg; Carbohydrate 3g (Dietary Fiber 0g); Protein 0g.*

VARY IT! For a different flavor, in Step 1, reduce the water to 1 cup and add ¼ cup milk.

Yogurt and Mint Drink (Dugh)

PREP TIME: ABOUT 10 MIN | COOK TIME: NONE | YIELD: 2 SERVINGS

INGREDIENTS

1 cup whole milk yogurt, beaten for 5 minutes

½ teaspoon chopped fresh mint

½ teaspoon dried oregano

½ teaspoon fine sea salt

¼ teaspoon freshly ground black pepper

1½ cups carbonated or still water, chilled

2 tablespoons freshly squeezed lime juice

4 ice cubes

DIRECTIONS

1 In a pitcher, add the yogurt, mint, oregano, salt, and pepper. Stir well.

2 Gradually add the water, stirring constantly. Add the lime juice, and stir well. Cover and place in the fridge for at least 30 minutes.

3 Serve chilled with cubes of ice. *Nush-e joon!*

PER SERVING: *Calories 79 (From Fat 36); Fat 4g (Saturated 2g); Cholesterol 12mg; Sodium 558mg; Carbohydrate 7g (Dietary Fiber 0g); Protein 4g.*

Vinegar and Mint Sherbet (Sharbat-e Sekanjebin)

PREP TIME: ABOUT 10 MIN	COOK TIME: 30 MIN	YIELD: 15 SERVINGS

INGREDIENTS

6 cups granulated sugar

2 cups water, plus extra for making the drink

1½ cups wine vinegar

4 sprigs fresh mint

4 cups crushed ice

1 cucumber, peeled and thinly sliced

2 limes, sliced

½ cup fresh mint leaves

½ cup fresh cilantro leaves

2 tablespoons dried rose petals or marigold flowers

DIRECTIONS

1 In a medium saucepan, add the sugar and water and bring to a boil. Simmer over medium heat, stirring occasionally, until the sugar has completely dissolved, about 10 minutes. Add the vinegar and boil over medium heat until a thick syrup forms, about 15 to 20 minutes. Add the mint sprigs. Remove from the heat and allow to cool. Discard the mint and pour the syrup into a clean, dry bottle. Seal tightly with a cork or screw cap until ready to use.

2 To make the drink, in a pitcher, mix 1 part syrup with 3 parts water and stir well. Fill half a glass with crushed ice, slices of cucumber, a slice of lime, a few mint and cilantro leaves, and a dried rose petal or marigold flower. Top up the glass with the diluted syrup from the pitcher. *Nush-e joon!*

PER SERVING: *Calories 322 (From Fat 1); Fat 0g (Saturated 0g); Cholesterol 0mg; Sodium 5mg; Carbohydrate 82g (Dietary Fiber 1g); Protein 0g.*

NOTE: The basis of sharbat was the ice and snow that ancient Iranians had learned to preserve during the hot summer months in spectacular domed ice wells on the edges of towns and along caravan routes. The flavorings were syrups, made by combining fruit or vegetable juice with honey, sugar, or date or grape molasses and boiling the mixture down to intensify the flavor. Sipped through a mound of crushed ice or snow, the syrup became a delightful drink. Sharbats could be either sweet or savory.

Sour Cherry Sherbet (Sharbat-e Albalu)

PREP TIME: ABOUT 5 MIN	COOK TIME: 35 MIN	YIELD: 15 SERVINGS

INGREDIENTS

3 pounds fresh sour cherries or pitted frozen sour/tart cherries

6 cups sugar

3 cups water

4 tablespoons lime juice

DIRECTIONS

1 In a large colander, rinse the cherries. Stem the cherries and discard any that are blemished.

2 In a large saucepan, add the sugar and water and bring to a boil.

3 Add the cherries to the saucepan. Bring back to a boil, reduce the heat to medium, and simmer for 35 minutes. Add the lime juice, remove from the heat, and allow to cool. Drain the syrup, using a sieve, into a spouted glass container (save the cherries to use later as a preserve).

4 Use a funnel to pour the syrup into a clean, dry bottle; cork tightly; and refrigerate.

5 To make the sherbet, in a pitcher, mix 1 part syrup and 3 parts cold water, and stir well. To serve, for each person, fill half a glass with crushed ice and top up the glass with the diluted sour cherry syrup in the pitcher. *Nush-e joon!*

PER SERVING: *Calories 352 (From Fat 2); Fat 2g (Saturated 2g); Cholesterol 0mg; Sodium 2mg; Carbohydrate 90g (Dietary Fiber 1g); Protein 1g.*

TIP: You can transfer the cherries to a jar and use them, as Persians do, as a preserve. Or use it as a sweetener in tea or with yogurt as a dessert.

6

The Part of Tens

Get practical tips on being more efficient in the kitchen.

Uncover the myths about Persian food and learn what's authentic.

Discover some of the conventions of Persian table etiquette that will make you both a better guest and a better host.

Chapter **22**

Ten (or So) Time-Saving Tips for the Kitchen

love to cook, but I don't want to spend most of my time in the kitchen, nor do I want you to have to spend hours preparing weekday meals.

Over the past 40 years, I've been busy — raising my kids, helping family from Iran get settled in the United States, and writing cookbooks. I had to manage my time in order to be able to create healthy, delicious, and economical meals for the family. In this chapter, I share the tips that have helped me over the years — tips that you, too, can apply when you're in the kitchen.

Figure Out the Proper Prep Order

When my children were quite small and needed more of my attention, I'd plan my weekday meals in advance and start the prep whenever I had time, not when I had to start to cook. For example, I'd write or print out the recipe I wanted to cook the next day, read it carefully, and put it on a sheet pan. Then I'd look for and gather all the ingredients for the recipe to be sure I had everything I needed, including kitchen tools such as peelers, graters, and any electric appliances. For the refrigerated ingredients, I'd put a check mark on the recipe, and if I needed any ingredients that I didn't have, I'd write a shopping list.

I learned early on that gathering all the ingredients for cooking a recipe, measuring them out, and putting them on the sheet pan is very helpful in accelerating the process and making cooking more fun. I like to peel and chop onions and garlic, puree tomatoes, and sauté herbs as I find time during the day or the day before I actually start to cook.

Wash and Chop Herbs

Persian cooking uses lots of herbs that need to be washed and chopped, which can be time-consuming. One way to save time is to do this in advance, whenever you have time and then store the thoroughly dried chopped herbs in an airtight glass container and keep them in the fridge until you need them.

You can always use a sharp knife and a cutting board for chopping vegetables and herbs. But using a food processor to chop herbs saves time.

You can also chop herbs in advance, and then label, date, and freeze them to use when needed. These days, frozen chopped herbs are available at the grocery store, and they're often high-quality because they're harvested and processed at their peak.

For braises that require large quantities of herbs, you can go through the process of washing, drying, chopping, and sautéing the herbs whenever you have time. Transfer to an airtight glass container and keep in the fridge for two days or in the freezer for up to three weeks.

Clean and Wash Barberries

Barberries (small tart berries), which are cherished and frequently called for in Persian recipes, need care and attention before using. This can be time-consuming so I recommend cleaning and caramelizing them ahead of time, and keeping them in a labeled airtight glass container in the fridge to use whenever you need them. (They keep for up to a week.)

Soak Legumes

I soak my dried legumes the night before I need them. This not only reduces the cooking time, but also helps the digestion. For a shortcut, you can use canned legumes, but be sure to drain and rinse them in cold water before using.

Peel Garlic

I peel batches of garlic whenever I have time (in front of the TV, for example) and then mince it in a food processor, cover it with olive oil, and store it in a labeled airtight glass container in the fridge to use as needed (for up to three weeks). Or you can just peel and dry the cloves thoroughly, to prevent any kind of mold, and keep them in a labeled airtight glass container in the fridge (for up to two weeks). These days, you can also buy peeled garlic cloves at the supermarket.

Cook Crispy Fried Onions in Batches

You can save time by cooking frequently used garnishes — such as crispy fried onions, mint, or toasted nuts — in batches head of time and store them in a labeled airtight glass container in the fridge to use as needed for up to three weeks.

Store Your Spices Efficiently

I like to buy whole spices, including peppercorns, and grind them in small batches in my electric spice grinder to use as needed. I store them in labeled airtight glass jars in the cupboard (out of the light). I keep three frequently used ones — fine sea salt, ground pepper, and ground turmeric — in small ceramic containers with lids next to the stove.

In this book, I include a recipe for making a Persian spice mix, *advieh* (see Chapter 6). You can make it in small batches yourself and store it in an airtight glass container in the cupboard. You can also buy readymade *advieh* from Persian markets or online, or you can use my version, Najmieh's Advieh, available at `https://persianbasket.com/advieh-najmieh-batmanglij-s-persian-spice-mix.html`.

Choose the Right Size Pan and Use a Lid

Using a good, medium-size, enameled, cast-iron braiser that is wide but not too deep will save you cooking time because your ingredients can be spread out and not crowded. The lid will seal in the simmering juices, keeping the ingredients moist while speeding up the time it takes for them to become tender.

Use a Rice Cooker, Multicooker, Food Processor, and Electric Mixer

Use a Persian-style rice cooker (the thermostats have been set to make a golden crust layer on the bottom of the pot) to save a lot of time and get consistently good results. You can even place all the ingredients called for in the recipe in the rice cooker ahead of time in the morning and just turn it on an hour before you want to eat.

Similarly, multicookers (like the Instant Pot), which have sautéing features and allow you to add the water or broth and cook under pressure, can halve the cooking time for braises that need to be slow-cooked over a long time.

I frequently use a food processor to save time preparing herbs in batches in advance.

A handheld electric mixer saves time when you need to partially puree ingredients in soups (which helps give body to the soup) without taking them out of the pot.

Finally, an electric mixer is a time-saver whenever you want to make breads and pastries.

Chapter **23**

Ten Myths about Persian Cooking

I n this chapter, I dispel ten common myths about Persian cooking.

Persian Food Is Different from Iranian Food

The words *Iran* and *Persia* refer to the same place. These days, the word *Iran* is used to refer to the country and *Persia* or *Persian* is used to refer to the culture. But Iranian food is Persian food, and Persian food is Iranian food. There is no difference.

That said, Iran is a large, ethnically diverse country (three times bigger than France). It's divided into several plateaus separated by high mountain ranges running west to east and north to south, with the Caspian Sea in the north and the Persian Gulf in the south. These regions have distinctly different climates and their own local ingredients and food culture. In northern and central Iran, food tends to be delicately spiced whereas in southern Iran, it's hot and spicy. So, not all Persian or Iranian cooking is the same.

Persian Cooking Doesn't Fit with Modern Cooking Practices

Persian cooking, with its emphasis on fresh, natural ingredients, fits beautifully with the trend in eating that's spreading across the United States. "Join the delicious revolution!" as chef Alice Waters says. "Eat simply, eat together, eat seasonally, shop at farmers markets." This is what Iranians have been doing for thousands of years!

Persian Food Is Only Kabobs

Much of Iran's cuisine is essentially vegetarian. Although kabobs are popular restaurant dishes, they represent only a small sampling of the dishes Iranians eat at home.

Persian Food Is Unhealthy

Persian food is the mother of the Mediterranean diet: mostly herbs, vegetables, fruits, grains, legumes, and only small amounts of meat, poultry, or fish. What could be healthier than that?

Persian Food Is Fattening

A staple of Persian food is rice, which can be a fattening carbohydrate, but when rice is cooked Persian-style (by parboiling, draining, and rinsing), much of the starch content is eliminated. Cooking it in this way, and using olive oil in the process, makes rice quite healthy.

Instead of taking medications, Persians often use food as a remedy, which is also becoming more common these days in the United States.

Persian Food Doesn't Look Good

For Persians, feasting your eyes is as important as feasting your taste buds. The look of Persian food replicates Persian miniatures and carpets, using colorful elements brought together in a delicate way. I may be biased, but I think the photos in this book speak for themselves!

Persian Food Takes Too Long to Cook

It's true that, like all good food, Persian food needs careful attention and takes time. But if you follow the recipes and my suggestions in this book, and use the steps as a road map, you'll save time when making a delicious Persian meal.

Persian Food Is Too Complicated to Make

If you follow the essential rules and basic steps in this book before starting to cook, you'll find that cooking most Persian dishes is not complicated and is actually quite simple.

Persian Food Is Expensive to Make

Most Persian dishes use rice, beans, vegetables, and fruits, and only small amounts of meat, poultry, or fish. You can use this book to cook a Persian feast that's very economical.

Persian Restaurants Represent Persian Cooking

Although rice and kabobs are popular fare in most Persian restaurants, they only represent a small sampling of what Iranians eat at home. And the recipes in this book reflect this.

» Avoiding double-dipping

» Honoring your host

» Loading up your plate

Chapter **24**

Ten Tips on Persian Table Manners

s the Persian poet Rumi said in the 13th century, "All is one," and we are all humans with similar desires and needs. Yet, every country has certain customs and habits according to geographical location, history, religion, and culture. A deeper appreciation and understanding of other cultures can be a big help in bringing the world together and avoiding misunderstandings. So, with that in mind, here are ten tips for serving and eating a Persian meal.

Eat with a Spoon and Maybe a Fork (not a Knife)

Most Iranians of all walks of life eat their meals with a spoon; some use a fork and a spoon. Traditionally, dishes were served in bowls, and because meat is usually cut into small pieces, using a spoon was quite functional.

Use Your Hands, Especially with Bone-in Kabobs

Using your hands to eat bone-in kabobs, such as lamb rib chops or chicken, is perfectly okay. For other kabobs, which are usually taken off the skewer over flatbreads, it's a treat to make a *loqmeh* (small mouthful), including some of the fresh herb and pickle trimmings, in a piece of flatbread such as lavash, and pop it in your mouth. For these dishes, using your hands is acceptable and even encouraged. I love to eat like this!

Use a Serving Utensil to Pick Up Food from a Communal Plate

Using your fingers to take food from a communal plate is a no-no in Persian culture. My mother always made sure that every dish had an appropriate spoon, fork, or ladle for serving.

Also, don't use your own fork or spoon for picking up food from a communal plate. And try not to lick your fingers no matter how delicious the food is — use a napkin instead.

Don't Double-Dip

Most Iranians don't eat from the same plate or drink from the same glass, except perhaps among close family. Lovers sometimes share a bowl using the same spoon as a sign of their love for each other.

Don't double-dip your vegetable, chips, or pieces of bread. I like to provide small plates so guests can use the serving spoon to put some of the dip on their plate and use that for dipping.

Don't Load Up Your plate

A Persian meal involves a main course and many small side dishes, but don't feel that you must put a lot of everything on your plate at once. Instead, take small amounts of each dish or a combination that you fancy — I find it useful to ask my host about any combinations of dishes that are intended to go together. You can always go back for more.

This practice also tends to leave enough food for everyone to enjoy. Plus, you'll often find that Persian hosts will encourage you to take seconds — you want to be sure you have room for seconds, so as not to disappoint your host.

Show Appreciation to Your Host

Iranians are very hospitable. For them, the guest is a friend of God! Be curious and ask about anything unfamiliar. Be genuine, but be sure to compliment the host for anything you enjoy.

If You Are the Host, Welcome Each Guest Individually and with Respect

When guests arrive, try to welcome each guest individually with equal attention and respect. Guests should never be made to feel that they're imposing or not welcome.

Be Grateful to Your Host

Arriving at a Persian party five or ten minutes late is not considered rude — in fact, it's even encouraged.

Don't bring cut flowers unless they're already in a vase. Bringing cut flowers without a vase makes work for the host, who will have to find a vase and arrange flowers in the middle of a party. (Of course, if you're the host, you may want to consider having a vase handy in case someone turns up with cut flowers.)

Also, if you don't know your hosts well, it's probably best not to arrive with wine or spirits — they may not drink alcohol.

Wash Your Hands

Before the meal, you may want to ask your hosts where you can wash your hands. This is hygienic not only for you but also for everyone else at the gathering — you never know what you may be handing to each other.

Don't Leave Too Early or Too Late

Iranians love to entertain and share their food and culture, so they go out of their way to please their guests from the moment they arrive to the moment they leave. So, don't eat and run, which is considered rude, but also don't overstay your welcome.

Iranians are generally polite and won't give you any hints that you should leave. They might even encourage you to stay longer even when it's time to leave.

Appendix

Metric Conversion Guide

Note: The recipes in this book weren't developed or tested using metric measurements. There may be some variation in quality when converting to metric units.

Common Abbreviations

Abbreviation(s)	What It Stands For
cm	Centimeter
C., c.	Cup
G, g	Gram
kg	Kilogram
L, l	Liter
lb.	Pound
mL, ml	Milliliter
oz.	Ounce
pt.	Pint
t., tsp.	Teaspoon
T., Tb., Tbsp.	Tablespoon

Volume

U.S. Units	Canadian Metric	Australian Metric
¼ teaspoon	1 milliliter	1 milliliter
½ teaspoon	2 milliliters	2 milliliters
1 teaspoon	5 milliliters	5 milliliters
1 tablespoon	15 milliliters	20 milliliters

U.S. Units	Canadian Metric	Australian Metric
¼ cup	50 milliliters	60 milliliters
⅓ cup	75 milliliters	80 milliliters
½ cup	125 milliliters	125 milliliters
⅔ cup	150 milliliters	170 milliliters
¾ cup	175 milliliters	190 milliliters
1 cup	250 milliliters	250 milliliters
1 quart	1 liter	1 liter
1½ quarts	1.5 liters	1.5 liters
2 quarts	2 liters	2 liters
2½ quarts	2.5 liters	2.5 liters
3 quarts	3 liters	3 liters
4 quarts (1 gallon)	4 liters	4 liters

Weight

U.S. Units	Canadian Metric	Australian Metric
1 ounce	30 grams	30 grams
2 ounces	55 grams	60 grams
3 ounces	85 grams	90 grams
4 ounces (¼ pound)	115 grams	125 grams
8 ounces (½ pound)	225 grams	225 grams
16 ounces (1 pound)	455 grams	500 grams (½ kilogram)

Length

Inches	Centimeters
0.5	1.5
1	2.5
2	5.0

Inches	Centimeters
3	7.5
4	10.0
5	12.5
6	15.0
7	17.5
8	20.5
9	23.0
10	25.5
11	28.0
12	30.5

Temperature (Degrees)

Fahrenheit	Celsius
32	0
212	100
250	120
275	140
300	150
325	160
350	180
375	190
400	200
425	220
450	230
475	240
500	260

Index

About the Author

Najmieh Batmanglij was born and raised in Iran. She came to the United States in the late 1960s for her college education. Seven years later, she earned her master's degree in education and returned to Iran. In 1979, when the Islamic Revolution took a fundamentalist turn, she and her husband fled to France. It was in France that Najmieh decided to follow her passion and become a cook. She wrote her first cookbook, *Ma Cuisine d'Iran*, in French.

Najmieh has spent the past 42 years cooking, traveling, and adapting authentic Persian recipes to tastes and techniques in the West. She has been hailed as "the guru of Persian cuisine" by *The Washington Post*, and Yotam Ottolenghi called her "The Goddess of Iranian Cooking." Her book *Food of Life: Ancient Persian and Modern Iranian Cooking and Ceremonies* was called "the definitive book on Iranian cooking" by the *Los Angeles Times*; her book *Silk Road Cooking: A Vegetarian Journey* was selected as one of the ten best vegetarian cookbooks of 2004 by *The New York Times*; and her book *From Persia to Napa: Wine at the Persian Table* won the Gourmand Cookbook Award for the best wine history book of 2007. Her most recent book, *Cooking in Iran: Regional Recipes and Kitchen Secrets*, was selected as one of the best cookbooks of Fall 2018 by *The New York Times*. In 2021, she was declared by *The New York Times* Book Review one of "Seven Immigrant Women Who Changed the Way Americans Eat."

Najmieh is a member of Les Dames d'Escoffier and lives in the Washington, D.C., area, where she teaches Persian cooking, and consults with restaurants around the world. Her website is www.najmieh.com and her Instagram handle is @najmieh.

Dedication

I dedicate this book to you, the reader, and to all those who are curious to learn more about Persian food, which has one of the oldest yet least known schools of cooking in the world.

Author's Acknowledgments

A big thanks to Tracy Boggier, who found me, encouraged me to do this project, and worked hard to make it happen — thank you, Tracy, for giving me this opportunity. Thanks to Vicki Adang, for the initial help turning my outline into a *For Dummies* table of contents. And, of course, thanks to my editor, Elizabeth Kuball, who, with grace and flexibility, has turned the text into *For Dummies* style.

Also, many thanks to Rachel Nix for her meticulous testing of the recipes and for analyzing their nutritional value. Thanks are also due to Elizabeth Kurtzman for her wonderful illustrations.

Finally, I'd like to thank Mojdeh Bahar and Tina Nejand for all the help and support they gave me for this book.

Publisher's Acknowledgments

Senior Acquisitions Editor: Tracy Boggier

Project Editor: Elizabeth Kuball

Copy Editor: Elizabeth Kuball

Technical Editor: Rachel Nix, RD

Recipe Tester: Rachel Nix, RD

Nutrition Analyst: Rachel Nix, RD

Production Editor: Mohammed Zafar Ali

Illustrator: Elizabeth Kurtzman

Cover Images: Courtesy of Najmieh Batmanglij

Take dummies with you everywhere you go!

Whether you are excited about e-books, want more from the web, must have your mobile apps, or are swept up in social media, dummies makes everything easier.

Find us online!

dummies
A Wiley Brand

Leverage the power

Dummies is the global leader in the reference category and one of the most trusted and highly regarded brands in the world. No longer just focused on books, customers now have access to the dummies content they need in the format they want. Together we'll craft a solution that engages your customers, stands out from the competition, and helps you meet your goals.

Advertising & Sponsorships

Connect with an engaged audience on a powerful multimedia site, and position your message alongside expert how-to content. Dummies.com is a one-stop shop for free, online information and know-how curated by a team of experts.

- Targeted ads
- Video
- Email Marketing
- Microsites
- Sweepstakes sponsorship

20 **MILLION**
PAGE VIEWS
EVERY SINGLE MONTH

15
MILLION
UNIQUE
VISITORS PER MONTH

43%
OF ALL VISITORS
ACCESS THE SITE
VIA THEIR MOBILE DEVICES

700,000 NEWSLETTER
SUBSCRIPTIONS
TO THE INBOXES OF
300,000 UNIQUE **INDIVIDUALS EVERY WEEK**

# of dummies

Custom Publishing

Reach a global audience in any language by creating a solution that will differentiate you from competitors, amplify your message, and encourage customers to make a buying decision.

- Apps
- Books
- eBooks
- Video
- Audio
- Webinars

Brand Licensing & Content

Leverage the strength of the world's most popular reference brand to reach new audiences and channels of distribution.

For more information, visit **dummies.com/biz**

PERSONAL ENRICHMENT

Staying Sharp
9781119187790
USA $26.00
CAN $31.99
UK £19.99

Facebook
9781119179030
USA $21.99
CAN $25.99
UK £16.99

Guitar
9781119293354
USA $24.99
CAN $29.99
UK £17.99

Investing
9781119293347
USA $22.99
CAN $27.99
UK £16.99

Beekeeping
9781119310068
USA $22.99
CAN $27.99
UK £16.99

Digital Photography
9781119235606
USA $24.99
CAN $29.99
UK £17.99

Meditation
9781119251163
USA $24.99
CAN $29.99
UK £17.99

Pregnancy
9781119235491
USA $26.99
CAN $31.99
UK £19.99

Samsung Galaxy S7
9781119279952
USA $24.99
CAN $29.99
UK £17.99

iPhone
9781119283133
USA $24.99
CAN $29.99
UK £17.99

Crocheting
9781119287117
USA $24.99
CAN $29.99
UK £16.99

Nutrition
9781119130246
USA $22.99
CAN $27.99
UK £16.99

PROFESSIONAL DEVELOPMENT

Windows 10
9781119311041
USA $24.99
CAN $29.99
UK £17.99

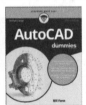
AutoCAD
9781119255796
USA $39.99
CAN $47.99
UK £27.99

Excel 2016
9781119293439
USA $26.99
CAN $31.99
UK £19.99

QuickBooks 2017
9781119281467
USA $26.99
CAN $31.99
UK £19.99

macOS Sierra
9781119280651
USA $29.99
CAN $35.99
UK £21.99

LinkedIn
9781119251132
USA $24.99
CAN $29.99
UK £17.99

Windows 10
9781119310563
USA $34.00
CAN $41.99
UK £24.99

SharePoint 2016
9781119181705
USA $29.99
CAN $35.99
UK £21.99

Fundamental Analysis
9781119263593
USA $26.99
CAN $31.99
UK £19.99

Networking
9781119257769
USA $29.99
CAN $35.99
UK £21.99

Office 2016
9781119293477
USA $26.99
CAN $31.99
UK £19.99

Office 365
9781119265313
USA $24.99
CAN $29.99
UK £17.99

Salesforce.com
9781119239314
USA $29.99
CAN $35.99
UK £21.99

Coding
9781119293323
USA $29.99
CAN $35.99
UK £21.99

Learning Made Easy

ACADEMIC

9781119293576
USA $19.99
CAN $23.99
UK £15.99

9781119293637
USA $19.99
CAN $23.99
UK £15.99

9781119293491
USA $19.99
CAN $23.99
UK £15.99

9781119293460
USA $19.99
CAN $23.99
UK £15.99

9781119293590
USA $19.99
CAN $23.99
UK £15.99

9781119215844
USA $26.99
CAN $31.99
UK £19.99

9781119293378
USA $22.99
CAN $27.99
UK £16.99

9781119293521
USA $19.99
CAN $23.99
UK £15.99

9781119239178
USA $18.99
CAN $22.99
UK £14.99

9781119263883
USA $26.99
CAN $31.99
UK £19.99

Available Everywhere Books Are Sold

dummies.com

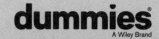

dummies®
A Wiley Brand

Small books for big imaginations

9781119177173
USA $9.99
CAN $9.99
UK £8.99

9781119177272
USA $9.99
CAN $9.99
UK £8.99

9781119177241
USA $9.99
CAN $9.99
UK £8.99

9781119177210
USA $9.99
CAN $9.99
UK £8.99

9781119262657
USA $9.99
CAN $9.99
UK £6.99

9781119291336
USA $9.99
CAN $9.99
UK £6.99

9781119233527
USA $9.99
CAN $9.99
UK £6.99

9781119291220
USA $9.99
CAN $9.99
UK £6.99

9781119177302
USA $9.99
CAN $9.99
UK £8.99

Unleash Their Creativity

dummies.com

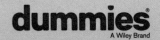

dummies®
A Wiley Brand